# The GARDENER'S Sourcebook

## SHEILA BUFF

L&B

Lyons & Burford, Publishers

Printed in the United States of America

10 9 8 7 6 5 4 3 2 1

Design by Elaine Streithof

Library of Congress Cataloging-in-Publication Data
Buff, Sheila.
    The gardener's sourcebook / Sheila Buff.
        p.    cm.
    ISBN 1-55821-515-8(cloth). — ISBN 1-55821-464-X (pbk.)
    1. Gardening—United States—Directories. 2. Nurseries (Horticulture)—United
States—Directories. 3. Gardening equipment industry—United States—Directories.
4. Gardening—Canada—Directories. 5. Nurseries (Horticulture)—Canada—Directories.
6. Gardening equipment industry—Canada—Directories. 7. Mail-order business—United
States—Directories. 8. Mail-order business—Canada—Directories. I. Title.
SB450.943.U6B84 1996
635'.025'7—dc20                                                                    96-22959
                                                                                              CIP

# Contents

# Introduction

THIS BOOK BEGAN innocently enough several years ago, when I decided that an arch covered by climbing roses would look nice at the entrance to my front garden. This is not the sort of decision a gardener enters into lightly. The search for the ideal arch and a climbing rosebush exactly like the one I remembered from my grandmother's garden took more than a year and revealed a perfectionist streak in my personality that left me a little surprised. I did find the ideal arch, eventually, and the right climbing rose. The quest was long, but I can't say it was particularly arduous. I wrote letters, mostly, and made some phone calls, and then settled back for a leisurely perusal of the catalogues that arrived dependably in the mail.

They kept coming, of course, and over time and additional quests (the one to find native water plants was particularly intriguing) many, many more joined the throng. Because garden catalogues make enjoyable and informative reading, and because freelance authors can rarely bring themselves to discard the written word, stacks of catalogues and brochures took over my workroom and spilled over to the rest of the house. The situation was familiar. So was the solution: Write a book.

It wasn't quite so easy, of course (it never is). To bring together a lot of scattered information into one book, and to make that book as thorough and complete as possible, I had to write a lot more letters and make a lot more phone calls, as well as spend a lot of time in libraries. The information in *The Gardener's Sourcebook* is as accurate and up to date as possible. The suppliers listed here are chiefly those that sell their plants and other products through the mail. Addresses and phone numbers sometimes change (although you wouldn't think it was so easy to move an entire nursery), but mail to an old address is usually forwarded promptly to the new, and a call to directory assistance will usually yield a new phone number.

This book focuses on horticulture—the cultivation of ornamental flowers. To list sources for vegetables, fruits, and herbs would add enormously to an already lengthy volume. Leaving aside the extensive listings of ornamental plant sources, however, food-growing gardeners will still find much of value here. Well over half this book provides sources for tools, supplies, and information of universal interest to every gardener.

A careful effort has been made to include as many nurseries, organizations, services, manufacturers, retailers, and other resources as completely and accurately as possible. Inclusion in this book is not an endorsement of any sort by the author or the publisher. Likewise, exclusion from this book is not deliberate in any way by the author or the publisher and does not imply a criticism of any sort.

Keeping up with the changes in the most popular hobby in America is difficult. There are doubtless some glaring omissions in this book, and as gardening continues to grow in popularity, additional services and suppliers are sure to appear. Corrections, updates, and additions for future editions of this book are encouraged. Please send them to me in care of the publisher.

# Plant Sources

$T$HIS LENGTHY SECTION of THE GARDENER'S SOURCEBOOK focuses on sources for specific plants. After the opening listing of plant emporiums, the chapter is organized alphabetically by common plant-family name. Each plant entry begins with a list of relevant organizations and other information (where available), then goes on to list plant sources alphabetically by nursery. The nurseries listed under each plant family specialize in that particular family, although not necessarily to the exclusion of others. They sell their plants through the mail—with a very few exceptions, nurseries that don't ship aren't listed in this book. For information and plant sources for specialty gardening areas such as bonsai, roses, and orchids, see chapter 2.

Nursery catalogues range from elaborate, four-color productions to simple plant lists. Related products such as books and tools are often listed along with the plants. The catalogues are often quite informative and always fun to read. Bear in mind, however, that even simple catalogues cost money to produce—and the price of paper has skyrocketed recently. Many nurseries must now charge a dollar or two (sometimes more) for their catalogues. The price is almost always refunded against your order.

Most nursery owners are hard-working people who love what they do. Because they are often outside working, they may be hard to reach on the telephone. If you need the answer to a plant question, be patient and keep trying. If you'd like a catalogue, it's best to request it by mail. Send a short note along with your check, stamps, or stamped, self-addressed envelope. Be sure your request gives your complete, legible mailing address.

In general, nurseries welcome visitors. Many maintain beautiful display gardens that are well worth a trip. If you'd like to visit, however, call ahead. Not all nurseries are open all the time—you may even need to make an appointment. You may also need detailed directions for finding the place.

The nurseries listed below sell healthy plants that can be shipped to you in the mail or by a delivery service. The plants will grow well if correctly planted and tended. To help avoid disappointments or problems, be sure to order early and specify delivery dates if necessary. Ask about the nursery's substitution policy if the plant you want is unavailable at shipping time. Keep a record of your order, including the date, whom you spoke with, what you ordered, and any special instructions you gave. Guarantee policies vary from firm to firm, but the vast majority will refund your money or replace the plant if it fails to grow properly. In the unlikely event that you can't resolve a problem with a nursery to your satisfaction, write to:

Garden Centers of America, 1250 I Street NW, Suite 500, Washington, DC 20005 (202) 789-2900

Over 3,500 retail nurseries belong to this trade association. A smaller organization consisting only of mail-order firms is:

Mailorder Gardening Association
Box 2129
Columbia, MD 21045
(410) 730-9713

Prices are in U.S. dollars unless otherwise noted.

## Plant Emporiums

The familiar names listed below are large firms offering a broad array of plants, seeds, supplies, and other products.

W. Atlee Burpee Company
300 Park Avenue
Warminster, PA 18974
(215) 674-4900
(800) 888-1447
Catalogue: free

DeGiorgi Seed Company
6011 N Street
Omaha, NE 68117
(402) 731-3901
Catalogue: $2.00

Henry Field Seed and Nursery Company
415 North Burnett
Shenandoah, IA 51602
(605) 665-9391
Catalogue: free

Gurney's Seed and Nursery Company
110 Capital Street
Yankton, SD 57079
(605) 665-1930
Catalogue: free

Johnny's Selected Seeds
Foss Hill Road
Albion, ME 04910
(207) 437-9294
Catalogue: free

Kelly Nurseries
410 8th Avenue NW
Faribault, MN 55021
(507) 334-1623
Catalogue: free

Lamb Nurseries
East 101 Sharp Avenue
Spokane, WA 99202
(509) 328-7956
Catalogue: $1.00

Mellinger's, Inc.
2310 West South Range Road
North Lima, OH 44452
(216) 549-9861
(800) 321-7444
Catalogue: free

Park Seed Company
Cokesbury Road
Greenwood, SC 29647
(803) 223-7333
(800) 845-3369
Catalogue: free

Pinetree Garden Seeds
Box 300
New Gloucester, ME 04260
(207) 926-3400
Catalogue: free

Shepherd's Garden Seeds
30 Irene Street
Torrington, CT 06790
(860) 482-3638

Stokes Seeds, Inc.
Box 548
Buffalo, NY 14240
(716) 695-6980
Catalogue: free

Thompson & Morgan, Inc.
Box 1308
Jackson, NJ 08527

(800) 274-7333
Catalogue: free

Wayside Gardens
Hodges, SC 29695
(800) 845-1124
Catalogue: free

White Flower Farm
Route 63
Litchfield, CT 06759
(203) 496-9600
Catalogue: $4.00

# African Violets and Other Gesneriads

*Organizations*

African Violet Society of America, Inc.
2375 North Street
Beaumont, TX 77702
(409) 839-4725
(800) 770-AVSA
Dues: $18.00
Publication: *African Violet*
(bimonthly magazine)

African Violet Society of Canada
c/o Bonnie Scanlan
1573 Arbourdale Avenue
Victoria, British Columbia V8N 5J1
(604) 477-7561
Dues: Canada $12.00; US $14.00
Publication: *Chatter* (quarterly)

American Gloxinia and Gesneriad
Society, Inc.
Horticultural Society of New York
128 West 58th Street
New York, NY 10019
Dues: $20.00
Publication: *The Gloxinian*
(bimonthly journal)

Gesneriad Correspondence Club
207 Wycoff Way West
East Brunswick, NJ 08816
Dues: $5.00
Publication: bimonthly newsletter

Gesneriad Hybridizers Association
Meg Stephenson
4115 Pillar Drive, Route 1
Whitmore Lake, MI 48189
Dues: $5.00
Publication: *Crosswords*

Gesneriad Research Foundation
1873 Oak Street
Sarasota, FL 34236

Gesneriad Society International
Richard Dunn
11510 124th Terrace North
Largo, FL 34648
(813) 585-4247
Dues: $16.50
Publication: *Gesneriad Journal*
(bimonthly)

Royal Saintpaulia Club
c/o Ms. A. Moffett
Box 198
Sussex, New Brunswick E0E 1P0

Saintpaulia and Houseplant Society
The Secretary
33 Church Road, Newbury Park
Ilford, Essex 1G2 7ET
England
(081) 590-3710
Dues: £5.00
Publication: quarterly bulletin

Saintpaulia International
1650 Cherry Hill Road South
State College, PA 16803
(814) 237-7410
Publication: *Saintpaulia International News*
(bimonthly)

## Supplies and Tools

CMI Plastics
Box 369
Cranbury, NJ 08512
(609) 395-1920
Product: Humidi-Grow plant trays
Catalogue: free

Dyna-Gro™ Corporation
1065 Broadway
San Pablo, CA 94806
(800) DYNA-GRO
Product: Dyna-Gro™ fertilizer
Catalogue: free

Innis Violets
8 Madison Lane
Lynnfield, MA 01904
Products: growing supplies
and terrariums
Catalogue: $1.00

JF Industries
CHR 65, Box 309
Pryor, OK 74361
(918) 434-6768
Product: leaf supports
Catalogue: long SASE

Source Technology Biologicals, Inc.
(800) 356-8733
Product: Phyton® 27 fungicide

V-Base
920 Leland Avenue
Lima, OH 45805
Product: plant-finding computer database

Violet Express
1440–41 Everett Road
Eagle River, WI 54521
(715) 479-3099
Products: general supplies
Catalogue: $2.75

The Violet House
Box 1274
Gainesville, FL 32602
(904) 377-8465
Products: general supplies
Catalogue: free

The Violet Showcase
3147 South Broadway
Englewood, CO 80110
(303) 761-1770
Products: violet grooming kit;
general supplies
Catalogue: $1.00

W. F. G. & Associates
3345 Owens Brook Way
Kennesaw, GA 30152
(770) 974-0883
Product: Freedom® Planter

## Plant Sources

A-mi Violettes
Box 630, 75 Marier Street
St.-Felix de Valois, Quebec J0K 2M0
(514) 889-8673
Catalogue: $2.00

African Queen
2351 Ballycastle Drive
Dallas, TX 75228
(214) 320-4944
Catalogue: $2.00

Alice's Violet Room
Route 6, Box 233
Waynesville, MO 65583
(314) 336-4763
Catalogue: long SASE

Belisle's Violet House
Box 111
Radisson, WI 54867
(715) 945-2687
Catalogue: $2.00

Big Sky Violets
10678 Schoolhouse Lane
Moiese, MT 59824
(406) 644-2296
Catalogue: $2.50

Cape Cod Violetry
28 Minot Street
Falmouth, MA 02540
(508) 548-2798
Catalogue: $2.00

Coda Gardens
Box 8417
Fredericksburg, VA 22404
Catalogue: $2.00

Florals of Fredericks
155 Spartan Drive
Maitland, FL 32751
Catalogue: $2.00

Hidden Valley Sinningias
Box 862
Indian Hills, CO 80454
(303) 697-4293
Catalogue: $1.00

JoS Violets
2205 College Drive
Victoria, TX 77901
(512) 575-1344
Catalogue: long SASE

Just Enough Sinningias
Patti Schwindt
Box 560493
Orlando, FL 32856
(407) 423-4750
Catalogue: $2.00

Karleens Achimenes
1407 West Magnolia
Valdosta, GA 31601
(912) 242-1368
Catalogue: $1.50

Kartuz Greenhouses
1408 Sunset Drive
Vista, CA 92083
(619) 941-3613
Catalogue: $2.00

Kent's Flowers
2501 East 23rd Avenue
Fremont, NE 68025
(402) 721-1478
Catalogue: 50¢

Lauray of Salisbury
432 Undermountain Road
Salisbury, CT 06068
(203) 435-2263
Catalogue: $2.00

Les Violettes Natalia
Box 206
Beecher Falls, VT 05902
(819) 889-3235
Catalogue: $2.00

Lyndon Lyon Greenhouses, Inc.
14 Mutchler Street
Dolgeville, NY 13329
(315) 429-8291
Catalogue: $2.00

McKinney's Glasshouse
89 Mission Road
Wichita, KS 67207
(316) 686-9438
Catalogue: $2.00

Mighty Minis
7318 Sahara Court
Sacramento, CA 95828
Catalogue: $2.00

Pat's Pets
Dunlap Enterprises
4189 Jarvis Road
Hillsboro, MO 63050
Catalogue: $1.00

Pleasant Hill African Violets
Route 1, Box 73
Brenham, TX 77833
(409) 836-9736
Catalogue: $1.50

Rob's Mini-o-lets
Box 9
Naples, NY 14512
(716) 374-8592
Catalogue: $1.00

Rozell Rose Nursery & Violet Boutique
12206 Highway 31 West
Tyler, TX 75709
(903) 595-5137
Catalogue: $1.00

Teas Nursery Company, Inc.
Box 1603
Bellaire, TX 77402
(800) 446-7723
Catalogue: $2.00

Tiki Nursery
Box 187
Fairview, NC 28730
(704) 628-2212
Catalogue: $2.00

Tinari Greenhouses
Box 190
2325 Valley Road
Huntington Valley, PA 19006
(215) 947-0144
Catalogue: $1.00

Travis' Violets
Box 42
Ochlocknee, GA 31773
(912) 574-5167
Catalogue: $1.00

Violet Creations
5520 Wilkins Road
Tampa, FL 33610

(813) 626-6817
Catalogue: free

Violet Express
1440–41 Everett Road
Eagle River, WI 54521
(715) 479-3099
Catalogue: $2.75

The Violet House
Box 1274
Gainesville, FL 32602
(904) 377-8465
Catalogue: free

Violets by Appointment
45 3rd Street
West Sayville, NY 11796
(516) 589-2724
Catalogue: $1.50

Violets Collectible
1571 Wise Road
Lincoln, CA 95648
(916) 645-3487
Catalogue: $2.00

The Violet Showcase
3147 South Broadway
Englewood, CO 80110
(303) 761-1770
Catalogue: $1.00

Volkmann Brothers Greenhouses
2714 Minert Street
Dallas, TX 75219
(214) 526-3484
Catalogue: $1.00

Weiss' Gesneriads
2293 South Taylor Road
Cleveland Heights, OH 44118
Catalogue: free

Jim Wildman
133 Rosemont Drive

Syracuse, NY 13205
(315) 492-2562
Catalogue: $1.00

## Alpine Plants
*See chapter 2,* **Alpine and Rock Gardening**

## Azaleas, Rhododendrons, and Woody Shrubs

*Organizations*

American Rhododendron Society
Barbara R. Hall, Executive Director
Box 1380
Gloucester, VA 23061
(804) 693-4433
Dues: $25.00
Publication: *Journal of the ARS* (quarterly)

Azalea Society of America, Inc.
Membership Chair
Box 34536
West Bethesda, MD 20827
(301) 585-5269
Dues: $20.00
Publication: *The Azalean* (quarterly)

Rhododendron Society of Canada
c/o R. S. Dickhout
5200 Timothy Crescent
Niagara Falls, Ontario L2E 5G3
(416) 357-5981
Note: *See* American Rhododendron Society

Rhododendron Species Foundation
Box 3798
Federal Way, WA 98063
(206) 838-4646
Dues: $30.00
Publication: *RSF Newsletter* (quarterly)

Woody Plant Society
c/o Betty Ann Mech
1315 66th Avenue NE

Minneapolis, MN 55432
(612) 574-1197
Dues: $15.00
Publication: *Bulletin* (biannual)

*Plant Sources*

Appalachian Gardens
Box 82
Waynesboro, PA 17268
(717) 762-4312
Catalogue: free

A Sandy Rhododendron
41610 SE Coalman Road
Sandy, OR 97055
(503) 668-4830
Catalogue: $5.00

Warren Baldsiefen
Box 88
Bellvale, NY 10912
Catalogue: $3.00

Barbour Bros., Inc.
RD 2
Stoneboro, PA 16153
Catalogue: free

Vernon Barnes & Son
Box 250
McMinnville, TN 37110
Catalogue: $3.00

Beaver Creek Nursery
Box 18243
Knoxville, TN 37928
(615) 922-3961
Catalogue: $1.00

Benjamin's Rhododendrons
Box 147
Sumner, WA 98390
Catalogue: $3.00

The Bovees Nursery
1737 SW Coronado
Portland, OR 97219
(800) 435-9250
Catalogue: $2.00

Briarwood Gardens
14 Gully Lane
East Sandwich, MA 02537
(508) 888-2146
Catalogue: $1.00

Broken Arrow Nursery
13 Broken Arrow Road
Hamden, CT 06518
(203) 288-1026
Catalogue: long SASE with three stamps

Brown's Kalmia and Azalea Nursery
8527 Semihamoo Drive
Blaine, WA 98230
(206) 371-2489
Catalogue: long SASE

Bull Valley Rhododendron Nursery
214 Bull Valley Road
Aspers, PA 17304
(717) 677-6313
Catalogue: $2.00

Camellia Forest Nursery
125 Carolina Forest
Chapel Hill, NC 27516
Catalogue: $1.00

Cape Cod Vireyas
405 Jones Road
Falmouth, MA 02540
(508) 548-1613
Catalogue: $3.00

Cardinal Nursery
Route 1, Box 316
State Road, NC 28676
Catalogue: $3.00

Carlson's Gardens
Box 305
South Salem, NY 10590
(914) 763-5958
Catalogue: $3.00

The Cummins Garden
22 Robertsville Road
Marlboro, NJ 07746
(908) 536-2591
Catalogue: $1.00

Phillip Curtis Farms
Box 640
Canby, OR 97013
Catalogue: $1.00

Eastern Plant Specialties
Box 226
Georgetown, ME 04548
(207) 371-2888
Catalogue: $3.00

Flora Lan Nursery
Route 1, Box 357
Forest Grove, OR 97116
Catalogue: $3.00

Forest Farm
990 Tetherow Road
Williams, OR 97544
(503) 846-7269
Catalogue: $3.00

Garver Gardens
Box 609
Laytonville, CA 95454
(707) 984-6724
Catalogue: free

Girard Nurseries
Box 428
Geneva, OH 44041
(216) 466-2881
Catalogue: free

Gossler Farms Nursery
1200 Weaver Road
Springfield, OR 97477
(503) 746-3922
Catalogue: $2.00

The Greenery
1451 West Burdickville Road
Maple City, MI 49664
(616) 228-7037
Catalogue: free

Greer Gardens
1280 Goodpasture Island Road
Eugene, OR 97401
(800) 548-0111
Catalogue: $3.00

Hager Nurseries
RFD 5, Box 2000
Spotsylvania, VA 22553
Catalogue: 50¢

Hall Rhododendrons
1280 Quince Drive
Junction City, OR 97448
Catalogue: $1.00

Hammond's Acres of Rhodys
25911 70th Avenue NE
Arlington, WA 98223
(206) 435-9206
Catalogue: $2.00

James Harris Hybrid Azaleas
538 Swanson Drive
Lawrenceville, GA 30243
(404) 963-7463
Catalogue: long SASE

Hillhouse Nursery
90 Kresson-Gibbsboro Road
Voorhees, NJ 08043
(609) 784-6203
Catalogue: free

Holbrook Farm and Nursery
Box 368
115 Lance Road
Fletcher, NC 28732
(704) 891-7790
Catalogue: free

Homeplace Garden Nursery
Box 300
Harden Bridge Road
Commerce, GA 30529
(706) 335-2892
Catalogue: $2.00

Kellygreen Rhododendron Nursery
6924 Highway 38
Drain, OR 97435
(503) 836-2290
Catalogue: $1.25

Lamtree Farm
RR 1, Box 162
2323 Copeland Road
Warrensville, NC 28693
(910) 385-6144
Catalogue: $2.00

E. B. Nauman and Daughter
688 St. Davids Lane
Schenectady, NY 12309
(518) 276-6726
Catalogue: $1.00

North Coast Rhododendron Nursery
Box 308
Bodega, CA 94922
(707) 829-0600
Catalogue: $1.00

Nuccio's Nurseries
Box 6160
3555 Chaney Trail
Altadena, CA 91003
(818) 794-3383
Catalogue: free

Oak Hill Farm
204 Pressly Street
Clover, SC 29710
(803) 222-4245
Catalogue: $1.00

Red's Rhodies
15920 SW Oberst Lane
Sherwood, OR 97140
(503) 625-6331
Catalogue: long SASE with two stamps

Schild Azalea Gardens and Nursery
1705 Longview Street
Hixson, TN 37343
(615) 842-9686
Catalogue: $1.00

F. W. Schumacher Company, Inc.
36 Spring Hill Road
Sandwich, MA 02563
(508) 888-0659
Catalogue: free

Shepherd Hill Farm
200 Peekskill Hollow Road
Putnam Valley, NY 10579
(914) 528-5917
Catalogue: free

Sonoma Horticultural Nursery
3970 Azalea Avenue
Sebastopol, CA 95472
Catalogue: $2.00

Sorum's Nursery
18129 SW Belton Road
Sherwood, OR 97140
(503) 628-2354
Catalogue: long SASE

Southern Plants
Box 232
Semmes, AL 36575
Catalogue: $1.50

Stubbs Shrubs
23225 SW Bosky Dell Lane
West Linn, OR 97068
(503) 638-5048
Catalogue: $2.00

Sun, Wind & Rain
Box 505
Silverton, OR 97381
(503) 873-5541
Catalogue: free

Transplant Nursery
Parkertown Road
Lavonia, GA 30553
(706) 356-8947
Catalogue: $1.00

Westgate Garden Nursery
751 Westgate Drive
Eureka, CA 95503
(707) 442-1239
Catalogue: $4.00

Whitney Gardens and Nursery
Box F
31600 Highway 101
Brinnon, WA 98320
(360) 796-4411
Catalogue: $4.00

# Bamboo

## Organization

American Bamboo Society
666 Wagnon Road
Sebastopol, CA 95472
(518) 765-3507
Dues: $20.00
Publications: *ABS Newsletter* (bimonthly);
*Journal of the ABS* (irregular)

## Publication

*Temperate Bamboo Quarterly*
30 Myers Road
Summertown, TN 38483
(615) 964-4151
Frequency: quarterly
Subscription: $24.00

## Plant Sources

A Bamboo Shoot
1462 Darby Road
Sebastopol, CA 95472
(707) 823-0131
Catalogue: $1.00

American Bamboo Company
345 West 2nd Street
Dayton, OH 45402
Catalogue: free

Bamboo Gardens of Washington
5015 192nd Place NE
Redmond, WA 98053
(206) 868-5166
Catalogue: $4.00

Bamboo Sourcery
666 Wagnon Road
Sebastopol, CA 95472
(707) 823-5866
Catalogue: $2.00

Kurt Bluemel, Inc.
2740 Greene Lane
Baldwin, MD 21013
(410) 557-7229
Catalogue: $3.00

Burt Associates Bamboo
Box 719
Westford, MA 01886
(508) 692-3240
Catalogue: $2.00

Endangered Species
Box 1830
Tustin, CA 92680
Catalogue: $6.00

New England Bamboo Company
Box 358
Rockport, MA 01966
(508) 546-3581
Catalogue: $2.00

Northern Groves
Box 86291
Portland, OR 97286
(503) 774-6353
Catalogue: $1.00

Raintree Nursery
393B Butts Road
Morton, WA 98356
(206) 496-6400
Catalogue: free

Steve Ray's Bamboo Gardens
909 79th Place South
Birmingham, AL 35206
(205) 833-2052
Catalogue: $2.00

Tornello Landscape
Box 788
Ruskin, FL 33570
(813)645-5445
Catalogue: $1.00

Tradewinds Nursery
28446 Hunter Creek Loop
Gold Beach, OR 97444
(503) 247-0835
Catalogue: long SASE

Upper Bank Nurseries
Box 486
670 South Ridley Creek Road
Media, PA 19063

(215) 566-0679
Catalogue: long SASE

# Begonias

## Organizations

American Begonia Society
c/o John Ingle, Jr.
157 Monument Road
Rio Bell, CA 95562
(707) 764-5407
Dues: $21.00
Publication: *The Begonian*
 (bimonthly magazine)

British Columbia Fuchsia and Begonia
Society
c/o Lorna Herchenson
2402 Swinburne Avenue
North Vancouver, British Columbia
V7H 1L2
(604) 929-5382
Dues: Canada $10.00
Publication: *The Eardrop*
 (11 times annually)

Canadian Begonia Society
70 Enfield Avenue
Toronto, Ontario M8W 1T9
Dues: Canada $20.00

## Plant Sources

Antonelli Brothers
2545 Capitola Road
Santa Cruz, CA 95062
(408) 475-5222
Catalogue: $1.00

B & K Tropicals
5300 48th Terrace North
St. Petersburg, FL 33709
(813) 522-8691
Catalogue: $1.00

Cruickshank's, Inc.
1015 Mount Pleasant Road
Toronto, Ontario M4P 2M1
(416) 488-8292
(800) 665-5605
Catalogue: $3.00

Daisy Farm
9995 SW 66th Street
Miami, FL 33173
(305) 274-9813
Catalogue: $2.00

Fairyland Begonia and Lily Garden
1100 Griffith Road
McKinleyville, CA 95521
(707) 839-3034
Specialties: hybrid lilies
Catalogue: 50¢

Golden Hills Nursery
Box 247, Macdoel, CA 96058
(916) 398-4023
Catalogue: $2.00

Kartuz Greenhouses
1408 Sunset Drive
Vista, CA 92083
(619) 941-3613
Catalogue: $2.00

Kay's Greenhouses
207 West Southcross
San Antonio, TX 78221
Catalogue: $2.00

Lauray of Salisbury
432 Undermountain Road
Salisbury, CT 06068
(203) 435-2263
Catalogue: $2.00

Logee's Greenhouses
141 North Street
Danielson, CT 06239
Catalogue: $3.00

Paul P. Lowe
5741 Dewberry Way
West Palm Beach, FL 33415
(407) 686-9392
Catalogue: long SASE

Miree's
70 Enfield Avenue
Toronto, Ontario M8W 1T9
(416) 251-6369
Catalogue: $2.00

Palos Verdes Begonia Farm
4111 242nd Street
Torrance, CA 90505
(800) 349-9299
Catalogue: $2.00

Sunshine State Tropicals
Box 1033
Port Richey, FL 34673
(813) 841-9618
Catalogue: $1.00

Van Bourgondien Bros.
245 Farmingdale Road
Babylon, NY 11702-0598
(516) 669-3500
(800) 622-9997
Catalogue: free

Vicki's Exotic Plants
522 Vista Park Drive
Eagle Point, OR 97524
(503) 826-6318
Catalogue: $1.00

White Flower Farm
Box 63
Litchfield, CT 06759
(203) 496-9600
Catalogue: $4.00

# Bog Plants
*See chapter 2,* **Water Gardening**

# Bonsai
*See chapter 2,* **Bonsai**

# Bromeliads and Epiphytic Plants
*See also chapter 2,* **Orchids**

## Organizations

Bromeliad Society, Inc.
2488 East 49th Street
Tulsa, OK 74105
Dues: $20.00
Publication: *BSI Journal* (bimonthly)

The Cryptanthus Society
2355 Rusk
Beaumont, TX 77702
(409) 835-0644
Dues: $10.00
Publications: *The Cryptanthus Journal*
 (quarterly); *Yearbook*

Epiphyllum Society of America
Betty Berg, Membership Secretary
Box 1395
Monrovia, CA 91017
(818) 447-9688
Dues: $10.00
Publication: *The Bulletin* (bimonthly)

Epiphytic Plant Study Group
c/o Dr. Seymour Linden
1535 Reeves Street
Los Angeles, CA 90035
(310) 556-1923
Dues: $12.50
Publication: *Epiphytes* (journal)

## Plant Sources

Alberts and Merkel Brothers
2210 South Federal Highway
Boynton Beach, FL 33435
(407) 732-2071
Catalogue: $1.00

Don Beadle
First Dirt Road
Venice, FL 34292
(813) 485-1096
Specialties: billbergias
Catalogue: SASE

Bird Rock Tropicals
6523 El Camino Real
Carlsbad, CA 92009
(619) 438-9393
Specialties: tillandsias
Catalogue: long SASE

Arthur Boe Distributor
Box 6655
New Orleans, LA 70114
Specialties: tillandsias
Catalogue: SASE

City Gardens
451 West Lincoln
Madison Heights, MI 48071
(313) 398-2660
Catalogue: $2.00

Colin's Nursery
448 North Lake Pleasant Road
Apopka, FL 32712
(407) 886-2982
Specialties: cryptanthus
Catalogue: $1.00

Cornelison Bromeliads
225 San Bernardino Street
North Fort Myers, FL 33903
(813) 995-4206
Catalogue: SASE

Dane Company
4626 Lamont Street
Corpus Christi, TX 78411
(512) 852-3806
Catalogue: long SASE

Epi World
10607 Glenview Avenue
Cupertino, CA 95014
(408) 865-0566
Catalogue: $2.00

Fox Orchids, Inc.
6615 West Markham Street
Little Rock, AR 72205
(501) 663-4246
Catalogue: free

Golden Lake Greenhouses
10782 Citrus Drive
Moorpark, CA 93021
(805) 529-3620
Catalogue: $2.00

Gray/Davis Epiphyllums
Box 710443
Santee, CA 92072
(619) 448-2540
Catalogue: $2.00

Holladay Jungle
Box 5727
1602 East Fountain Way
Fresno, CA 93755
(209) 229-9858
Specialties: tillandsias
Catalogue: free

Kenner & Sons
10919 Explorer Road
La Mesa, CA 91941
(619) 660-0161
Catalogue: free

Lauray of Salisbury
432 Undermountain Road
Salisbury, CT 06068
(203) 435-2263
Catalogue: $2.00

Ann Mann's Orchids
9045 Ron-Den Lane

Windermere, FL 34786
(407) 876-2625
Catalogue: $1.00

Marilyn's Garden
13421 Sussex Place
Santa Ana, CA 92705
(714) 633-1375
Catalogue: $2.00

Michael's Bromeliads
1365 Canterbury Road North
St. Petersburg, FL 33710
(813) 347-0349
Catalogue: long SASE

Northwest Epi Center
2735 SE Troutdale Road
Troutdale, OR 97060
(503) 666-4171
Catalogue: $2.00

Oak Hill Gardens
Box 25
Dundee, IL 60118
(708) 428-8500
Catalogue: $1.00

Pineapple Place
3961 Markham Woods Road
Longwood, FL 32779
(407) 333-0445
Catalogue: long SASE

Rainbow Gardens Nursery and Bookshop
1444 East Taylor Street
Vista, CA 92084
(619) 758-4290
Catalogue: $2.00

Rainforest Flora
1927 West Rosecrans Avenue
Gardena, CA 90249
(310) 515-5200
Catalogue: $2.00

Russell's Bromeliads
1690 Beardall Avenue
Sanford, FL 32771
(800) 832-5632
Specialties: tillandsias
Catalogue: SASE

Shelldance Nursery
2000 Highway 1
Pacifica, CA 94044
(415) 355-4845
Catalogue: $1.00

Southern Exposure
35 Minor Street
Beaumont, TX 77702
(409) 835-0644
Specialties: cryptanthus
Catalogue: $5.00

Tropiflora
3530 Tallevast Road
Sarasota, FL 34243
(813) 351-2267
Specialties: tillandsias
Catalogue: free

# Bulbs
*See also* **Daffodils**

## Organization

International Bulb Society
Box 4928
Culver City, CA 90230
Dues: $30.00
Publication: *Herbertia* (annual journal)

## Plant Sources

Jacques Amand
Box 59001
Potomac, MD 20859
(301) 762-2942
(800) 452-5414

Specialties: spring and summer bloomers
Catalogue: $2.00

Amaryllis, Inc.
Box 318
1452 Glenmore Avenue
Baton Rouge, LA 70821
(504) 924-5560
Specialties: amaryllis
Catalogue: $1.00

Autumn Glade Botanicals
46857 West Ann Arbor Trail
Plymouth, MI 48170
Specialties: summer bloomers
Catalogue: free

Bio-Quest International
Box 5752
Santa Barbara, CA 93150
(805) 969-4072
Specialties: South African bulbs
Catalogue: $2.00

Breck's
U.S. Reservation Center
6523 North Galena Road
Peoria, IL 61656
(800) 722-9069
Specialties: spring bloomers
Catalogue: free

The Bulb Crate
2560 Deerfield Road
Riverwoods, IL 60015
(708) 317-1414
Catalogue: $1.00

Bundles of Bulbs
112 Greenspring Valley Road
Owings Mills, MD 21117
(410) 363-1371
Specialties: spring bloomers
Catalogue: $1.00

Cruickshank's, Inc.
1015 Mount Pleasant Road
Toronto, Ontario M4P 2M1
(416) 488-8292
(800) 665-5605
Specialties: spring and summer bloomers
Catalogue: $3.00

The Daffodil Mart
1004 Daffodil Lane
Route 3, Box 794
Gloucester, VA 23601
(804) 693-3966
Catalogue: free

Peter deJager Bulb Company
Box 2010
188 Asbury Street
South Hamilton, MA 01982
(508) 468-4707
Specialties: Dutch bulbs
Catalogue: free

Dick's Flower Farm
North 5028 Delaney Road
Delavan, WI 53115
(414) 724-5682
Specialties: summer bloomers
Catalogue: $1.00

Jim Duggan Flower Nursery
1817 Sheridan
Leucadia, CA 92024
(619) 943-1658
Specialties: South African bulbs
Catalogue: $2.00

Dunford Farms
Box 238
Sumner, WA 98390
Specialties: agapanthus, alstromerias,
cyclamens
Catalogue: $1.00

Dutch Gardens, Inc.
Box 200
Adelphia, NJ 07710
(908) 780-2713
(800) 818-3861
Specialties: Dutch bulbs, summer
bloomers
Catalogue: free

Flowers & Greens
Box 1802
Davis, CA 95617
(916) 756-9238
Specialties: alstromerias, gladioli, freesias
Catalogue: $2.00

Howard B. French Bulb Importer
Route 100
Pittsfield, VT 05762
(802) 746-8148
Specialties: spring bloomers
Catalogue: free

Russell Graham, Purveyor of Plants
4030 Eagle Crest Road NW
Salem, OR 97304
(503) 362-1135
Specialties: species bulbs
Catalogue: $2.00

GreenLady Gardens
1415 Eucalyptus Drive
San Francisco, CA 94132
(415) 753-3332
Specialties: spring and summer bloomers
Catalogue: $3.00

Growers Service Company
10118 Crouse Street
Hartland, MI 48353
Specialties: species and exotic bulbs
Catalogue: $5.00

Holland Bulb Farm
354 Old Hook Road
Westwood, New Jersey 06765

(201) 391-3499
Catalogue: free

Holland Bulb Farm, Inc.
Box 220
Tatamy, PA 18085
(800) 283-5082
Catalogue: free

Jackson & Perkins Company
2518 South Pacific Highway
Medford, OR 97501
(800) 292-4769
Specialties: spring bloomers
Catalogue: free

Kelly's Plant World
10266 East Princeton
Sanger, CA 93657
(209) 294-7676
Specialties: summer bloomers
Catalogue: $1.00

John D. Lyon
143 Alewife Brook Parkway
Cambridge, MA 02140
Catalogue: $3.00

Mad River Imports
RR 1, Box 1695
Rankin Road
Moretown, VT 05660
(802) 496-3004
Specialties: spring bloomers
Catalogue: free

McClure & Zimmerman
Box 368
108 West Winnebago
Friesland, WI 53935
(414) 326-4220
Specialties: Dutch and species bulbs
Catalogue: free

Messelaar Bulb Company
Box 269
Ipswich, MA 01938
(508) 356-3737
Specialties: Dutch bulbs
Catalogue: free

Michigan Bulb Company
1950 Waldorf NW
Grand Rapids, MI 49550
Specialties: Dutch bulbs
Catalogue: free

Charles H. Mueller Company
7091 North River Road
New Hope, PA 18938
(215) 862-2033
Specialties: spring and summer bloomers
Catalogue: free

New Holland Bulb Company
Box 335
Rockport, IL 62370
Catalogue: free

Old House Gardens
536 3rd Street
Ann Arbor, MI 48103
(313) 995-1486
Specialties: historical bulbs
Catalogue: $1.00

Robinett Bulb Farm
Box 1306
Sebastopol, CA 95473
(707) 829-2729
Specialties: West Coast–native bulbs
Catalogue: free

John Scheepers, Inc.
Box 700
Bantam, CT 06750
(203) 567-0838
Specialties: spring and summer bloomers
Catalogue: free

Schipper & Co., USA
Box 7584
Greenwich, CT 06836-7584
(203) 625-0638
(800) 877-8637
Specialties: spring bloomers
Catalogue: free

Skolaski's Glads and Field Flowers
4821 County Highway Q
Waunakee, WI 53597
(608) 836-4822
Specialties: summer bloomers
Catalogue: free

Sunsweet Bulb Company
Box Z
Sumner, GA 31789
(912) 386-2211
Catalogue: $1.00

Ty Ty Plantation Bulbs
Box 159
Ty Ty, GA 31795
(912) 382-0404
Specialties: spring and summer bloomers
Catalogue: $2.00

Van Bourgondien Bros.
Box 1000
245 Farmingdale Road
Babylon, NY 11702
(516) 669-3500
(800) 622-9997
Specialties: spring and summer bloomers
Catalogue: free

Van Dyck's Flower Farms, Inc.
Box 430-4033
Brightwaters, NY 11718-9831
(800) 248-2852
Specialties: spring bloomers
Catalogue: free

Van Engelen, Inc.
Stillbrook Farm

313 Maple Street
Litchfield, CT 06759
(203) 567-8734
Catalogue: free

VanLierop Bulb Farm
13407 80th Street East
Puyallup, WA 98372
(206) 848-7272
Catalogue: $1.00

Mary Mattison van Schaik
Box 32
Cavendish, VT 05412
(802) 226-7653
Specialties: Dutch bulbs
Catalogue: $1.00

Veldheer Tulip Gardens
12755 Quincy Street
Holland, MI 49424
(616) 399-1900
Specialties: Dutch bulbs
Catalogue: free

Mary Walker Bulb Company
Box 256
Omega, GA 31775
(912) 386-1919
Catalogue: $1.00

The Waushara Gardens
N5491 5th Drive
Plainfield, WI 54966
(715) 335-4462
Specialties: summer bloomers
Catalogue: $1.00

White Flower Farm
Route 63
Litchfield, CT 06759
(203) 469-9600
Specialties: spring and summer bloomers
Catalogue: $4.00

Wildflower Nursery
1680 Highway 25-70
Marshall, NC 28753
(704) 656-2681
Specialties: Southeast-native plants
Catalogue: $1.00

# Cacti and Succulents

## Organizations

British Cactus and Succulent Society
Mr. P. A. Lewis, FBCSS
Firgrove, 1 Springwoods, Courtmoor
Fleet, Hants. GU13 9SU
England
Dues: £13.00
Publications: *British Cactus and Succulent Journal* (quarterly); *Bradleya* (annual)

Cactus and Succulent Society of America
c/o Dr. Seymour Linden
1535 Reeves Street
Los Angeles, CA 90035
(310) 556-1923
Dues: $30.00
Publication: *Cactus & Succulent Journal* (bimonthly)

Desert Plant Society of Vancouver
6200 McKay Avenue, Box 145-790
Barnaby, British Columbia V5H 4MY
(604) 525-5315
Dues: Canada $15.00

Toronto Cactus and Succulent Club
David Naylor
RR 2
9091 8th Line Road
Georgetown, Ontario L7G 4S5
(416) 877-6013
Dues: Canada $20.00
Publication: *Cactus Factus*

## Publications

*The Amateur's Digest*
Marina Welham, Editor
8591 Lochside Drive
Sidney, British Columbia V8L 1M5
Frequency: bimonthly
Subscription: US $20.00

*Desert Plants*
Boyce Thompson Southwestern
Arboretum
Box AB
Superior, AZ 85273
(602) 689-2723
Frequency: quarterly
Subscription: $15.00

## Other Information and Sources

*A free directory of California's cactus nurseries
(wholesale and retail) is available from:*

California Cactus Growers Association
11152 Palm Terrace Lane
Riverside, CA 92505

*Software for managing your cactus collection is
available from:*

Lucio Mondolfo
6563 College Hill Road
Clinton, NY 13323
Programs: CactusBase database; Lexicon
of Cactus Names
System requirements: IBM DOS 3.1+,
4MB RAM

## Plant Sources

Abbey Garden Cactus
Box 2249
La Habra, CA 90632
(805) 684-5112
Catalogue: $3.00

Arid Lands Greenhouses
3560 West Bilby Road
Tucson, AZ 85746
(520) 883-9404
Catalogue: SASE

Aztekakti/Desertland Nursery
Box 26126
11306 Gateway East
El Paso, TX 79926
(915) 858-1130
Catalogue: $1.00

B & B Cactus Farm
11550 East Speedway
Tucson, AZ 85748
(602) 721-4687
Catalogue: SASE

Betsy's Brierpatch
1610 Ellis Hollow Road
Ithaca, NY 14850
(607) 273-6266
Catalogue: long SASE

Blossom Creek Greenhouse
Box 598
North Plain, OR 97133
(503) 647-0915
Catalogue: $2.00

Cactus by Dodie
934 Mettler Road
Lodi, CA 95242
(209) 368-3692
Catalogue: $2.00

Cactus by Mueller
10411 Rosedale Highway
Bakersfield, CA 93312
(805) 589-2674
Catalogue: $2.00

Cactus Farm
Route 5, Box 1610
Nacogdoches, TX 75961

(409) 560-6406
Catalogue: free

Christa's Cactus
529 West Pima
Coolidge, AZ 85228
(602) 723-4185
Catalogue: $1.00

Desert Moon Nursery
Box 600
Veguita, NM 87062
(505) 864-0614
Catalogue: $1.00

Desert Nursery
1301 South Copper
Deming, NM  88030
(505) 546-6264
Catalogue: free

Desert Theatre
17 Behler Road
Watsonville, CA 95076
(408) 728-5513
Catalogue: $2.00

The Great Petaluma Desert
5010 Bodega Avenue
Petaluma, CA 94952
(707) 778-8278
Catalogue: $3.00

Grigsby Cactus Gardens
2326 Bella Vista
Vista, CA 92084
(619) 727-1323
Catalogue: $2.00

Henrietta's Nursery
1345 North Brawley
Fresno, CA 93722
(209) 275-2166
Catalogue: $1.00

Highland Succulents
1446 Bear Run Road
Gallipolis, OH 45631
(614) 256-1428
Catalogue: $2.00

Intermountain Cactus
1478 North 750 East
Kaysville, UT 84037
(801) 546-2006
Catalogue: long SASE

K & L Cactus and Succulent Nursery
9500 Brook Ranch Road East
Ione, CA 95640
(209) 274-0360
Catalogue: $3.00

Lauray of Salisbury
432 Undermountain Road
Salisbury, CT 06068
(203) 435-2263
Catalogue: $2.00

Living Stones Nursery
2936 North Stone
Tucson, AZ 85705
(602) 628-8773
Specialties: lithops and mesembs
Catalogue: $2.00

Loehman's Cactus Patch
Box 871
Paramount, CA 90723
(310) 428-4501
Catalogue: $1.00

Mesa Garden
Box 72
Belen, NM 87002
(505) 864-3131
Catalogue: two stamps

Midwest Cactus
Box 163
New Melle, MO 63365

(314) 828-5389
Specialties: opuntias
Catalogue: $1.00

Miles' To Go
Box 6
Cortaro, AZ 85652
Catalogue: free

Nature's Curiosity Shop
3551 Evening Canyon Road
Oceanside, CA 92056
Specialties: succulents
Catalogue: $1.00

New Mexico Cactus Research
Box 787
1132 East River Road
Belen, NM 87002
(505) 864-4027
Catalogue: $1.00

New Mexico Desert Garden
10231 Belnap NW
Albuquerque, NM 87114
(505) 898-0121
Catalogue: $2.00

Northridge Gardens
9821 White Oak Avenue
Northridge, CA 91325
(818) 349-9798
Specialties: succulents
Catalogue: $1.00

Plantasia Cactus Gardens
867 Filer Avenue West
Twin Falls, ID 83301
(208) 734-7959
Specialties: winter-hardy cacti
Catalogue:two stamps

Plants of the Southwest
Agua Fria
Route 6, Box 11
Santa Fe, NM 87505

(800) 788-SEED
Catalogue: $3.50

Rainbow Gardens Nursery and Bookshop
1444 Taylor Street
Vista, CA 92084
(619) 758-4290
Catalogue: $2.00

Rare Plant Research
13245 SE Harold
Portland, OR 97236
Specialties: rare succulents
Catalogue: $2.00

Redlo Cacti
2315 NW Circle Boulevard
Corvallis, OR 97330
(503) 752-2910
Catalogue: $2.00

Schulz Cactus Growers
1095 Easy Street
Morgan Hill, CA 95037
(408) 683-4489
Catalogue: free

Scotty's Desert Plants
Box 1017
Selma, CA 93662
(209) 891-1026
Catalogue: $1.00

The Seed Shop
Tongue River Stage
Miles City, MT 59301
Specialties: seeds
Catalogue: $2.00

Shein's Cactus
3360 Drew Street
Marina, CA 93933
(408) 384-7765
Catalogue: $1.00

Bob Smoley's Gardenworld
4038 Watters Lane
Gibsonia, PA 15044
(412) 443-6770
Catalogue: SASE

Southwestern Exposure
10310 East Fennimore
Apache Junction, AZ 85220
(602) 986-7771
Catalogue: two stamps

Strong's Alpine Succulents
Box 50115
Parks, AZ 86018
(602) 526-5784
Catalogue: $1.00

Succulenta
Box 480325
Los Angeles, CA 90048
(213) 933-1552
Catalogue: $1.00

Sunrise Nursery
13705 Pecan Hollow
Leander, TX 78641
(512) 259-1877
Catalogue: $1.00

Winter Country Cacti
Box 296
Littleton, CO 80160
Catalogue: $2.00

# Caladiums

*Plant Sources*

Caladium World
Drawer 629
Sebring, FL 33871
(813) 385-7661
Catalogue: free

Fancy Leaf Caladiums
704 County Road 621 East
Lake Placid, FL 33852
(813) 465-0044
Catalogue: free

Rainbow Acres
Box 1362
Avon Park, FL 33825
(813) 382-4449
Catalogue: free

Spaulding Bulb Farm
1811 Howey Road
Sebring, FL 33872
Catalogue: $1.00

# Camellias

*Organizations*

American Camellia Society
Massee Lane Gardens
1 Massee Lane
Fort Valley, GA 31030
(912) 967-2358
Dues: $20.00
Publication: *The Camellia Journal*
(quarterly)

International Camellia Society
c/o Thomas H. Perkins III
Box 750
Brookhaven, MS 39601
(601) 833-7351
Dues: $13.00
Publication: *International Camellia Journal*
(annual)

Southern California Camellia Society
c/o Mrs. Bobbie Belcher
7457 Brydon Road
La Verne, CA 91750

## Plant Sources

Camellia Forest Nursery
125 Carolina Forest
Chapel Hill, NC 27516
Catalogue: $1.00

Erinon Nursery
Box 325
Plymouth, FL 32768
(407) 886-7917
Catalogue: SASE

Fairweather Gardens
Box 330
Greenwich, NJ 08323
(609) 451-6261
Catalogue: $3.00

Nuccio's Nurseries
Box 6160
3555 Chaney Trial
Altadena, CA 91003
(818) 794-3383
Catalogue: free

Valdosta Camellia Scions
2436 Meadowbrook Drive
Valdosta, GA 31602
(912) 242-1390
Catalogue: send want list

Wheelers Nursery, Inc.
Route 20
Macon, GA 31211
(912) 745-3131
Note: no shipping
Catalogue: SASE

Woodlanders, Inc.
1128 Colleton Avenue
Aiken, SC 29801
(803) 648-7522
Catalogue: $2.00

# Campanulas

## Plant Source

Campanula Connoisseur
702 Traver Trail
Glenwood Springs, CO 81601
Catalogue: $1.00

# Cannas

## Plant Sources

Brudy's Exotics
Box 820874
Houston, TX 77282
(800) 926-7333
Catalogue: free

Kelly's Plant World
10266 East Princeton
Sanger, CA 93657
(209) 294-7676
Catalogue: $1.00

Wheel View Farm
212 Reynolds Road
Shelburne, MA 01370
Catalogue: $1.00

# Carnivorous Plants

## Organizations

The Carnivorous Plant Society
174 Baldwins Lane
Croxley Green, Hertfordshire WD3 3LQ
England
Dues: £13.00
Publication: *Journal of the Carnivorous Plant Society* (quarterly)

International Carnivorous Plant Society
Fullerton Arboretum

California State University
Fullerton, CA 92634
(714) 773-2766
Dues: $15.00
Publication: *Carnivorous Plant Newsletter*
(quarterly)

## Plant Sources

Acid-Wetland Flora
1705 North Quebec Street
Arlington, VA 22207
(703) 524-3181
Catalogue: $1.50

Botanique Nursery
Route 1, Box 183
Stanardsville, VA 22973
Catalogue: $1.00

California Carnivores
7020 Trenton-Healdsburg Road
Forestville, CA 95436
(707) 838-1630
Catalogue: $2.00

Carolina Exotic Gardens
Route 5, Box 238A
Greenville, NC 27834
(919) 758-2600
Catalogue: $1.00

Glasshouse Works
Box 97, Church Street
Stewart, OH 45778
(614) 662-2142
Catalogue: $2.00

Hungry Plants
1216 Cooper Drive
Raleigh, NC 27607
(919) 829-3751
Catalogue: free

Lee's Botanical Garden
Box 669

LaBelle, FL 33935
(813) 675-8728
Catalogue: free

Marie's Orchids and Carnivorous Plants
6400 Cedarbrook Drive
Pinellas Park, FL 34666
(813) 546-7882
Catalogue: $1.00

Orgel's Orchids
18950 SW 136th Street
Miami, FL 33196
(305) 233-7168
Catalogue: free

Peter Paul's Nursery
4665 Chapin Road
Canandaigua, NY 14424
(716) 394-7397
Catalogue: free

Chuck Powell
2932 Sunburst Drive
San Jose, CA 95111
(408) 363-0926
Catalogue: $1.00

Southern Carnivores
Box 864081
Marietta, GA 30060
Catalogue: $2.00

Tropiflora
3530 Tallevast Road
Sarasota, FL 34243
(813) 351-2267
Catalogue: free

# Chrysanthemums

## Organizations

Canadian Chrysanthemum and Dahlia
Society

c/o Karen Ojaste
17 Granard Boulevard
Scarborough, Ontario M1M 2E2
(416) 269-6960
Dues: Canada $10.00

National Chrysanthemum Society (UK)
H. B. Locke
2 Lucas House, Craven Road
Rugby, Warwickshire CV21 3HY
England
(0788) 56-9039
Dues: $15.00
Publications: fall and spring bulletins;
yearbook

National Chrysanthemum Society, Inc.
(US)
Galen L. Goss
10107 Homar Pond Drive
Fairfax Station, VA 22039
(703) 978-7981
Dues: $12.50
Publication: *The Chrysanthemum* (quarterly)

## Publication

*Chrysanthemum Corner with Peony Highlights*
Box 5635
Dearborn, MI 48128
Frequency: bimonthly
Subscription: $18.00

## Plant Sources

Dooley Mum Gardens
210 North High Drive NE
Hutchinson, MN 55350
(612) 587-3050
Catalogue: $2.00

Huff's Garden Mums
710 Juniatta
Burlington, KS 66839
(316) 364-2765
(800) 279-4675

Catalogue: $2.00

King's Mums
20303 East Liberty Road
Clements, CA 95227
(209) 759-3571
Catalogue: $2.00

Mums by Paschke
12286 East Main Road
North East, PA 16428
(814) 725-9860
Catalogue: free

Sunnyslope Gardens
8638 Huntington Drive
San Gabriel, CA 91775
(818) 287-4071
Catalogue: free

# Clematis

## Organization

The British Clematis Society
Mrs. B. Risdon, Membership Secretary
The Tropical Bird Gardens, Rode
Bath, Somerset BA3 6QW
England
(0373) 83-0326
Dues: £12.00
Publication: *The Clematis Journal* (annual)

## Plant Sources

Clifford's Perennial and Vine
Route 2, Box 320
East Troy, WI 53120
(414)968-4040

The Compleat Garden—Clematis Nursery
217 Argilla Road
Ipswich, MA 01938-2614
Catalogue: $2.00

Garden Scapes
1840 West 48th Street
Davenport, IA 52806
(800) 690-9858
Catalogue: $3.00

D. S. George Nurseries
2491 Penfield
Fairport, NY 14450
Catalogue: $1.00

Homestead Farms
Route 2, Box 31A
Owensville, MO 65066
(314) 437-4277
Catalogue: free

Arthur H. Steffen, Inc.
Box 184
Fairport, NY 14450
(716) 377-1665
Catalogue: $2.00

# Coleus

*Plant Source*

Color Farm Growers
2710 Thornhill Road
Auburndale, FL 33823
(813) 967-9895
Catalogue: $1.00

# Cyclamens
*See also* **Bulbs**

*Organization*

Cyclamen Society
Dr. D. V. Bent
Little Pilgrims, 2 Pilgrims Way East
Otford, Sevenoaks, Kent TN14 5QN
England
(0959) 52-2322

Dues: £7.00
Publication: *Cyclamen* (semiannual)

*Plant Sources*

Hansen Nursery
Box 446
Donald, OR 97020
(503) 678-5409
Catalogue: long SASE

Kline Nursery Company
Box 23161
Tigrad, OR 97281
(503) 244-3910
Catalogue: $2.00

# Daffodils
*See also* **Bulbs**

*Organizations*

American Daffodil Society, Inc.
c/o Mary Lou Gripshover
1686 Grey Fox Trails
Milford, OH 45150
(513) 248-9137
Dues: $20.00
Publication: *Daffodil Journal* (quarterly)

The Daffodil Society (UK)
c/o Don Barnes
32 Montgomery Avenue
Sheffield S7 1NZ
England
Dues: $15.00

*Plant Sources*

Bonnie Brae Gardens
110 SE Christensen Road
Corbett, OR 97019
(503) 695-5190
Catalogue: long SASE

Cascade Daffodils
Box 10626
White Bear Lake, MN 55110
(612) 426-9616
Catalogue: $2.00

The Daffodil Mart
7463 Heath Trail
Gloucester, VA 23601
(804) 693-3966
Catalogue: $1.00

Grant E. Mitsch Novelty Daffodils
Box 218
Hubbard, OR 97032
(503) 651-2742
Catalogue: $3.00

Oregon Trail Daffodils
41905 SE Louden Road
Corbett, OR 97019
(503) 695-5513
Catalogue: free

Sisters' Bulb Farm
Route 2, Box 170
Gibsland, LA 71028
(318) 843-6379
Catalogue: free

Nancy R. Wilson
6525 Briceland–Thorn Road
Garberville, CA 95542
(707) 923-2407
Specialties: narcissi
Catalogue: $1.00

# Dahlias

## Organizations

American Dahlia Society
Terry Shaffer, Membership Chair
422 Sunset Boulevard
Toledo, OH 43612

(419) 478-4159
Dues: $20.00
Publication: *Bulletin* (quarterly)

Canadian Chrysanthemum and Dahlia
Society
c/o Karen Ojaste
17 Granard Boulevard
Scarborough, Ontario M1M 2E2
(416) 269-6960
Dues: Canada $10.00

Puget Sound Dahlia Association
Roger L. Walker
Box 5602
Bellevue, WA 98005
Dues: $15.00
Publication: *PSDA Bulletin*

## Plant Sources

Almand Dahlia Gardens
2541 West Avenue 133
San Leandro, GA 94577
Catalogue: $1.00

Alpen Gardens
173 Lawrence Lane
Kalispell, MT 59901
(406) 257-2540
Catalogue: free

Bedford Dahlias
65 Leyton Road
Bedford, OH 44146
(216) 232-2852
Catalogue: one stamp

Blue Dahlia Gardens
San Jose, IL 62682
Catalogue: $1.00

Bowles Nursery
292 Terry Road
Smithtown, NY 11787
Catalogue: one stamp

Clacks Dahlia Patch
5585 North Myrtle Road
Myrtle Creek, OR 97457
Catalogue: SASE

Connell's Dahlias
10216 40th Avenue East
Tacoma, WA 98446
(206) 531-0292
Catalogue: $2.00

Dahlias by Phil Traff
10717 SR 162
Puyallup, WA 98374
Catalogue: $1.00

Dan's Dahlias
994 South Bank Road
Oakville, WA 98568
(206) 482-2607
Catalogue: $2.00

Evergreen Acres Dahlia Gardens
682 Pulaski Road
Greenlawn, NY 11740
(516) 262-9423
Catalogue: long SASE with two stamps

Ferncliff Gardens
Box 66
Sumas, WA 98295
(604) 826-2447
Catalogue: free

Frey's Dahlias
12054 Brick Road
Turner, OR 97392
(503) 743-3910
Catalogue: one stamp

Garden Valley Dahlias
406 Lower Garden Valley Road
Roseburg, OR 97470
(503) 673-8521
Catalogue: one stamp

Golden Rule Dahlia Farm
3460 Route 48 North
Lebanon, OH 45036
(513) 932-3805
Catalogue: $1.00

Heartland Dahlias
804 East Vistula
Bristol, IN 46507
Catalogue: $2.00

Homestead Gardens
125 Homestead Road
Kalispell, MT 59901
(406) 756-6631
Catalogue: free

J. T. Dahlias
Box 20967
Greenfield, WI 53220
Catalogue: long SASE

Gordon Le Roux Dahlias
5021 View Drive
Everett, WA 98023
(206) 252-4991
Catalogue: $1.00

Pleasant Valley Glads and Dahlias
Box 494
163 Senator Street
Agawam, MA 01001
(413) 789-0307
Catalogue: free

Sea-Tac Dahlia Gardens
20020 Des Moines Memorial Drive
Seattle, WA 98198
(206) 824-3846
Catalogue: long SASE

Shackleton's Dahlias
30535 Division Drive
Troutdale, OR 97060
(503) 663-7057
Catalogue: one stamp

Swan Island Dahlias
Box 700
995 NW 22nd Avenue
Canby, OR 97013
(503) 266-7711
Catalogue: $3.00

Phil Traff Dahlia Gardens
1316 132nd Avenue East
Sumner, WA 98390
Catalogue: $1.00

Wisley Dahlia Farm
9076 County Road 87
Hammondsport, NY 14840
(607) 569-3578
Catalogue: free

# Daylilies

## Organization

American Hemerocallis Society
c/o Elly Launius, Executive Secretary
1454 Rebel Drive
Jackson, MS 39211
(601) 366-4362
Dues: $18.00
Publication: *The Daylily Journal* (quarterly)

## Plant Sources

A & D Peony and Perennial Nursery
6808 180th Street SE
Snohomish, WA 98290
(206) 485-2487
Catalogue: $1.50

Adamgrove
Route 1, Box 246
California, MO 65018
Catalogue: $3.00

Alcovy Daylily Farm
775 Cochran Road

Covington, GA 30209
(404) 787-7177
Catalogue: $1.00

Alpine Valley Gardens
2627 Calistoga Road
Santa Rosa, CA 95404
(707) 539-1749
Catalogue: long SASE

American Daylily and Perennials
Box 210
Grain Valley, MO 64029
(816) 224-2852
(800) 770-2777
Catalogue: $3.00

American Hostas, Daylilies and
Perennials
1288 Gatton Rocks Road
Bellville, OH 44813
Catalogue: $5.00

Artemis Gardens
170 Moss Bridge Road
Bozeman, MT 59715
Catalogue: $1.00

Ater Nursery
3803 Greystone Drive
Austin, TX 78731
(512) 345-3225
Specialties: diploids and tetraploids
Catalogue: one stamp

Babbette's Gardens
Babbette Sandt
40975 North 172nd Street East
Lancaster, CA 93535
Catalogue: $1.00

Balash Gardens
26595 H Drive North
Albion, MI 49224
(517) 629-5997
Catalogue: $1.00

Bayberry Row
Box 1439
Hopewell, VA 23860
Catalogue: $1.00

Bell's Daylily Garden
1305 Griffin Road
Sycamore, GA 31790
(912) 567-4284
Catalogue: free

John Benz
12195 6th Avenue
Cincinnati, OH 45249
Catalogue: $1.00

Big Tree Daylily Garden
777 General Hutchison Parkway
Longwood, FL 32750
(407) 831-5430
Catalogue: $2.00

Bloomingfields Farm
Route 55
Gaylordsville, CT 06755
(203) 345-6951
Catalogue: free

Blossom Valley Gardens
15011 Oak Creek Road
El Cajon, CA 92021
Catalogue: $1.00

Borboleta Gardens
Route 5, 15980 Canby Avenue
Faribault, MN 55021
(507) 334-2807
Catalogue: $3.00

Brookwood Gardens, Inc.
303 Fir Street
Michigan City, IN 46360
(800) 276-6593
Catalogue: $3.00

Busse Gardens
13579 10th Street NW
Cokato, MN 55321
(612) 286-2654
Catalogue: $2.00

C & C Nursery
Route 3, Box 422
Murray, KY 42071
(502) 753-2993
Catalogue: $1.00

Caprice Farm Nursery
15425 SW Pleasant Hill Road
Sherwood, OR 97140
(503) 625-7241
Catalogue: $2.00

Cascade Bulb and Seed
Box 271, 2333 Crooked Finger Road
Scotts Mills, OR 97375
Catalogue: long SASE

Chaparral Gardens
7221 Chaparral Drive
Latrobe, CA 95682
(916) 676-7918
Catalogue: $1.00

Coburg Planting Fields
573 East 600 North
Valparaiso, IN 46383
(219) 462-4288
Catalogue: $2.00

Cooper's Garden
2345 Decatur Avenue North
Golden Valley, MN 55427
(612) 591-0495
Catalogue: $1.00

Cordon Bleu Farms
Box 2033
418 Buena Creek Road
San Marcos, CA 92079
Catalogue: $1.00

Corner Oaks Garden
6139 Blanding Boulevard
Jacksonville, FL 32244
(904) 771-0417
Note: AHS display garden
Catalogue: SASE

Covered Bridge Gardens
1821 Honey Run Road
Chico, CA 95928
(916) 342-6661
Note: AHS display garden
Catalogue: $1.00

Crintonic Gardens
County Line Road
Gates Mills, OH 44040
(216) 423-3349
Catalogue: $1.00

Crochet Daylily Garden
Box 425
Prairieville, LA 70769
Catalogue: $1.00

Day Bloomers Garden
Box 869
Loughman, FL 33858
(941) 424-3949
Catalogue: $1.00

Daylilies in the Pines
1551 Cedar Street
Ramona, CA 92065
(619) 789-5790
Catalogue: SASE

Daylily Discounters
One Daylily Plaza
Alachua, FL 32615
(904) 462-1539
Catalogue: $2.00

Daylily Farms
Route 1, Box 89A
Bakersville, NC 28705-9714
Catalogue: $2.00

Daylily World
Box 1612
260 North White Cedar Road
Sanford, FL 32772
(407) 322-4034
Catalogue: $5.00

Helen Deering
2847 64th Street
Byron Center, MI 49315
Catalogue: $1.00

Edith's Daylilies
Route 1, Box 1840
Clarkesville, GA 30523
(706) 947-3683
Note: AHS display garden
Catalogue: free

Enchanted Valley Gardens
9123 North Territorial Road
Evansville, WI 53536
(608) 882-4200
Catalogue: free

Albert C. Faggard
3840 LeBleu Street
Beaumont, TX 77707
Catalogue: $1.00

Farmhouse Daylily Garden
591 Strickland Road
Whigham, GA 31797
(912) 762-3135
Catalogue: SASE

Floyd Cove Nursery
725 Longwood-Markham Road
Sanford, FL 32771
(407) 324-9229
Catalogue: $2.00

Forestlake Gardens
HC 72 LOW Box 535
Locust Grove, VA 22508
(703) 972-2890
Specialties: seeds
Catalogue: free

Four Winds Garden
Box 141
South Harpswell, ME 04079
Catalogue: $1.00

Gardenimport
Box 760
Thornhill, Ontario L3T 4A5
Catalogue: $4.00

Garden Path Daylilies
Box 8524
Clearwater, FL 34618
(813) 442-4730
Catalogue: $1.00

Garden Perennials
Route 1, Wayne, NE 68787
(402) 375-3615
Catalogue: $1.00

Gleber's Daylily Garden
17163 Swearingen Road
Kentwood, LA 70444
(504) 229-3740
Catalogue: $1.00

Goravani Growers
1730 Keane Avenue
Naples, FL 33964
(813) 455-4287
Catalogue: $2.00

G. R.'s Perennials
465 North 660 West
West Bountiful, UT 84708
(801) 292-8237
Note: AHS display garden
Catalogue: SASE

Grace Gardens North
N 3739 County Highway K
Granton, WI 54436
(715) 238-7122
Catalogue: free

Greenwood Daylily Gardens
5595 East 7th Street
Long Beach, CA 90804
(310) 494-8944
Catalogue: $5.00

Guidry's Daylily Garden
1005 East Vermilion Street
Abbeville, LA 70510
(318) 893-0812
Catalogue: free

Hahn's Rainbow Iris Garden
200 North School Street
Desloge, MO 63601
(314) 431-3342
Catalogue: $1.50

Hem'd Inn
Lucille Warner
534 Aqua Drive
Dallas, TX 75218
Catalogue: $1.00

Hermitage Gardens
Route 2
Raleigh, NC 27610
Catalogue: $1.00

Herrington Daylily Garden
204 Winfield Road
Dublin, GA 31021
Catalogue: $1.00

Hickory Hill Gardens
RR 1, Box 11
Loretto, PA 15940
Catalogue: $2.50

Howard J. Hite
370 Gallogly Road
Pontiac, MI 48055
Catalogue: $1.00

Hobby Garden, Inc.
38164 Monticello Drive
Prairieville, LA 70769
(504) 673-3623
Catalogue: free

Homestead Farms
Route 2, Box 31A
Owensville, MO 65066
(314) 437-4277
Catalogue: free

Iron Gate Gardens
Route 3, Box 250
Kings Mountain, NC 28086
(704) 435-6178
Catalogue: $3.00

Jaggers Bayou Beauties
15098 Knox Ferry Road
Bastrop, LA 71220
(318) 283-2252
Catalogue: free

Jernigan Gardens
Route 6, Box 593
Dunn, NC 28334
(919) 567-2135
Catalogue: long SASE

Johnson Daylily Garden
70 Lark Avenue
Brooksville, FL 34601
(904) 544-0330
Catalogue: SASE

Joiner Gardens
9630 Whitfield Avenue
Savannah, GA 31406
Catalogue: free

Klehm Nursery
4210 North Duncan Road
Champaign, IL 61821
(800) 553-3715
Catalogue: $4.00

Ladybug Beautiful Gardens
857 Leopard Trail
Winter Springs, FL 32708
Note: AHS display garden
Catalogue: $2.00

Lake Norman Gardens
580 Island Forest Drive
Davidson, NC 28036
Catalogue: $1.00

Lakeside Acres
8119 Roy Lane
Ooltewah, TN 37363
(615) 238-4534
Catalogue: $2.00

Larkdale Farms
4058 Highway 17 South
Green Cove Springs, FL 32043
Catalogue: $1.00

Lee's Gardens
Box 5
25986 Sauder Road
Tremont, IL 61568
(309) 925-5262
Catalogue: $2.00

Le Petit Jardin
Box 55, McIntosh, FL 32664
(904) 591-3227
Specialties: tetraploids
Catalogue: free

Little River Farm
7815 NC 39
Middlesex, NC 27557
(919) 965-9507
Catalogue: $2.00

Little River Gardens
1050 Little River Lane
Alpharetta, GA 30201
(404) 740-1371
Specialties: hybrids
Catalogue: $1.00

Louisiana Nursery
Route 7, Box 43
Opelousas, LA 70570
(318) 948-3696
Specialties: diploids and tetraploids
Catalogue: $4.00

Majestic Gardens
2100 North Preble County Line Road
West Alexandria, OH 45381
(513) 833-5100
Note: AHS display garden
Catalogue: free

Maple Tree Gardens
Box 547
Ponca, NE 68770
Catalogue: 50¢

Marietta Gardens
Box 70
Marietta, NC 28362
(910) 628-9466
Note: AHS display garden
Catalogue: SASE

McMillen's Iris Garden
RR 1
Norwich, Ontario N0J 1P0
(519) 468-6508
Catalogue: $2.00

Meadowlake Gardens
Route 4, Box 709
Walterboro, SC 29488
(803) 844-2524
Catalogue: $2.00

Mercers Garden
6215 Maude Street
Fayetteville, NC 28306
Catalogue: $1.00

Metamora Country Gardens
1945 Dryden Road
Metamora, MI 48455
(810) 678-3519
Catalogue: $1.00

Mid-America Iris Gardens
3409 North Geraldine Avenue
Oklahoma City, OK 73112
(405) 946-5743
Catalogue: $2.00

Mike's Daylilies
426 Copeland Road
Powell, TN 37849
(615) 947-9419
Catalogue: free

Bryant K. Millikan
6610 Sunny Lane
Indianapolis, IN 46220
Catalogue: $1.00

Moldovan's Gardens
38830 Detroit Road
Avon, OH 44011
Catalogue: $1.00

Monarch Daylily Garden
Route 2, Box 182
Edison, GA 31746
(912) 835-2636
Catalogue: SASE

Nicholls Gardens
4724 Angus Drive
Gainesville, VA 22065
(703) 754-9623
Catalogue: $1.00

Oakes Daylilies
8204 Monday Road
Corryton, TN 37721
(615) 687-3770
(800) 532-9545
Catalogue: $2.00

Olallie Daylily Gardens
HCR 63, Box 1
Marlboro Branch Road
South Newfane, VT 05351
(802) 348-6614
Catalogue: free

Oxford Gardens
3022 Oxford Drive
Durham, NC 27707
Catalogue: $1.00

Petree Gardens
4447 Cain Circle
Tucker, GA 30084
Catalogue: $1.00

Pinecliffe Daylily Gardens
6604 Scottsville Road
Floyds Knob, IN 47119
(812) 923-8113
Catalogue: $2.00

Powell's Gardens
9468 US Highway 70E
Princeton, NC 27569
(919) 936-4421
Catalogue: $3.00

Ramona Gardens
2178 El Paso Street
Ramona, CA 92065
(619) 789-6099
Catalogue: $2.00

Renaissance Gardens
1047 Baron Road
Weddington, NC 28173
Catalogue: $1.00

Roderick Hillview Garden
3862 Highway 0
Farmington, MO 63640
(314) 431-5711
Catalogue: one stamp

Rollingwood Gardens
21234 Rollingwood Trail
Eustis, FL 32726
(904) 589-8765
Catalogue: $3.00

Roycroft Nursery
Belle Isle Road, Route 6, Box 70
Georgetown, SC 29440
Catalogue: $1.00

Sandstone Gardens
1323 Sandstone Place
Green Bay, WI 54313
(414) 498-2895
Catalogue: SASE

Saxton Gardens
1 1st Street
Saratoga Springs, NY 12866
(518) 584-4697
Catalogue: two stamps

Schmid Gardens
847 Westwood Boulevard
Jackson, MI 49203
(517) 787-5275
Catalogue: $1.00

Scott Daylily Farm
5830 Clark Road
Harrison, TN 37341
(615) 344-9113
Catalogue: SASE

Seaside Daylily Farm
Box 807I
West Tisbury, MA 02575
(508) 693-3276
Catalogue: free

R. Seawright
201 Bedford Road
Carlisle, MA 01741
(508) 369-2172
Catalogue: $2.00

Serendipity Gardens
3210 Upper Bellbrook Road
Bellbrook, OH 45305
(513) 426-6596
Catalogue: SASE

Shields Gardens
Box 92, Westfield, IN 46074
(317) 896-3925
Catalogue: $1.00

Singing Oaks Garden
Box 56, Abell Road
Blythwood, SC 29016
(803) 786-1351
Note: AHS display garden
Catalogue: free

Sir Williams Gardens
2852 Jackson Boulevard
Highland, MI 48356
(313) 887-4779
Catalogue: $2.00

Snow Creek Daylily Gardens
330 P Street
Port Townsend, WA 98368
Catalogue: $2.00

Soules Garden
5809 Rahke Road
Indianapolis, IN 46217
(317) 786-7839
Catalogue: $1.00

The Split Rail Daylily Farm
Route 1, Box 849
High Springs, FL 32643
(904) 752-4654
Catalogue: $1.00

Spring Creek Daylily Garden
25150 Gosling
Spring, TX 77389
Catalogue: free

Springlake Ranch Gardens
Route 2, Box 360
De Queen, AR 71832
Catalogue: $1.00

Starlight Daylily Gardens
2515 Scottsville Road
Borden, IN 47106
(812) 923-3735
Catalogue: $2.00

Sterrett Gardens
Box 85
Craddockville, VA 23341
(804) 442-4606
Note: AHS display garden
Catalogue: free

Sunnyridge Gardens
1724 Drinnen Road
Knoxville, TN 37914
(615) 933-0723
Catalogue: $1.00

Sunshine Hollow
198 CR 52, Athens, TN 37303
(615) 745-4289
Catalogue: $1.00

Swann's Daylily Garden
Box 7687
Warner Robins, GA 31095
(912) 953-4778
Note: AHS display garden
Catalogue: free

Dave Talbott Nursery
4038 Highway 17 South
Green Cove Springs, FL 32043
(904) 284-9874
Catalogue: $2.00

Thoroughbred Daylilies
Box 21864
Lexington, KY 40522
(606) 268-4462
Specialties: seeds
Catalogue: free

Thundering Springs Daylily Garden
1056 South Lake Drive
Thundering Springs Lake
Dublin, GA 31021
(912) 272-1526
Note: AHS display garden
Catalogue: $1.00

Tranquil Lake Nursery, Inc.
45 River Street
Rehoboth, MA 02769
(508) 242-4002
Catalogue: $1.00

Valente Gardens
RFD 2, Box 234
Dillingham Road
East Lebanon, ME 04027
(207) 457-2076
Catalogue: two stamps

Andre Viette Farm and Nursery
Route 1, Box 16
Fishersville, VA 22939
(703) 942-2118
Catalogue: $3.00

Water Mill Daylily Garden
56 Winding Way
Water Mill, NY 11976
(516) 726-9640
Catalogue: free

Gilbert H. Wild and Son, Inc.
Box 338
1112 Joplin Street
Sarcoxie, MO 64862
(417) 548-3514
Catalogue: $3.00

Wimberlyway Gardens
7024 NW 18th Avenue
Gainesville, FL 32605
(904) 331-4922
Catalogue: $3.00

Windmill Gardens
Box 351
Luverne, AL 36049
Catalogue: $1.00

Woodside Garden
824 Williams Lane
Chadds Ford, PA 19317
Catalogue: $1.00

# Delphiniums

## Organization

The Delphinium Society
Mrs. Shirley E. Bassett
"Takakkaw," Ice House Wood
Oxted, Surrey RH8 9DW
England
Dues: $10.00
Publication: *Delphinium Year Book*

## Plant Source

Thompson & Morgan, Inc.
Box 1308
Jackson, NJ 09527
(908) 363-2225
Catalogue: free

# Epimediums

## Plant Sources

Collector's Nursery
1602 NE 162nd Avenue
Vancouver, WA 98684
Catalogue: $1.00

Cricklewood Nursery
11907 Nevers Road
Snohomish, WA 98290
(206) 568-2829
Catalogue: $2.00

Robyn's Nest Nursery
7802 NE 63rd Street
Vancouver, WA 98662
(206) 256-7399
Catalogue: $2.00

Siskiyou Rare Plant Nursery
2825 Cummings Road
Medford, OR 97501
(503) 772-6846
Catalogue: $2.00

We-Du Nurseries
Route 5, Box 724
Marion, NC 28752
(704) 738-8300
Catalogue: $2.00

## Epiphytic Plants
*See* **Bromeliads and Epiphytic Plants**

## Exotic and Tropical Plants

### *Organization*

Peperomia and Exotic Plant Society
c/o Anita Baudean
100 Neil Avenue
New Orleans, LA 70131
(504) 394-4146
Dues: $7.50
Publication: *The Gazette*
(three times annually)

### *Plant Sources*

Autumn Glade Botanicals
46857 Ann Arbor Trail

Plymouth, MI 48170
(800) 331-7969
Catalogue: free

The Banana Tree
715 Northampton Street
Easton, PA 18042
(215) 253-9589
Catalogue: $3.00

Bob's
Route 2, Box 42
Wingate, TX 79566
Catalogue: $1.00 plus SASE

Brudy's Exotics
Box 820874
HR 595
Houston, TX 77282
(800) 926-7333
Catalogue: free

Crockett's Tropical Plants
Box 389
Harlingen, TX 78551
(210) 423-1747
Catalogue: $3.00

D'anna B'nana
15-1293 Auina Road
Pahoa, HI 96778
(808) 965-6262
Catalogue: free

Endangered Species
Box 1830
Tustin, CA 92680
Catalogue: $6.00

Exotics Hawaii, Ltd.
1344 Hoakoa Place
Honolulu, HI 96821
Catalogue: SASE

Glasshouse Works
Box 97, Church Street

Stewart, OH 45778
(614) 662-2142
Catalogue: $2.00

Heliconia and Ginger Gardens
Box 79161
Houston, TX 77279
Catalogue: $2.00

Jerry Horne Rare Plants
10195 SW 70th Street
Miami, FL 33173
(305) 270-1235
Catalogue: long SASE

Olive Road Nursery
1615 Olive Road
Pensacola, FL 32514
(904) 477-9862
Catalogue: free

The Plumeria People
910 Leander Drive
Leander, TX 78641
(713) 496-2352
Catalogue: $3.00

Rainbow Tropicals
Box 4038
Hilo, HI 96720
(808) 959-4565
Catalogue: free

Southern Exposures
35 Minor Street
Beaumont, TX 77702
(409) 835-0644
Catalogue: $5.00

Stallings Nursery
910 Encinitas Boulevard
Encinitas, CA 92024
(619) 753-3079
Catalogue: $3.00

Sunshine Farms
Box 289
Mountain View, HI 96771
(808) 968-6312
Catalogue: SASE

Two Strikes
819 West Main Street
Blytheville, AR 72315
Catalogue: SASE with two stamps

Valhalla Nursery
204 Nixon Place
Chula Vista, CA 91910
(619) 425-7754
Catalogue: $2.00

Guy Wrinkle Exotic Plants
11610 Addison Street
North Hollywood, CA 91601
(310) 670-8637
Specialties: cycads
Catalogue: $1.00

# Ferns

## Organizations

American Fern Society
c/o Richard Hauke
456 McGill Place
Atlanta, GA 30312
(404) 525-3147
Dues: $15.00
Publications: *American Fern Journal*
(quarterly); *Fiddlehead Forum* (bimonthly
newsletter)

Hardy Fern Foundation
Box 166
Medina, WA 98039
(206) 747-2998
Dues: $20.00
Publication: quarterly newsletter

International Tropical Fern Society
8720 SW 34th Street
Miami, FL 33165
(305) 221-0502

Los Angeles International Fern Society
Box 90943
Pasadena, CA 91109
Dues: $20
Publication: *LAIFS Journal* (bimonthly)

## Plant Sources

Fancy Fronds
Box 1090
Gold Bar, WA 98251
(360)793-1472
Catalogue: $1.00

Timothy D. Field Ferns and Wildflowers
395 Newington Road
Newington, NH 03801
(603) 436-0457
Catalogue: free

Foliage Gardens
2003 128th Avenue SE
Bellevue, WA 98005
(206) 747-2998
Catalogue: $2.00

Fox Orchids, Inc.
6615 West Markham Street
Little Rock, AR 72205
(501) 663-4246
Catalogue: free

Gardens of the Blue Ridge
Box 10
US 221 North
Pineola, NC 28662
(704) 733-2417
Catalogue: $3.00

Ann Mann's Orchids
9045 Ron-Den Lane

Windermere, FL 34786
(407) 876-2625
Catalogue: $1.00

Oak Hill Gardens
Box 25
West Dundee, IL 60118
(708) 428-8500
Catalogue: $1.00

Oakridge Nursery
Box 182
East Kingston, NH 03827
(603) 642-8227
Catalogue: free

Orchid Gardens
2232 139th Avenue NW
Andover, MN 55744
Catalogue: 75¢

Orgel's Orchids
18950 SW 136th Street
Miami, FL 33196
(305) 233-7168
Catalogue: free

Palestine Orchids
Route 1, Box 312
Palestine, WV 26160
(304) 275-4781
Catalogue: free

Shady Lace Nursery
Box 266
Olive Branch, MS 38654
(800) 335-8657
Catalogue: free

Shady Oaks Nursery
112 10th Avenue SE
Waseca, MN 56903
(507) 835-5033
Catalogue: $3.00

Varga's Nursery
2631 Pickertown Road
Warrington, PA 19876
(610) 343-0646
Catalogue: $1.00

Wild Earth Native Plant Nursery
49 Mead Avenue
Freehold, NJ 07728
(908)308-9777
Catalogue: $1.00

# Geraniums

## Organizations

British and European Geranium Society
Leyland Cox
Norwood Chine, 26 Crabtree Lane
Sheffield, Yorkshire S5 7AV
England
(0742) 426-2000
Dues: $15.00
Publications: *The Geranium Gazette*
(three times annually);
*The Geranium Yearbook*

British Pelargonium and Geranium
Society
c/o Carol Helyar
134 Montrose Avenue
Welling, Kent DA16 2QY
(081) 856-6137
Dues: $12.00
Publications: *Pelargonium News*
(three times annually); *Yearbook*

Canadian Pelargonium and Geranium
Society
Kathleen Gammer, Membership
Secretary
101-2008 Fullerton Avenue
North Vancouver, British Columbia
V7P 3G7
(604) 926-2190

Dues: Canada $10.00
Publication: *Storksbill* (quarterly)

The Geraniaceae Group
c/o Penny Clifton
9 Waingate Bridge Cottages
Haverigg, Cumbria LA18 4NF
England
Dues: $16.00
Publication: *The Geraniaceae Group News*
(quarterly)

International Geranium Society
Membership Secretary
Box 92734
Pasadena, CA 91109
(818) 908-8867
Dues: $12.50
Publication: *Geraniums Around the World*
(quarterly journal)

## Plant Sources

A Scented Geranium
Box 123
Washington, KY 41096
Catalogue: $3.50

Brawner Geraniums
Route 4, Box 525A
Buckhannon, WV 26201
(304) 472-4203
Specialties: pelargoniums
Catalogue: $2.00

Cook's Geranium Nursery
712 North Grand
Lyons, KS 67554
(316) 257-5033
Catalogue: $1.00

Davidson-Wilson Greenhouses, Inc.
RR 2, Box 168
Crawfordsville, IN 47933-9426
(317) 364-0556
Catalogue: $3.00

Fischer Geraniums
24500 SW 167th Avenue
Homestead, FL 33031
(305) 245-9464
Catalogue: $1.00

Highfield Garden
4704 NE Cedar Creek Road
Woodland, WA 98674
(800) 669-9956
Catalogue: $1.00

Holbrook Farm and Nursery
Box 368
Fletcher, NC 28732
(704) 891-7790
Catalogue: free

Lake Odessa Greenhouse
1123 Jordan Lake Street
Lake Odessa, MI 48849
(616) 374-8488
Catalogue: free

Logee's Greenhouse
141 North Street
Danielson, CT 06239
(203) 774-8038
Catalogue: $1.00

Oglevee, Ltd.
150 Oglevee Lane
Connellsville, PA 15425
(412) 628-8360
Catalogue: $1.00

Shady Hill Gardens
821 Walnut Street
Batavia, IL 60510
(708) 879-5679
Catalogue: $2.00

Shepherd Geraniums
13851 Christensen Road
Galt, CA 95632
Catalogue: $1.00

Sunnybrook Farms Nursery
Box 6
9448 Mayfield Road
Chesterland, OH 44026
(216) 729-7232
Catalogue: $1.00

Wheeler Farm Gardens
171 Bartlett Street
Portland, CT 06480
(203) 342-2374
(800) 934-3341
Catalogue: free

Willamette Valley Gardens
Box 285A
Lake Oswego, OR 97034
(503) 636-6517
Catalogue: $1.00

# Gesneriad

*See* **African Violets and
Other Gesneriads**

# Gladioli

*Organizations*

All-America Gladiolus Selections
11734 Road 33½
Madera, CA 93638
(209) 645-5329

Canadian Gladiolus Society
c/o W. L. Turbuck
3073 Grant Road
Regina, Saskatchewan S4S 5G9
Dues: Canada $10.00
Publication: *Canadian Gladiolus Annual*

North American Gladiolus Council
c/o William Strawser
701 South Hendricks Avenue
Marion, IN 46953

(317) 664-3857
Dues: $10.00
Publication: *Bulletin* (quarterly)

*Plant Sources*

Pleasant Valley Glads and Dahlias
Box 494
163 Senator Street
Agawam, MA 01001
(413) 789-0307
Catalogue: free

Skolaski's Glads & Field Flowers
4821 County Highway Q
Waunakee, WI 53597
(608) 836-4822
Catalogue: free

Summerville Gladiolus
RD 1, Box 449
1330 Ellis Mill Road
Glassboro, NJ 08028
(609) 881-0704
Catalogue: free

The Waushara Gardens
5491 North 5th Drive
Plainfield, WI 54966
(715) 335-4462
Catalogue: $1.00

# Ground Covers

*Plant Sources*

Barbour Bros. Inc.
RD 2, Stoneboro, PA 16153
Catalogue: free

Double D Nursery
2215 Dogwood Lane
Arnoldsville, GA 30619
(706) 742-7417
Catalogue: free

Gilson Gardens, Inc.
Box 277
Perry, OH 44081
(216) 259-5252
Catalogue: free

Joyce's Garden
64640 Old Bend-Redmond Highway
Bend, OR 97701
(503) 388-4680
Catalogue: $2.00

Nichols Garden Nursery
1190 North Pacific Highway
Albany, OR 97321
(503) 928-9280
Catalogue: free

Peekskill Nurseries
Box 428
Shrub Oak, NY 10588
(914) 245-5595
Catalogue: free

Pinky's Plants
Box 126
442 G Street
Pawnee City, NE 68420
(800) 94-PINKY
Catalogue: $3.50

Prentiss Court Ground Covers
Box 8662
Greenville, SC 29604
(803) 277-4037
Catalogue: $2.00

Silver Springs Nursery
HCR 62, Box 86
Moyle Springs, ID 83845
(208) 267-5753
Catalogue: 50¢

Andre Viette Farm and Nursery
Route 1, Box 16
Fishersville, VA 22939

(703) 942-2118
Catalogue: $3.00

Woodlanders, Inc.
1128 Colleton Avenue
Aiken, SC 29801
(803) 648-7522
Catalogue: $2.00

# Heathers and Heaths

*Organizations*

The Heather Society
c/o Mrs. A. Small
Denbeigh, All Saints Road,
Creeting St. Mary
Ipswich, Suffolk 1P6 8PJ
England
(0449) 71-1220
Dues: £6.00
Publications: *Bulletin* (three times
annually); yearbook

North American Heather Society
c/o Pauline Croxton
3641 Indian Creek Road
Placerville, CA 95667
Dues: $10.00
Publication: *Heather News* (quarterly)

Northeast Heather Society
Walter K. Wornick
Box 101, Highland View
Alstead, NH 03602
(603) 835-6165
Dues: $5.00
Publication: *Heather Notes*

*Plant Sources*

Ericaceae
Box 293
Deep River, CT 06417
Catalogue: free

Heaths and Heathers
Box 850
1199 Monte–Elma Road
Elma, WA 98541
(206) 482-3258
Catalogue: long SASE

Rock Spray Nursery
Box 693
Depot Road
Truro, MA 02666
(508) 349-6769
Catalogue: $1.00

# Hibiscus

*Organization*

American Hibiscus Society
Jeri Grantham, Executive Secretary
Box 321540
Cocoa Beach, FL 32932
(407) 783-2576
Dues: $17.50
Publication: *The Seed Pod* (quarterly)

*Plant Sources*

Air Expose
4703 Leffingwell Street
Houston, TX 77026
Catalogue: long SASE

Fancy Hibiscus
1142 SW 1st Avenue
Pompano Beach, FL 33060
(305) 782-0741
Catalogue: $2.00

Florida Colors Nursery
23740 SW 147th Avenue
Homestead, FL 33032
(305) 258-1086
Catalogue: free

Reasoner's, Inc.
Box 1881
2501 53rd Avenue East
Oneco, FL 34264
(813) 756-1881
Catalogue: $1.00

# Hostas

## Organization

American Hosta Society
c/o Robyn Duback
7802 NE 63rd Street
Vancouver, WA 98662
Dues: $19.00
Publication: *Hosta Journal* (semiannual)

## Publication

*The Hosta Digest*
Meadowbrook Hosta Farm
81 Meredith Road
Tewksbury, MA 01876
(508) 851-8943
Frequency: quarterly
Subscription: $20.00

## Plant Sources

A & D Peony and Perennial Nursery
6808 180th Street SE
Snohomish, WA 98290
(206) 485-2487
Catalogue: $1.50

Adrian's Flowers of Fashion Nursery
855 Parkway Boulevard
Alliance, OH 44601
(216) 823-1964
Catalogue: SASE with two stamps

Akin' Back Farm
Box 158H
Buckner, KY 40010

(502) 222-5791
Catalogue: $2.00

Ambergate Gardens
8015 Krey Avenue
Waconia, MN 55387
(612) 443-2248
Catalogue: $2.00

American Hostas, Daylilies and
Perennials
1288 Gatton Rocks Road
Bellville, OH 44813
Catalogue: $5.00

Anderson Iris Gardens
22179 Keather Avenue North
Forest Lake, MN 55025
(612) 433-5268
Catalogue: $2.00

The Azalea Patch
2010 Mountain Road
Joppa, MD 21085
(410) 679-0762
Catalogue: $1.00

Brookwood Gardens, Inc.
303 Fir Street
Michigan City, IN 46360
(800) 276-6593
Catalogue: $3.00

Busse Gardens
13579 10th Street NW
Cokato, MN 55321
(612) 286-2654
Catalogue: $2.00

C & C Nursery
Route 3, Box 422
Murray, KY 42071
(502) 753-2993
Catalogue: $1.00

Caprice Farm Nursery
15425 SW Pleasant Hill Road
Sherwood, OR 97140
(503) 625-7241
Catalogue: $2.00

Coastal Gardens and Nursery
4611 Socastee Boulevard
Myrtle Beach, SC 29575
(803) 293-2000
Catalogue: $2.00

Cooks Nursery
10749 Bennett Road
Dunkirk, NY 14048
(716) 366-8844
Catalogue: $1.00

Daylily Farms
Route 1, Box 89A
Bakersville, NC 28705-9714
Catalogue: $2.00

Donnelly's Nursery
705 Charlotte Highway
Fairview, NC 28730
Catalogue: $1.00

Hildenbrandt's Iris Gardens
HC 84, Box 4
Lexington, NE 68850
(308) 324-4334
Catalogue: $1.00

Holbrook Farm and Nursery
Box 368
115 Lance Road
Fletcher, NC 28732
(704) 891-7790
Catalogue: $1.00

Homestead Farms
Route 2, Box 31A
Owensville, MO 65066
(314) 437-4277
Catalogue: free

Honeysong Farm
51 Jared Place
Seaford, DE 19973
Catalogue: $1.00

Hosta Haven
10302 Nantucket Court
Fairfax, VA 22032
(800) 354-0503
Catalogue: $1.00

House of Hosta
2320 Elmwood Road
Green Bay, WI 54313
(414) 434-2847
Catalogue: one stamp

Iron Gate Gardens
Route 3, Box 250
Kings Mountain, NC 28086
(704) 435-6178
Catalogue: $3.00

Kuk's Forest Nursery
10174 Barr Road
Brecksville, OH 44141
(216) 526-5271
Catalogue: $2.00

Lakeside Acres
8119 Roy Lane
Ooltewah, TN 37363
(615) 238-4534
Catalogue: $2.00

Laurie's Landscaping
2959 Hobson Road
Downers Grove, IL 60517
(708) 969-1270
Catalogue: long SASE

Lee's Gardens
Box 5, 25986 Sauder Road
Tremont, IL 61568
(309) 925-5262
Catalogue: $2.00

Mary's Plant Farm
2410 Lanes Mill Road
Hamilton, OH 45013
(513) 894-0022
Catalogue: $1.00

Matterhorn Nursery Inc.
227 Summit Park Road
Spring Valley, NY 10977
(914) 354-5986
Catalogue: $5.00

Meadowbrook Hosta Farm
81 Meredith Road
Tewksbury, MA 01876
(508) 851-8943
Catalogue: free

Mid-America Iris Gardens
3409 North Geraldine Avenue
Oklahoma City, OK 73112
(405) 946-5743
Catalogue: $2.00

Piccadilly Farm
1971 Whippoorwill Road
Bishop, GA 30621
Catalogue: $1.00

Plant Delights Nursery
9241 Sauls Road
Raleigh, NC 27603
(919) 772-4794
Catalogue: $3.50

Plant Hideaway
Route 3, Box 259
Franklinton, NC 27525
(919) 494-7178
Catalogue: free

Powell's Gardens
9468 US Highway 70 E
Princeton, NC 27569
(919) 936-4421
Catalogue: $3.00

Savory's Gardens, Inc.
5300 Whiting Avenue
Edina, MN 55439
(612) 941-8755
Catalogue: $2.00

Schmid Gardens
847 Westwood Boulevard
Jackson, MI 49203
(517) 787-5275
Catalogue: $1.00

R. Seawright
201 Bedford Road
Carlisle, MA 01741
(508) 369-2172
Catalogue: $2.00

Shady Oaks Nursery
112 10th Avenue SE
Waseca, MN 56903
(507) 835-5033
Catalogue: $3.00

Silvermist
1986 Harrisville Road
Stoneboro, PA 16153
(814) 786-9219
Catalogue: free

Soules Garden
5809 Rahke Road
Indianapolis, IN 46217
(317) 786-7839
Catalogue: $1.00

Stark Gardens
631 G24 Highway
Norwalk, IA 50211
(515) 981-4780
Catalogue: one stamp

Sunnybrook Farms Nursery
Box 6
9448 Mayfield Road
Chesterland, OH 44026

(216) 729-7232
Catalogue: $1.00

Tower Perennial Gardens
3412 East 64th Court
Spokane, WA 99223
(509) 448-5837
Catalogue: free

Triple Creek Farm
8625 West Banks Mill Road
Winston, GA 30187
(404) 489-8022
Catalogue: $1.00

Walden-West
5744 Crooked Finger Road
Scotts Mills, OR 97375
(503) 873-6875
Catalogue: SASE

White Oak Nursery
6145 Oak Point Court
Peoria, IL 61614
(309) 693-1354
Catalogue: $1.00

# Hydrangeas

*Plant Sources*

Bell Family Nursery
6543 South Zimmerman Road
Aurora, OR 97002
(503) 651-2887
Catalogue: $3.50

Wilkerson Mill Gardens
9595 Wilkerson Mill Road
Palmetto, GA 30268
Catalogue: $1.00

# Irises

*Organizations*

American Iris Society
Marilyn Harlow, Membership Secretary
Box 8455
San Jose, CA 95155
(408) 971-0444
Dues: $12.50
Publication: *Bulletin of the AIS* (quarterly)

## AMERICAN IRIS SOCIETY SECTIONS

Dwarf Iris Society of America
Lynda S. Miller
3167 East US 224
Ossian, IN 46777
(219) 597-7403
Dues: AIS dues plus $3.00
Publication: *Dwarf Iris Society Newsletter*

Historic Iris Preservation Society (HIPS)
Ada Godfrey
9 Bradford Street
Foxborough, MA 01035
Dues: AIS dues plus $5.00
Publication: *Roots Journal*

Median Iris Society
Deborah Outcalt
Route 1, Box CW 20
Spencer, IN 47460
Dues: AIS dues plus $5.00
Publication: journal

Reblooming Iris Society
Charlie Brown
3114 South FM 131
Denison, TX 75020
Dues: AIS dues plus $5.00
Publication: bulletin

Society for Japanese Irises
Carol Warner
16815 Falls Road

Upperco, MD 21155
(410) 374-4788
Dues: AIS dues plus $3.50
Publication: *The Review*

Society for Pacific Coast Native Iris
Adele Lawyer
4333 Oak Hill Road
Oakland, CA 94605
Dues: AIS dues plus $5.00
Publication: *SPCNI Almanac*

The Society for Siberian Irises
Howard L. Brookins
N 75 W14247 North Point Drive
Menomonee Falls, WI 53051
(414) 251-5292
Dues: AIS dues plus $5.00
Publication: *The Siberian Iris*

Species Iris Group of North America
(SIGNA)
Colin Rigby
18341 Paulson SW
Rochester, WA 98579
Dues: AIS dues plus $5.00
Publication: *SIGNA*

Spuria Iris Society
Floyd W. Wickenkamp
10521 Bellarose Drive
Sun City, AZ 85351
(602) 977-2354
Dues: AIS dues plus $5.00
Publication: *Spuria Newsletter*

## AMERICAN IRIS SOCIETY COOPERATING SOCIETIES

Aril Society International
Audrey Roe
2816 Charleston NE
Albuquerque, NM 87110
Dues: $5.00
Publication: yearbook

Society for Louisiana Irises
Elaine Bourque
1812 Broussard Road East
Lafayette, LA 70508
Dues: $7.50
Publications: newsletter; special bulletins

## OTHER ORGANIZATIONS

British Iris Society
Mrs. E. M. Wise
197 The Parkway, Iver Heath
Iver, Bucks. SL0 0RQ
England
Publication: *The Iris Year Book*

Canadian Iris Society
c/o Verna Laurin
199 Florence Avenue
Willowdale, Ontario M2N 1G5
(416) 225-1088
Dues: Canada $5.00
Publication: *CIS Newsletter* (quarterly)

## Iris Products and Supplies

House of Iris
The Mills Falls Marketplace
Route 3, Box 16
Meredith, NH 03253
(603) 279-8155
Specialties: iris crafts, jewelry, gifts

## Plant Sources

Abbey Gardens
32009 South Ona Way
Molalla, OR 97038
(503) 829-2928
Catalogue: $1.00

Adamgrove
Route 1, Box 246
California, MO 65018
Catalogue: $3.00

Aitken's Salmon Creek Garden
608 NW 119th Street
Vancouver, WA 98685
(206) 573-4472
Specialties: bearded irises
Catalogue: $2.00

Amberway Gardens
5803 Amberway Drive
St. Louis, MO 63128
(314) 842-6103
Catalogue: $1.00

Anderson Iris Gardens
22179 Keather Avenue North
Forest Lake, MN 55025
(612) 433-5268
Specialties: tall bearded irises
Catalogue: $2.00

Artemis Gardens
170 Moss Bridge Road
Bozeman, MT 59715
Specialties: bearded irises
Catalogue: $1.00

Babbette's Gardens
Babbette Sandt
40975 North 172nd Street East
Lancaster, CA 93535
Specialties: tall bearded irises
Catalogue: $1.00

Bay View Gardens
1201 Bay Street
Santa Cruz, CA 95060
Catalogue: $2.00

Bluebird Haven Iris Garden
6940 Fairplay Road
Somerset, CA 95684
(209) 245-5017
Catalogue: $1.00

Blue Iris Country Gardens
20791 Woodbury Drive

Grass Valley, CA 95949
(916) 346-2905
Catalogue: $1.00

Bois d'Arc Gardens
1831 Bull Run
Schriever, LA 70395
(504) 446-2329
Specialties: Louisiana irises
Catalogue: $1.00

Borboleta Gardens
Route 5
15980 Canby Avenue
Faribault, MN 55021
(507) 334-2807
Specialties: bearded and Siberian irises
Catalogue: $3.00

Borglum's Iris
2202 Austin Road
Geneva, NY 14456
Catalogue: $1.00

Bridge in Time Iris Gardens
10116 Scottsville Road
Alvaton, KY 42122
Specialties: reblooming irises
Catalogue: one stamp

George C. Bush
1739 Memory Lane Extension
York, PA 17402
(717) 755-0557
Specialties: beardless irises
Catalogue: one stamp

Cal-Dixie Iris Gardens
14115 Pear Street
Riverside, CA 92508
Specialties: bearded irises
Catalogue: two stamps

Cape Iris Gardens
822 Rodney Vista Boulevard
Cape Girardeau, MO 63701

(314) 334-3383
Catalogue: $1.00

Caprice Farm Nursery
15425 SW Pleasant Hill Road
Sherwood, OR 97140
(503) 625-7241
Specialties: Japanese and Siberian irises
Catalogue: $2.00

Cascade Bulb and Seed
Box 271
2333 Crooked Finger Road
Scotts Mills, OR 97375
Specialties: Siberian irises
Catalogue: long SASE

Chuck Chapman Iris
11 Harts Lane
Guelph, Ontario N1L 1B1
Catalogue: $2.00

Chehalem Gardens
Box 693
Newberg, OR 97132
(503) 538-8920
Specialties: spuria and Siberian irises
Catalogue: $2.00

Comanche Acres Iris Gardens
Route 1, Box 258
Gower, MO 64454
(816) 424-6436
Catalogue: $3.00

Contemporary Gardens
Box 534
Blanchard, OK 73010
Specialties: Australian imports
Catalogue: $1.00

Cooley's Gardens
Box 126
11553 Silverton Road NE
Silverton, OR 97381-0126
(503) 873-5463

(800) 225-5391
Specialties: tall bearded irises
Catalogue: $4.00

Cooper's Garden
2345 Decatur Avenue North
Golden Valley, MN 55427
(612) 591-0495
Specialties: species irises
Catalogue: $1.00

Cordon Bleu Farms
Box 2033
418 Buena Creek Road
San Marcos, CA 92079
Specialties: Louisiana and spuria irises
Catalogue: $1.00

Cottage Gardens
266 17th Avenue
San Francisco, CA 94121
(415) 387-7145
Specialties: median and tall bearded irises
Catalogue: free

C. Criscola Iris Garden
Route 2, Box 183
Walla Walla, WA 99362
(509) 525-4841
Specialties: bearded irises
Catalogue: two stamps

D. and J. Gardens
7872 Howell Prairie Road NE
Silverton, OR 97381
Catalogue: $1.00

David Iris Farm
Route 1
Fort Dodge, IA 50501
Catalogue: one stamp

Draycott Gardens
16815 Falls Road
Upperco, MD 21155
(410) 374-4788

Specialties: Siberian and Japanese irises
Catalogue: $1.00

Enchanted Iris Garden
715 Central Canyon
Nampa, ID 83651
(208) 465-5713
Specialties: tall bearded irises
Catalogue: $1.00

Ensata Gardens
9823 East Michigan Avenue
Galesburg, MI 49053
(616) 665-7500
Specialties: Japanese irises
Catalogue: $2.00

Fleur de Lis Gardens
185 NE Territorial Road
Canby, OR 97013
Specialties: tall bearded irises
Catalogue: $2.00

Foxes' Iris Patch
RR 5, Box 382
Huron, SD 57350
Catalogue: $3.00

Friendship Gardens
2590 Wellworth Way
West Friendship, MD 21794
Specialties: reblooming and
tall bearded irises
Catalogue: $1.00

Garden of the Enchanted Rainbow
Route 4, Box 439
Killen, AL 35645
Catalogue: $1.00

Grace Gardens North
N 3739 County Highway K
Granton, WI 54436
(715) 238-7122
Catalogue: free

Hahn's Rainbow Iris Garden
200 North School Street
Desloge, MO 63601
(314) 431-3342
Catalogue: $1.50

Hildenbrandt's Iris Gardens
75741 Road 431
Lexington, NE 68850
(308) 324-4334
Specialties: tall bearded and dwarf irises
Catalogue: $1.00

Holly Lane Iris Gardens
10930 Holly Lane
Osseo, MN 55369
Specialties: bearded irises
Catalogue: long SASE with two stamps

Huggins Farm Irises
Route 1, Box 348
Hico, TX 76457
(817) 796-4041
Specialties: bearded irises
Catalogue: $1.00

Illini Iris
Route 3, Box 5
Monticello, IL 61856
(217) 762-3446
Specialties: Siberian irises
Catalogue: SASE

Iris Acres
Route 4, Box 189
Winamac, IN 46996
(219) 946-4197
Specialties: bearded irises
Catalogue: $1.00

Iris City Gardens
502 Brighton Place
Nashville, TN 37205
(615) 386-3778
Catalogue: free

Iris Country
6219 Topaz Street NE
Brooks, OR 97035
(503) 393-4739
Specialties: bearded irises
Catalogue: $1.00

Iris Farm
Box 336
Ojo Caliente, NM 87539
Specialties: tall bearded irises
Catalogue: $1.00

The Iris Garden
Route 1, Box CW 20
Spencer, IN 47460
Specialties: tall bearded and median irises
Catalogue: two stamps

Iris Hill Farm
7280 Tassajara Creek Road
Santa Margarita, CA 93453
(805) 438-3070
Specialties: tall bearded irises
Catalogue: $1.00

The Iris Pond
7311 Churchill Road
McLean, VA 22101
Catalogue: $1.00

Iris Test Gardens
1010 Highland Park Drive
College Place, WA 99324
(509) 525-8804
Specialties: tall bearded irises
Catalogue: 50¢

Joni's Dance-in-the-Wind Garden
810 South 14th Street
Tekamah, NE 68061
Catalogue: $1.00

Keith Keppel
Box 18154
Salem, OR 97305

(503) 391-9241
Specialties: tall bearded and median irises
Catalogue: $2.00

Knee-Deep in June
708 North 10th Street
St. Joseph, MO 64501
Catalogue: $1.00

Laurie's Garden
41856 McKenzie Highway
Springfield, OR 97478
(503) 896-3756
Specialties: beardless irises
Catalogue: long SASE

Lee's Gardens
Box 5, 25986 Sauder Road
Tremont, IL 61568
(309) 925-5262
Catalogue: $2.00

Lone Star Iris Gardens
5637 Saddleback Road
Garland, TX 75043
Specialties: Louisiana irises
Catalogue: $2.00

Long's Gardens
Box 19
Boulder, CO 80306
(303) 442-2353
Specialties: tall bearded irises
Catalogue: free

Lorraine's Iris Patch
20272 Road 11 NW
Quincy, WA 98848
Catalogue: free

Louisiana Nursery
Route 7, Box 43
Opelousas, LA 70570
(318) 948-3696
Specialties: Louisiana irises
Catalogue: $4.00

M. A. D. Garden
4828 Jella Way
North Highland, CA 95660
Specialties: Bob and Mary Dunn intro-
ductions
Catalogue: SASE

Manchester Garden
614 Nandale Lane
Manchester, MO 63021
Catalogue: free

Maple Tree Gardens
Box 547
Ponca, NE 68770
Specialties: tall bearded and median irises
Catalogue: 50¢

Maryott's Gardens
1073 Bird Avenue
San Jose, CA 95125
(408) 971-0444
Specialties: bearded irises
Catalogue: long SASE

Maxim's Greenwood Gardens
2157 Sonoma Street
Redding, CA 96001
(916) 241-0764
Catalogue: $1.00

McAllister's Iris Gardens
Box 112
Fairacres, NM 88033
Specialties: aril irises
Catalogue: $1.00

McMillen's Iris Garden
RR 1
Norwich, Ontario N0J 1P0
(519) 468-6508
Catalogue: $2.00

Mid-America Iris Gardens
3409 North Geraldine Avenue
Oklahoma City, OK 73112

(405) 946-5743
Specialties: bearded and reblooming
irises
Catalogue: $2.00

Millar Mountain Nursery
RR 3
5086 McLay Road
Duncan, British Columbia V9L 2X1
(604) 748-0487
Catalogue: $2.00

Mill Creek Gardens
210 Parkway
Lapeer, MI 48446
(810) 664-5525
Catalogue: $1.00

Miller's Manor Gardens
3167 East US 224
Ossian, IN 46777
(219) 597-7403
Catalogue: $1.00

Misty Hill Farms—Moonshine Gardens
5080 West Soda Rock Lane
Healdsburg, CA 95448
(707) 433-8408
Specialties: reblooming irises
Catalogue: free

Monument Iris Garden
50029 Sunflower Road
Mitchell, NE 69357
Specialties: tall bearded irises
Catalogue: $1.00

Mountain View Gardens
2435 Middle Road
Columbia Falls, MT 59912
Specialties: Siberian irises
Catalogue: one stamp

Mountain View Iris Gardens
6307 Irwin Avenue
Lawton, OK 73503

(405) 492-5183
Catalogue: $1.50

Napa Country Iris Gardens
9087 Steele Canyon Road
Napa, CA 94558
Specialties: tall bearded irises
Catalogue: one stamp

Newburn's Iris Gardens
1415 Meadow Dale Drive
Lincoln, NE 68505
Specialties: tall bearded irises
Catalogue: free

Nicholls Gardens
4724 Angus Drive
Gainesville, VA 22065
(703) 754-9623
Catalogue: $1.00

Nicholson's Woodland Iris Gardens
2405 Woodland Avenue
Modesto, CA 95358
(209) 578-4184
Catalogue: $1.00

North Forty Iris
93 East 100 South
Logan, UT 84321
Specialties: tall bearded irises
Catalogue: $1.00

North Pine Iris Gardens
Box 595
Norfolk, NE 68701
Specialties: tall bearded and median irises
Catalogue: $1.00

O'Brien Iris Garden
3223 Canfield Road
Sebastopol, CA 95472
Catalogue: two stamps

Ohio Gardens
102 Laramie Road

Marietta, OH 45750
Catalogue: $1.00

Pacific Coast Hybridizers
Box 972, 1170 Steinway Avenue
Campbell, CA 95009
(408) 370-2955
Catalogue: $1.00

Pederson's Iris Patch
Sibley Road
Dazey, ND 58429
Catalogue: one stamp

Pine Ridge Gardens
832 Sycamore Road
London, AR 72847
(501) 293-4359
Specialties: beardless irises
Catalogue: $1.00

Pleasure Iris Gardens
425 East Luna
Chaparral, NM 88021
(505) 824-4299
Specialties: aril irises
Catalogue: $1.00

Portable Acres
2087 Curtis Drive
Penngrove, CA 94951
Specialties: Pacific Coast native irises
Catalogue: long SASE with two stamps

Powell's Gardens
9468 US Highway 70 E
Princeton, NC 27569
(919) 936-4421
Catalogue: $3.00

Ramona Gardens
2178 El Paso Street
Ramona, CA 92065
(619) 789-6099
Specialties: bearded irises
Catalogue: $2.00

Rancho de los Flores
8000 Balcom Canyon Road
Moorpark, CA 93021
Specialties: reblooming irises
Catalogue: free

Riverdale Iris Gardens
Box 524
Rockford, MN 55373
(612) 477-4859
Specialties: dwarf and median irises
Catalogue: $1.00

Roderick Hillview Garden
3862 Highway 0
Farmington, MO 63640
(314) 431-5711
Specialties: tall bearded irises
Catalogue: one stamp

Roris Gardens
8195 Bradshaw Road
Sacramento, CA 95829
(916) 689-7460
Specialties: tall bearded irises
Catalogue: $3.00

Royal Rainbow Gardens
2311 Torquay
Royal Oak, MI 48073
Catalogue: two stamps

Ruth's Iris Garden
1621 Adams Road
Yuba City, CA 95993
Catalogue: two stamps

Schreiner's Iris Gardens
3629 Quinaby Road
Salem, OR 97303
(800) 525-2367
Catalogue: $4.00

Shepard Iris Garden
3342 West Orangewood
Phoenix, AZ 85051

(602) 841-1231
Specialties: bearded and spuria irises
Catalogue: two stamps

Shiloh Gardens
Route 1, Box 77
Pawnee, IL 62558
Catalogue: two stamps

Sir Williams Gardens
2852 Jackson Boulevard
Highland, MI 48356
(313) 887-4779
Catalogue: $2.00

Sourdough Iris Gardens
109 Sourdough Ridge Road
Bozeman, MT 59715
Catalogue: long SASE

Spruce Gardens
2317 3rd Road
Wisner, NE 68791
(402) 529-6860
Specialties: tall bearded irises
Catalogue: $1.00

Stanley Iris Garden
3245 North Wing Road
Star, ID 83669
(208) 286-7079
Specialties: tall bearded irises
Catalogue: $1.00

Stephens Lane Gardens
Route 1, Box 136
Bells, TN 38006
Catalogue: $1.00

Sunnyridge Gardens
1724 Drinnen Road
Knoxville, TN 37914
(615) 933-0723
Catalogue: $1.00

Superstition Iris Gardens
2536 Old Highway
Cathey's Valley, CA 95306
Specialties: bearded irises
Catalogue: $1.00

Sutton's Green Thumber
16592 Road 208
Porterville, CA 93257
Catalogue: $1.00

TB's Place
1513 Ernie Lane
Grand Prairie, TX 75052
Catalogue: SASE

Tranquil Lake Nursery, Inc.
45 River Street
Rehoboth, MA 02769-1395
(508) 242-4002
Specialties: Japanese and Siberian irises
Catalogue: $1.00

Uranium Country Gardens
728 1675 Road
Delta, CO 81416
Catalogue: $1.00

Valley Gardens
4896 Granada Lane
Linden, CA 95236
Specialties: tall bearded and reblooming
irises
Catalogue: $1.00

York Hill Farm
18 Warren Street
Georgetown, MA 01833
Specialties: Japanese and Siberian irises
Catalogue: $1.00

Zebra Gardens
2511 West 10950 South
South Jordan, UT 84095
(801) 254-2536
Catalogue: $1.00

# Ivies

## Organization

American Ivy Society
Daphne Pfaff, Membership Chair
696 16th Avenue South
Naples, FL 33940
(813) 261-0388
Dues: $15.00
Publications: *The Ivy Journal* (annual);
*Between the Vines* (semiannual newsletter)

## Plant Sources

Ivies of the World
Box 408
Weirsdale, FL 32195
(904) 821-2201
Catalogue: $1.50

Sunnybrook Farms Nursery
Box 6
9448 Mayfield Road
Chesterland, OH 44026
(216) 729-7232
Catalogue: $1.00

# Lilacs

## Organization

International Lilac Society
The Holden Arboretum
9500 Sperry Road
Mentor, OH 44060
(216) 946-4400
Dues: $15.00
Publication: *Lilac Journal* (quarterly)

## Plant Sources

Ameri-Hort Research
Box 1529
Medina, OH 44258

(216) 723-4966
Catalogue: $2.00

Fox Hill Nursery
347 Lunt Road
Freeport, ME 04032
(207) 729-1511
Catalogue: $2.00

Heard Gardens, Ltd.
5355 Merle Hay Road
Johnston, IA 50131
(515) 276-4533
Catalogue: $2.00

Wedge Nursery
Route 2, Box 144
Albert Lea, MN 56007
(507) 373-5225
Catalogue: free

# Lilies

## *Organizations*

American Calochortus Society
c/o H. P. McDonald
Box 1128
Berkeley, CA 94701
Dues: $4.00
Publication: *Mariposa* (quarterly)

British Columbia Lily Society
Del Knowlton, Secretary/Treasurer
5510 239th Street
Langley, British Columbia V3A 7N6
(604) 534-4729
Dues: Canada $5.00
Publication: *BCLS Newsletter* (quarterly)

Canadian Prairie Lily Society
M. E. Driver, Secretary
22 Red River Road
Saskatoon, Saskatchewan S7K 1G3
(306) 242-5329

Dues: Canada $5.00
Publication: *Newsletter* (quarterly)

International Aroid Society
Box 43-1853
Miami, FL 33143
(305) 271-3767
Dues: $18.00
Publications: *IAS Newsletter* (bimonthly);
*Aroideana* (annual)

North American Lily Society, Inc.
Dr. Robert Gilman, Executive Secretary
Box 272
Owatonna, MN 55060
(507) 451-2170
Dues: $12.50
Publications: *Lily Yearbook;* quarterly bulletin

Pacific Northwest Lily Society
Dick Malpass
10804 NW 11th Avenue
Vancouver, WA 98685
(503) 656-1575
Dues: $8.00
Publication: bulletin

## *Plant Sources*

Ambergate Gardens
8015 Krey Avenue
Waconia, MN 55387
(612) 443-2248
Specialties: Martagnon lilies
Catalogue: $2.00

B & D Lilies
330 P Street
Port Townsend, WA 98368
(206) 385-1738
Catalogue: $3.00

Borboleta Gardens
Route 5
15980 Canby Avenue

Faribault, MN 55021
(507) 334-2807
Catalogue: $3.00

Fairyland Begonia and Lily Garden
1100 Griffith Road
McKinleyville, CA 95521
(707) 839-3034
Specialties: hybrid lilies
Catalogue: 50¢

Hartle-Gilman Gardens
RR 4, Box 14
Owatona, MN 55060-9416
(507) 451-3191
Specialties: hybrid lilies
Catalogue: free

Honeywood Lilies
Box 68
Parkside, Saskatchewan S0J 2A0
(306) 747-3296
Catalogue: $2.00

The Lily Garden
36752 SE Bluff Road
Boring, OR 97009
(503) 668-5291
Catalogue: free

The Lily Nook
Box 657
Rolla, ND 58367
(204) 476-3225
Catalogue: $2.00

The Lily Pad
5102 Scott Road
Olympia, WA 98502
(206) 866-0291
Catalogue: $2.00

Lindel Lilies
5510 239th Street
Langley, British Columbia V3A 7N6
(604) 534-4729

Specialties: hybrid lilies
Catalogue: free

Olympic Coast Garden
84 Eaton Lane
Sequim, WA 98382
Catalogue: $1.00

Rex Bulb Farms
Box 774
Port Townsend, WA 98368
Catalogue: $1.00

Riverside Gardens
RR 5
Saskatoon, Saskatchewan S7K 3J8
Specialties: hybrid Asiatic lilies
Catalogue: $1.00

# Native Plants
*See also* **Prairie Plants; Wildflowers**

*Organizations*
See chapter 8, **Native Plant Societies
and Botanical Clubs**

*Plant Sources*

A High Country Garden
2902 Rufina Street
Santa Fe, NM 87505
(800) 925-9387
Specialties: xeric plants
Catalogue: free

Alplains
32315 Pine Crest Court
Kiowa, CO 80117
(303) 621-2247
Specialties: Rocky Mountains
Catalogue: $1.00

Amanda's Garden
8410 Harpers Ferry Road
Springwater, NY 14560

Specialties: perennials
Catalogue: free

Cherokee Rose
9382 Island Road
St. Francisville, LA 70775
Specialties: Southeast
Catalogue: $1.00

Comstock Seed
8520 West 4th Street
Reno, NV 89523
(702) 746-3681
Specialties: Great Basin
Catalogue: free

Desert Moon Nursery
Box 600
Veguita, NM 87062
(505) 864-0614
Specialties: desert plants
Catalogue: $1.00

Edge of the Rockies
133 Hunna Road
Bayfield, CO 81122
Specialties: Rocky Mountains
Catalogue: $2.00

Frosty Hollow
Box 53
Langley, WA 98260
(206) 221-2332
Specialties: Northwest
Catalogue: long SASE

Goodness Grows
Box 311
Lexington, GA 30648
(706) 743-5055
Specialties: Southeast
Catalogue: free

Great Basin Natives
770 West 400 South
Provo, UT 84601

Specialties: Great Basin
Catalogue: $1.00

Wallace W. Hansen
2158 Bower Court SE
Salem, OR 97301
(503) 581-2638
Specialties: Pacific Northwest
Catalogue: $2.00

High Altitude Gardens
Box 419
Ketchum, ID 83340
(800) 874-7333
Specialties: high-altitude plants
Catalogue: $3.00

Holman Brothers Seed
Box 337
Glendale, AZ 85311
(602) 244-1650
Specialties: Sonoran and Mojave Desert
Catalogue: two stamps

Kiowa Creek Botanicals
520 North Grant Avenue
Fort Collins, CO 80521
Specialties: Plains and prairies seeds
Catalogue: $1.00

Las Pilitas Nursery
Star Route, Box 23X
Las Pilitas Road
Santa Margarita, CA 93453
(805) 438-5992
Specialties: California
Catalogue: $1.00

Little Valley Farm
Route 3, Box 544
Spring Green, WI 53588
(608) 935-3324
Specialties: Midwest
Catalogue: one stamp

Mostly Natives Nursery
Box 258, 27235 Highway 1
Tomales, CA 94971
(707) 878-2009
Specialties: West Coast and xeric plants
Catalogue: $3.00

Native Gardens
5737 Fisher Lane
Greenback, TN 37742
(615) 856-0220
Catalogue: $2.00

Native Plants, Inc.
417 Wakara Way
Salt Lake City, UT 84108
(800) 533-8498
Catalogue: $1.00

Niche Gardens
1111 Dawson Road
Chapel Hill, NC 27516
(919) 967-0078
Specialties: Southeast
Catalogue: $3.00

Northwest Native Seed
915 Davis Place South
Seattle, WA 98144
(206) 329-5804
Specialties: Northwest
Catalogue: $1.00

NWN Nursery
Box 1143
DeFuniak Springs, FL 32433
(904) 638-7572
Specialties: Southeast
Catalogue: free

Ben Pace Nursery
Route 1, Box 925
Pine Mountain, GA 31822
(706) 663-2346
Specialties: Southeast
Catalogue: free

Theodore Payne Foundation Nursery
10459 Tuxford Street
Sun Valley, CA 91352
(818) 768-1802
Specialties: California
Catalogue: $3.00

Pine Ridge Gardens
832 Sycamore Road
London, AR 72847
Catalogue: $1.00

Plants of the Southwest
Agua Fria
Route 6, Box 11
Santa Fe, NM 87505
(800) 788-SEED
Specialties: Southwest
Catalogue: $3.50

Rouge House Seed
250 Maple Street
Central Point, OR 97502
Specialties: Pacific Northwest
Catalogue: $1.00

Sharp Brothers Seed Company
Box 140
Healy, KS 67850
(316) 398-2231
Specialties: Midwest
Catalogue: $5.00

Shooting Star Nursery
444 Bates Road
Frankfort, KY 40601
(502) 223-1679
Specialties: east of the Rockies
Catalogue: $2.00

Southwestern Exposure
10310 East Fennimore
Apache Junction, AZ 85220
(602) 986-7771
Specialties: Southwest
Catalogue: two stamps

Southwestern Native Seeds
Box 50503
Tucson, AZ 85703
Specialties: Southwest
Catalogue: $1.00

Tripple Brook Farm
37 Middle Road
Southampton, MA 01073
(413) 527-4626
Specialties: Northeast
Catalogue: free

Western Native Seed
Box 1281
Canon City, CO 81215
(719) 275-8414
Specialties: West
Catalogue: long SASE

Wild Earth Native Plant Nursery
49 Mead Avenue
Freehold, NJ 07728
(908) 780-5661
Catalogue: $2.00

Wild Seed
Box 27751
Tempe, AZ 85285
(602) 345-0669
Specialties: Southwest
Catalogue: free

Yucca Du Nursery
Box 655
Waller, TX 77484
(409) 826-6363
Specialties: Texas and Mexico
Catalogue: $4.00

# Orchids
*See chapter 2*

# Ornamental Grasses

*Plant Sources*

Ambergate Gardens
8015 Krey Avenue
Waconia, MN 55387
(612) 443-2248
Catalogue: $2.00

Baylands Nursery
2835 Temple Court
East Palo Alto, CA 94303
Catalogue: $1.00

Kurt Bluemel, Inc.
2740 Greene Lane
Baldwin, MD 21013
(410) 557-7229
Catalogue: $3.00

Coastal Gardens and Nursery
4611 Socastee Boulevard
Myrtle Beach, SC 29575
(803) 293-2000
Catalogue: $2.00

Endangered Species
Box 1830
Tustin, CA 92681
Catalogue: $6.00

Flowerplace Plant Farm
Box 4865
Meridian, MS 39304
(601) 482-5686
Catalogue: $3.00

Garden Place
Box 388
6780 Heisley Road
Mentor, OH 44061
(216) 255-3705
Catalogue: $1.00

Gardens North
34 Helena Street
Ottawa, Ontario K1Y 3M8
Catalogue: $3.00

Greenlee Nursery
301 East Franklin Avenue
Pomona, CA 91766
(714) 629-9045
Catalogue: $5.00

Holbrook Farm and Nursery
Box 368
115 Lance Road
Fletcher, NC 28732
(704) 891-7790
Catalogue: free

Landscape Alternatives
1465 North Pascal Street
St. Paul, MN 55108
(612) 488-1342
Specialties: Minnesota wildflowers
Catalogue: $1.00

Limerock Ornamental Grasses, Inc.
RD 1, Box 111C
Port Matilda, PA 16870
(814) 692-2272
Catalogue: $3.00

Matterhorn Nursery, Inc.
227 Summit Park Road
Spring Valley, NY 10977
(914) 354-5986
Catalogue: $5.00

Neufeld Nursery
1865 California Street
Oceanside, CA 92054
Catalogue: $1.00

Pacific Coast Seed
7074D Commerce Circle
Pleasanton, CA 94566
Catalogue: $1.00

Paradise Water Gardens
14 May Street
Whitman, MA 02382
(617) 447-4711
Catalogue: $3.00

Pinky's Plants
Box 126
442 G Street
Pawnee City, NE 68420
(800) 94-PINKY
Catalogue: $3.50

Rice Creek Gardens
11506 Highway 65
Blaine, MN 55434
Catalogue: $1.00

Sunlight Gardens
174 Golden Lane
Andersonville, TX 77805
Catalogue: $3.00

Wavecrest Nursery and Landscaping
Company
2509 Lakeshore Drive
Fennville, MI 49408
(616) 542-4175
Catalogue: $1.00

Wildlife Nurseries
Box 2724
Oshkosh, WI 54903
(414) 231-3780
Catalogue: $1.00

Wildwood Nursery
3975 Emerald Avenue
LaVerne, CA 91750
Catalogue: $1.00

Woodlanders, Inc.
1128 Colleton Avenue
Aiken, SC 29801
(803) 648-7522
Catalogue: $2.00

Ya-Ka-Ama Nursery
6215 Eastside Road
Forestville, CA 95436
Catalogue: $1.00

# Peonies

## Organizations

American Peony Society
c/o Greta Kessenich
250 Interlachen Road
Hopkins, MN 55343
(612) 938-4706
Dues: $10.00
Publication: *Bulletin* (quarterly)

Canadian Peony Society
1246 Donlea Crescent
Oakville, Ontario L6J 1V7
(416) 845-5380

## Publication

*Chrysanthemum Corner with Peony Highlights*
Box 5635
Dearborn, MI 48128
Frequency: bimonthly
Subscription: $18.00

## Plant Sources

A & D Peony and Perennial Nursery
6808 180th Street SE
Snohomish, WA 98290
(206) 485-2487
Catalogue: $1.50

Bigger Peony Farm
201 Northeast Rice Road
Topeka, KS 66616
Catalogue: free

Brand Peony Farm
Box 842

St. Cloud, MN 56302
Catalogue: $1.00

C & C Nursery
Route 3, Box 422
Murray, KY 42071
(502) 753-2993
Catalogue: $1.00

Caprice Farm Nursery
15425 SW Pleasant Hill Road
Sherwood, OR 97140
(503) 625-7241
Catalogue: $2.00

Cricket Hill Garden
670 Walnut Hill Road
Thomaston, CT 06787
(203) 283-4707
Specialties: tree peonies
Catalogue: $2.00

Ellery Nurseries
Box 68
Smyrna, DE 19977
Catalogue: free

Don Hollingsworth Peonies
RR 3, Box 27
Maryville, MO 64468
(816) 562-3010
Catalogue: $1.00

Homestead Farms
Route 2, Box 31A
Owensville, MO 65066
(314) 437-4277
Catalogue: free

Klehm Nursery
4210 North Duncan Road
Champaign, IL 61821
(800) 553-3715
Catalogue: $4.00

Laurie's Landscaping
2959 Hobson Road
Downers Grove, IL 60517
(708) 969-1270
Catalogue: long SASE

The New Peony Farm
Box 18235
St. Paul, MN 55118
(612) 457-8994
Catalogue: free

Nicholls Gardens
4724 Angus Drive
Gainesville, VA 22065
(703) 754-9623
Catalogue: $1.00

Reath's Nursery
County Road 577, Box 247
Vulcan, MI 49892
(906) 563-9777
Catalogue: $1.00

Sevald Nursery
4937 3rd Avenue South
Minneapolis, MN 55409
(612) 822-3279
Specialties: herbaceous peonies
Catalogue: $1.00

Gilbert H. Wild and Son, Inc.
Box 338
1112 Joplin Street
Sarcoxie, MO 64862-0338
(417) 548-3514
Catalogue: $3.00

# Perennials

## Organization

The Perennial Plant Association
Department of Horticulture
Ohio State University

2001 Fyffe Court
Columbus, OH 43210

## Plant Sources

Ambergate Gardens
8015 Krey Avenue
Waconia, MN 55387
(612) 443-2248
Catalogue: $2.00

Bluestone Perennials, Inc.
7211 Middle Ridge Road
Madison, OH 44057
(800) 852-5243
Catalogue: free

Busse Gardens
13579 10th Street NW
Cokato, MN 55321
(612) 286-2654
Catalogue: $2.00

Burch Estate
650 Dodds Lane
Gladwyne, PA 19035
(215) 649-8944
Catalogue: $1.00

Canyon Creek Nursery
3527 Dry Creek Road
Oroville, CA 95965
(916) 533-2166
Catalogue: $2.00

Carroll Gardens
Box 310
Westminster, MD 21157
(800) 638-6334
Catalogue: $3.00

Coastal Gardens and Nursery
4611 Socastee Boulevard
Myrtle Beach, SC 29575
(803) 293-2000
Catalogue: $2.00

The Crownsville Nursery
Box 797
1241 Generals Highway
Crownsville, MD 21032
(410) 923-2212
Catalogue: $2.00

Daisy Fields
12635 SW Brighton Lane
Hillsboro, OR 97123
Catalogue: $1.00

Digging Dog Nursery
Box 471
Albion, CA 95410
(707) 937-1130
Catalogue: $3.00

Donaroma's Nursery
Box 2189
Edgartown, MA 02539
(508) 627-3036
Catalogue: $1.00

Englearth Gardens
2461 22nd Street
Hopkins, MI 49328
(616) 793-7196
Catalogue: 50¢

Fieldstone Gardens, Inc.
620 Quaker Lane
Vassalboro, ME 04989
(207) 923-3826
Catalogue: $2.00

Fir Grove Perennial Nursery
19917 NE 68th Street
Vancouver, WA 98682
(206) 944-8384
Catalogue: $2.00

Flowerplace Plant Farm
Box 4865, Meridian, MS 39304
(601) 482-5686
Catalogue: $3.00

Foothill Cottage Gardens
13925 Sontag Road
Grass Valley, CA 95945
(916) 272-4362
Catalogue: $3.00

Forestfarm
990 Tetherow Road
Williams, OR 97544
(503) 846-7269
Catalogue: $3.00

Garden Perennials
Route 1
Wayne, NE 68787
(402) 375-3615
Catalogue: $1.00

Garden Place
Box 388
6780 Heisley Road
Mentor, OH 44061
(216) 255-3705
Catalogue: $1.00

The Gathering Garden
Route 1, Box 41E
Efland, NC 27243
Catalogue: $1.00

Goodwin Creek Gardens
Box 83, Williams, OR 97544
(503) 846-7357
Catalogue: $1.00

Hauser's Superior View Farm
Route 1, Box 199
Bayfield, WI 54814
(715) 779-5404
Catalogue: free

Heronswood Nursery
7530 288th Street NE
Kingston, WA 98346
(360) 297-4172
Catalogue: $4.00

Hillary's Garden
Box 378
Sugar Loaf, NY 10981
Catalogue: $2.00

Hillside Gardens
515 Litchfield Road
Norfolk, CT 06058
(203) 542-5345
Note: No mail order
Catalogue: $3.00

Holbrook Farm and Nursery
Box 368
115 Lance Road
Fletcher, NC 28732
(704) 891-7790
Catalogue: $1.00

Indigo Marsh Nursery
2236 Iseman Road
Darlington, SC 29532
Catalogue: $2.00

International Growers Exchange, Inc.
17142 Lasher Road
Detroit, MI 48219
Catalogue: $3.00

Ivy Garth
Box 606
Gates Mills, OH 44040
Catalogue: free

Joy Creek Nursery
20300 NW Watson Road
Scappoose, OR 97056
(503) 543-7474
Catalogue: $2.00

Judy's Perennials
1206 Maple Avenue
Downers Grove, IL 60615
(708) 969-6514
Catalogue: free

Klehm Nursery
4210 North Duncan Road
Champaign, IL 61821
(800) 553-3715
Catalogue: $4.00

Lamb Nurseries
Route 1, Box 460B
Long Beach, WA 98631
(360) 642-4856
Catalogue: $1.50

Ledgecrest Greenhouses
1029 Storrs Road
Storrs, CT 06268
(203) 487-1661
Catalogue: free

Mary's Plant Farm
2410 Lanes Mill Road
Hamilton, OH 45013
(513) 894-0022
Catalogue: $1.00

Matterhorn Nursery
227 Summit Park Road
Spring Valley, NY 10977
(914) 354-5986
Catalogue: $5.00

Meadow View Farms
Box 3146
Central Point, OR 97502
Catalogue: $3.00

Milaeger's Gardens
4838 Douglas Avenue
Racine, WI 53402
(414) 639-2371
Catalogue: $1.00

Montrose Nursery
Box 957
Hillsborough, NC 27278
(919) 732-7787
Catalogue: $2.00

Niche Gardens
111 Dawson Road
Chapel Hill, NC 27516
(919) 967-0078
Catalogue: $1.00

Owen Farms
RR 3, Box 158
2951 Curve-Nankipoo Road
Ripley, TN 38063
(901) 635-1588
Catalogue: $2.00

The Perennial Connection
Box 3002-115
Newburyport, MA 01950
Catalogue: $1.00

The Perfect Season
Box 191
McMinnville, TN 37110
(615) 668-3225
Catalogue: $2.00

Pine Ridge Gardens
832 Sycamore Road
London, AR 72847
Catalogue: $1.00

Pinky's Plants
Box 126, 442 G Street
Pawnee City, NE 68420
(800) 94-PINKY
Catalogue: $3.50

Plant Delights Nursery
9241 Sauls Road
Raleigh, NC 27603
(919) 772-4794
Catalogue: $3.50

Powell's Gardens
9468 US Highway 70 E
Princeton, NC 27569
(919) 936-4421
Catalogue: $3.00

The Primrose Path
RD 2, Box 110
Scottdale, PA 15683
(412) 887-6756
Catalogue: $2.00

Riverhead Perennials
5 Riverhead Lane
East Lyme, CT 06333
(203) 437-7828
Catalogue: $2.00

Rolling Green Landscaping and Nursery
Box 760
64 Breakfast Hill Road
Greenland, NH 03840
(603) 436-2732
Catalogue: SASE

Roslyn Nursery
211 Burrs Lane
Dix Hills, NY 11746
(516) 543-9347
Catalogue: $3.00

Sunlight Gardens
174 Golden Lane
Andersonville, TX 77805
Catalogue: $3.00

Sunset Ridge Farm
Box 131
Sharptown, MD 21861
(410) 883-2347
Catalogue: $1.00

Surry Gardens
Box 145
Route 172
Surry, ME 04684
(207) 667-4493
Catalogue: free

H. R. Talmage & Sons
Horticultural Goddess
36 Sound Avenue

Riverhead, NY 11901
(516) 727-0124
Catalogue: $1.00

Andre Viette Farm and Nursery
Route 1, Box 16
Fishersville, VA 22939
(703) 942-2118
Catalogue: $3.00

Wayside Gardens
Box 1
Hodges, SC 29695
(800) 845-1124
Catalogue: $1.00

We-Du Nurseries
Route 5, Box 724
Marion, NC 28752
(704) 738-8300
Catalogue: $2.00

Weiss Brothers Perennial Nursery
11690 Colfax Highway
Grass Valley, CA 95945
(916) 272-7657
Catalogue: free

White Flower Farm
Route 63, Litchfield, CT 06759
(203) 469-9600
Catalogue: $4.00

Woodside Gardens
1191 Egg & I Road
Chimcum, WA 98325
(206) 732-4754
Catalogue: $2.00

# Prairie Plants
*See also* **Native Plants; Wildflowers**

*Organizations*
*See chapter* 8, **Native Plant Societies and
Botanical Clubs**

*Plant Sources*

Bamert Seed Company
Route 3, Box 1120
Muleshoe, TX 79347
(800) 262-9892
Catalogue: free

Bluestem Prairie Nursery
Route 2, Box 106A
Hillsboro, IL 62049
(217) 532-6344
Catalogue: free

Dyck Arboretum of the Plains
Seed Exchange
Hesston College
Box 3000
Hesston, KS 67062
(316) 327-8127
Catalogue: long SASE

Holland Wildflower Farms
290 O'Neal Lane
Elkins, AR 72727
(501) 643-2622
Catalogue: long SASE with two stamps

Kiowa Creek Botanicals
520 North Grant Avenue
Fort Collins, CO 80521
Catalogue: $1.00

LaFayette Home Nursery
RR #1, Box 1A
LaFayette, IL 61449
(309) 995-3311
Catalogue: free

Landscape Alternatives
1465 North Pascal Street
St. Paul, MN 55108
(612) 488-1342
Catalogue: $1.00

Milaeger's Gardens
4838 Douglas Avenue
Racine, WI 53402
(414) 639-2371
Catalogue: $1.00

The Natural Garden
38 W443 Highway 64
St. Charles, IL 60174
(708) 584-0150
Catalogue: $2.00

Nesta Prairie Perennials
1019 Miller Road
Kalamazoo, MI 49001
(800) 233-5025
Catalogue: free

Prairie Moon Nursery
Route 3, Box 163
Winona, MN 55987
(507) 452-1362
Catalogue: $2.00

Prairie Nursery
Box 306
Westfield, WI 53964
(608) 296-3679
Catalogue: $3.00

Prairie Restoration, Inc.
Box 327
Princeton, MN 55371
(612) 389-4342
Catalogue: free

Prairie Ridge Nursery
9738 Overland Road
Mount Horeb, WI 53572
(608) 437-5245
Catalogue: $3.00

Prairie Seed Source
Box 83
North Lake, WI 53064
Catalogue: $1.00

Shooting Star Nursery
444 Bates Road
Frankfort, KY 40601
(502) 223-1679
Catalogue: $2.00

Stock Seed Farms, Inc.
28008 Mill Road
Murdock, NE 68407
(402) 867-3771
Catalogue: free

# Rare and Unusual Plants and Seeds

*Plant Sources*

Dr. A. N. Berkutenko
c/o Louise Ann Zurbrick
Box 210562
Anchorage, AK 99521
Specialties: seeds from Siberia
and the Russian far east
Catalogue: $1.00

J. L. Hudson, Seedsman
Box 1058
Redwood City, CA 94064
Specialties: rare seeds
Catalogue: $1.00

Karmix Exotix Nursery
Box 146
Shelburne, Ontario L0N 1SO
Specialties: wild-collected
international seeds
Catalogue: $2.00

Rare Plant Research
13245 SE Harold
Portland, OR 97236
Specialties: caudiciforms
Catalogue: $2.00

Rare Seed Locators, Inc.
Drawer 2479

2140 Shattuck Avenue
Berkeley, CA 94704
Catalogue: long SASE

SBE Seeds
3421 Bream Street
Gautier, MS 39553
(601) 497-6544
Catalogue: three stamps

Siskiyou Rare Plant Nursery
2825 Cummings Road
Medford, OR 97501
(503) 772-6846
Catalogue: $2.00

Sunquest Seed Company
2411 Aquarius Road
Orange Park, FL 32073
Catalogue: free

# Rhododendrons

*See* **Azaleas, Rhododendrons, and Woody Shrubs**

# Rock Garden Plants

*See chapter 2*

# Roses

*See chapter 2*

# Shade Plants

*Plant Sources*

Busse Gardens
13579 10th Street NW
Cokato, MN 55321
(612) 286-2654
Catalogue: $2.00

Heronswood Nursery
7530 288th Street NE
Kingston, WA 98436
(360) 297-4172
Catalogue: $4.00

Nature's Garden
40611 Highway 226
Scio, OR 97374
Catalogue: long SASE with two stamps

Pinky's Plants
Box 126
442 G Street
Pawnee City, NE 68420
(800) 94-PINKY
Catalogue: $3.50

Rainforest Gardens
13139 224th Street
Maple Ridge, British Columbia V2X 7E7
(604) 467-4218
Catalogue: $2.00

Shady Oaks Nursery
112 10th Avenue SE
Waseca, MN 56903
(507) 835-5033
Catalogue: $3.00

Spring Hill Gardens
110 West Elm Street
Tipp City, OH 45371
(800) 582-8527
Catalogue: $3.00

Stocklein's Nursery
135 Critchlow Road
Renfrew, PA 16053
(412) 586-7882
Catalogue: $1.00

Sunlight Gardens
174 Golden Lane
Andersonville, TX 77805
Catalogue: $3.00

Underwood Shade Nursery
Box 1386
North Attleboro, MA 02763
Catalogue: $2.00

## Succulents
See **Cacti and Succulents**

## Tulips
See **Bulbs**

## Violas

*Plant Source*

Canyon Creek Nursery
3527 Dry Creek Road
Oroville, CA 95965
(916) 533-2166
Catalogue: $2.00

## Water Garden Plants
See *Chapter 2*

## Wildflowers

*Organizations*
See also *chapter 8*, **Native Plant Societies
and Botanical Clubs**

National Wildflower Research Center
4801 La Crosse Boulevard
Austin, TX 78739
(512) 292-4100
Dues: $25.00
Publications: *Wildflower Journal; Wildflower*
newsletter

New England Wild Flower Society
Garden in the Woods
180 Hemenway Road

Framingham, MA 01701
(508) 877-7630
Dues: $35.00
Publication: *From the Garden* newsletter
(three times annually)

*Plant Sources*

Agua Fria Nursery
1409 Agua Fria Street
Santa Fe, NM 87501
Specialties: western wildflowers
Catalogue: free

Agua Viva Seed Ranch
Route 1, Box 8
Taos, NM 87571
(800) 248-9080
Specialties: xeric plants
Catalogue: free

Appalachian Wildflower Nursery
Route 1, Box 275A
Reedsville, PA 17804
(717) 667-6998
Catalogue: $2.00

Applewood Seed Company, Inc.
Box 10761, Edgemont Station
Golden, CO 80401
(303) 431-6283
Catalogue: free

Bentley Seeds, Inc.
16 Railroad Avenue
Cambridge, NY 12816
(518) 677-2603
Catalogue: $1.00

Boothe Hill Wildflower Seeds
23B Boothe Hill
Chapel Hill, NC 27514
(919) 967-4091
Catalogue: $2.00

Brookside Wildflowers
Route 3, Box 740
Boone, NC 28607
(704) 963-5548
Catalogue: $2.00

Cattail Meadows, Ltd.
Box 39391
Solon, OH 44139
Catalogue: free

Donaroma's Nursery
Box 2189
Edgartown, MA 02539
(508) 627-3036
Catalogue: $1.00

Earthly Goods, Ltd.
903 East 15th Street
New Albany, IN 47150
Catalogue: $2.00

Ernst Crownvetch Farms
RD 5, Box 806
Meadville, PA 16335
(800) 873-3321
Specialties: Northeast
Catalogue: free

Timothy D. Field Ferns and Wildflowers
395 Newington Road
Newington, NH 03801
(603) 436-0457
Catalogue: free

Flowerplace Plant Farm
Box 4865
Meridian, MS 39304
(601) 482-5686
Catalogue: $3.00

Gardens of the Blue Ridge
Box 10, US 221 North
Pineola, NC 28662
(704) 733-2417
Catalogue: $3.00

Green Horizons
218 Quinland
Kerrville, TX 78028
(210) 257-5141
Specialties: Texas
Catalogue: long SASE

Groveland Botanicals
422 Clymer
Penwater, MI 49449
Catalogue: $1.00

High Altitude Gardens
Box 419
Ketchum, ID 83340
(800) 874-7333
Specialties: Northwest
Catalogue: $3.00

Holbrook Farm and Nursery
Box 368
115 Lance Road
Fletcher, NC 28732
(704) 891-7790
Catalogue: $1.00

J. L. Hudson, Seedsman
Box 1058
Redwood City, CA 94064
Specialties: California
Catalogue: $1.00

Landscape Alternatives
1465 North Pascal Street
St. Paul, MN 55108
(612) 488-1342
Specialties: Minnesota wildflowers
Catalogue: $1.00

Larner Seeds
Box 407
Bolinas, CA 94924
(415) 868-9407
Specialties: western wildflowers
Catalogue: $3.00

Midwest Wildflowers
Box 64
Rockton, IL 61072
Catalogue: $1.00

Missouri Wildflowers Nursery
9814 Pleasant Hill Road
Jefferson City, MO 65109
Catalogue: $1.00

Moon Mountain Wildflowers
Box 725
Carpinteria, CA 93014
(805) 684-2565
Catalogue: $2.00

Native Gardens
5737 Fisher Lane
Greenback, TN 37742
(615) 856-0220
Catalogue: $2.00

Native Seeds, Inc.
14590 Triadelphia Mill Road
Dayton, MD 21036
(301) 596-9818
Catalogue: free

New England Wild Flower Society
Garden-in-the-Woods Gift Shop
180 Hemenway Road
Framingham, MA 01701
(617) 237-4924
Catalogue: $2.50

Niche Gardens
1111 Dawson Road
Chapel Hill, NC 27516
(919) 967-0078
Specialties: southeastern wildflowers
Catalogue: $3.00

Northwest Native Seed
915 Davis Place South
Seattle, WA 98144
(206) 329-5804

Specialties: Northwest
Catalogue: $1.00

Oakridge Nursery
Box 182
East Kingston, NH 03827
(603) 642-8227
Catalogue: free

Orchid Gardens
2232 139th Avenue NW
Andover, MN 55744
Catalogue: 75¢

Theodore Payne Foundation Nursery
10459 Tuxford Street
Sun Valley, CA 91352
(818) 768-1802
Specialties: California
Catalogue: $3.00

Plants of the Southwest
Agua Fria
Route 6, Box 11
Santa Fe, NM 87505
(800) 788-SEED
Specialties: Southwest
Catalogue: $3.50

Clyde Robin Seed Company, Inc.
Box 2366
Castro Valley, CA 94546
(510) 785-0425
Catalogue: $2.00

Rocky Mountain Rare Plants
Box 20483
Denver, CO 80220
Specialties: drought-tolerant seeds and
plants
Catalogue: $1.00

Seeds of Alaska
Box 3127
Kenai, AK 99611
(907) 262-5267

Specialties: Alaska wildflowers
Catalogue: $3.00

Shooting Star Nursery
444 Bates Road
Frankfort, KY 40601
(502) 223-1679
Specialties: east of the Rockies
Catalogue: $2.00

Sunlight Gardens
174 Golden Lane
Andersonville, TX 77805
Catalogue: $3.00

The Vermont Wildflower Farm
Route 7, Box 5
Charlotte, VT 05445
(802) 425-3500
Catalogue: $1.00

We-Du Nurseries
Route 5, Box 724
Marion, NC 28752
(704) 738-8300
Catalogue: $2.00

Wild and Crazy Seed Company
Box 895
Durango, CO 81302
(303) 780-5661
Specialties: Southwest
Catalogue: $2.00

Wild Earth Native Plant Nursery
49 Mead Avenue
Freehold, NJ 07728
(908) 780-5661
Catalogue: $2.00

Wildflower Seed Company
Box 406
St. Helena, CA 94574
Catalogue: $1.00

Wild Seed
Box 27751
Tempe, AZ 85285
(602) 345-0669
Specialties: Southwest
Catalogue: free

Wildseed Farms
Box 308
1101 Campo Rosa Road
Eagle Lake, TX 77434
(800) 848-0078
Catalogue: $2.00

The Wildwood Flower
Route 3, Box 165
Pittsboro, NC 27312
(919) 542-4344
Catalogue: long SASE

# Zinnias

*Plant Source*

Van Dyke Zinnias
5910 Corey Road
Perry, MI 48872
Catalogue: $1.00

# Specialty Gardening

THIS SECTION OF THE GARDENER'S SOURCEBOOK *contains listings for specialty garden areas: alpine and rock gardens, bonsai, butterfly gardening, fragrance gardens, historical gardens, orchids, roses, and water gardens. A section on rare-seed exchanges is also included. As in chapter 1, the sections for the different specialty garden types start with organizations and other sources of information and products; they go on to list plant sources alphabetically by nursery. With very few exceptions, only nurseries that specialize in these areas and can ship their plants are listed. Specialty nurseries that don't sell by mail often do exhibit at local and regional plant and flower shows. If you join an organization dedicated to your area of interest, you'll be kept informed about upcoming exhibits.*

## Alpine and Rock Gardening

*See also* **Bonsai**

### *Organizations*

Alpine Garden Club of British Columbia
Main Post Office Box 5161
Vancouver, British Columbia V6B 4B2
Publication: *Alpine Garden Club Bulletin*
(five times annually)

Alpine Garden Society
The Secretary
AGS Centre
Avon Bank, Pershore
Worcestershire WR10 3JP
England
(0386) 55-4790
Dues: £18.00
Publications: quarterly bulletin;
newsletter

American Rock Garden Society

Secretary
Box 67
Millwood, NY 10546
(914) 762-2948
Dues: $25.00
Publication: *Rock Garden Quarterly*

Newfoundland Alpine and
Rock Garden Club
Memorial University Botanical Garden
University of Newfoundland
St. John's, Newfoundland A1C 5S7
(709) 737-8590

Ontario Rock Garden Society
c/o Andrew Osyany
Box 146
Shelburne, Ontario L0N 1S0

Saxifrage Society
Adrian Young, Secretary
31 Eddington Road
London SW16 5BS

England
Dues: £10.00

Scottish Rock Garden Club
c/o Mrs. J. Thomlinson
1 Hillcrest Road
Bearsden, Glasgow G61 2EB
Scotland
Dues: $28.00
Publication: *The Rock Garden*
(semiannual journal)

## Supplies

Dorothy Bonitz
Herb & Flower Thyme
146 Great Oak Drive
Hampstead, NC 28443
Product: trough kit
Catalogue: free

Earthworks
Box 67
Hyattville, WY 82428
Product: hypertufa troughs
Catalogue: long SASE

Karen Harris
200 East Genesee Street
Fayetteville, NY 13066
Product: hypertufa troughs
Catalogue: SASE

Old World Garden Troughs®
Box 1253
Carmel, IN 46032
Product: troughs
Catalogue: $2.00

## Plant Sources

Alpenflora Gardens
17985 40th Avenue
Surrey, British Columbia V3S 4N8
Catalogue: $1.00

Alpine Gardens
12446 County F
Stitzer, WI 53825
(608) 822-6382
Catalogue: $2.00

Alplains
32315 Pine Crest Court
Kiowa, CO 80117
(303) 621-2247
Catalogue: $1.00

Appalachian Wildflower Nursery
Route 1, Box 275A
Reedsville, PA 17084
(717)667-6998
Catalogue: $2.00

Arrowhead Alpines
Box 857, Fowlerville, MI 48836
(517) 223-3581
Catalogue: $2.00

Bijou Alpines
13921 240th Street East
Graham, WA 98338
(206) 893-6191
Catalogue: $1.00

Boulder Wall Gardens
McLean Road
Walpole, NH 03608
(603) 756-9056
Catalogue: $1.00

The Bovees Nursery
1737 SW Coronado
Portland, OR 97219
(800) 435-9250
Catalogue: $2.00

Sam Bridge Nursery N' Greenhouses
437 North Street
Greenwich, CT 06830
(203) 869-3418
Note: No shipping

Chehalis Rare Plant Nursery
Route 3, Box 363
Lebanon, MO 65536
(206) 748-7627
Specialties: auricula seed
Catalogue: $1.00

Collector's Nursery
1602 NE 162nd Avenue
Vancouver, WA 98684
Catalogue: $1.00

Colorado Alpines
Box 2708
Avon, CO 81620
(303) 949-6464
Catalogue: $2.00

Country Cottage
10502 North 135th Street West
Sedgwick, KS 67135
Catalogue: 50¢

Cricklewood Nursery
11907 Nevers Road
Snohomish, WA 98290
(206) 568-2829
Catalogue: $2.00

The Cummins Garden
22 Robertsville Road
Marlboro, NJ 07746
(908) 536-2591
Catalogue: $2.00

Daystar
Route 2, Box 250
Litchfield, ME 04350
(207) 724-3369
Catalogue: $1.00

Dilworth Nursery
1200 Election Road
Oxford, PA 19363
(610) 932-0347
Catalogue: $1.00

Eastern Plant Specialties
Box 226
Georgetown, ME 04548
(207) 371-2888
Catalogue: $3.00

Ericaceae
Box 293
Deep River, CT 06417
Catalogue: free

Evergreen Gardenworks
430 North Oak Street
Ukiah, CA 95482
(707) 462-8909
Catalogue: $2.00

Field House Alpines
6730 West Mercer Way
Mercer Island, WA 98040
Catalogue: $2.00

Fieldstone Gardens, Inc.
620 Quaker Lane
Vassalboro, ME 04989
(207) 923-3826
Catalogue: $2.00

Fir Grove Perennial Nursery
19917 NE 68th Street
Vancouver, WA 98682
(206) 944-8384
Catalogue: $2.00

Joy Creek Nursery
20300 NW Watson Road
Scappoose, OR 97056
(503) 543-7474
Catalogue: $2.00

Lamb Nurseries
East 101 Sharp Avenue
Spokane, WA 99202
(509) 328-7956
Catalogue: $1.00

Miniature Plant Kingdom
4125 Harrison Grade Road
Sebastopol, CA 95472
(707) 874-2233
Catalogue: $2.50

Montrose Nursery
Box 957
Hillsborough, NC 27278
(919) 732-7787
Catalogue: $2.00

Mt. Tahoma Nursery
28111 112th Avenue East
Graham, WA 98338
(206) 847-9827
Catalogue: $1.00

Nature's Garden
40611 Highway 226
Scio, OR 97374
Catalogue: one stamp

Porterhowse Farms
41370 SE Thomas Road
Sandy, OR 97055
(503) 668-5834
Catalogue: $6.00

The Primrose Path
RD 2, Box 110
Scottdale, PA 15683
(412) 887-6756
Catalogue: $2.50

Rare Plant Research
13245 SE Harold
Portland, OR 97236
(503) 762-0289
Specialties: lewisia
Catalogue: $2.00

Rice Creek Gardens
11506 Highway 65
Minneapolis, MN 55434
Catalogue: $1.00

Robyn's Nest Nursery
7802 NE 63rd Street
Vancouver, WA 98662
(206) 256-7399
Catalogue: $2.00

Rocknoll Nursery
7812 Mad River Road
Hillsboro, OH 45133
(513) 393-5545
Catalogue: $1.00

Rocky Mountain Rare Plants
Box 20483
Denver, CO 80220
Catalogue: $1.00

Roslyn Nursery
211 Burrs Lane
Dix Hills, NY 11746
(516) 543-9347
Catalogue: $3.00

Siskiyou Rare Plant Nursery
2825 Cummings Road
Medford, OR 97501
(503) 772-6846
Catalogue: $2.00

Skyline Nursery
4772 Sequim-Dungeness Way
Sequim, WA 98382
Catalogue: $2.00

Springvale Farm Nursery
Mozier Hollow Road
Hamburg, IL 62045
(618) 232-1108
Catalogue: $2.00

Squaw Mountain Gardens
36212 SE Squaw Mountain Road
Estacada, OR 97023
(503) 630-5458
Catalogue: $2.00

Strong's Alpine Succulents
Box 2264
Flagstaff, AZ 86003
(602) 526-5784
Catalogue: $1.00

Surry Gardens
Box 145
Route 172
Surry, ME 04684
(207) 667-4493
Catalogue: free

Trennoll Nursery
3 West Page Avenue
Trenton, OH 45067
(513) 988-6121
Catalogue: $2.00

We-Du Nurseries
Route 5, Box 724
Marion, NC 28752
(704) 738-8300
Catalogue: $2.00

Wildginger Woodlands
Box 1091
Webster, NY 14580
Catalogue: $1.00

Willamette Valley Gardens Nursery
Box 285
Lake Oswego, OR 97034
(503) 636-6517
Catalogue: one stamp

Woodland Rockery
6210 Klam Road
Otter Lake, MI 48464
Catalogue: $1.00

Wrightman Alpines
RR 3
Kerwood, Ontario N0M 2B0
(519) 247-3751
Catalogue: $2.00

# Bonsai

## *Organizations*

The American Bonsai Society
Executive Office
2901 31st Court SE
Puyallup, WA 98374
Dues: $20.00
Publications: BONSAI: *Journal of The American Bonsai Society; ABStracts newsletter*

Bonsai Canada
12 Beardmore Crescent
Willowdale, Ontario M2K 2P5
Publication: *Bonsai Canada*

Bonsai Clubs International
c/o Virginia Ellermann
2636 West Mission Road
Tallahassee, FL 32304
(904) 575-1442
Dues: $25.00
Publication: *Bonsai*
(bimonthly magazine)

Bonsai Society of Greater New York
Membership Secretary
Box 565
Glen Oaks, NY 11004
(516) 293-9246
Dues: $17.00
Publication: *The Bonsai Bulletin*
(quarterly)

Toronto Bonsai Society
Eva Rae Davidson
190 McAllister Road
Downsview, Ontario M3H 2N9
(416) 590-9969
Dues: Canada $10.00
Publication: journal

## Publications

*Bonsai Today*
Stone Lantern Publishing Company
Box 816, Sudbury, MA 01776
Frequency: bimonthly
Subscription: $42.00

*International Bonsai*
International Bonsai Arboretum
Box 23894
Rochester, NY 14692
(716) 334-2595
Frequency: quarterly
Subscription: $24.00

Bonsai Institute of California
Box 6268
Whittier, CA 90609
Note: Publisher of books on bonsai

## Tools and Supplies

Artistic Plants
608 Holly Drive
Burleson, TX 76028
(817) 295-0802
Catalogue: $1.00

Jim Barrett
480 Oxford Drive
Arcadia, CA 91006
(818) 445-4529
Catalogue: free

Bennett's Bonsai Nursery
1816 Fairfax Avenue
Metairie, LA 70003
(504) 888-7994
Catalogue: free

Bonsai Associates, Inc.
3000 Chestnut Avenue
Baltimore, MD 21211
(410) 235-5336
Catalogue: $2.00

Bonsai Mountain Garden
Box 241
Helotes, TX 78023
Catalogue: $5.00

Bonsai Northwest
5021 South 144th Street
Seattle, WA 98168
(206) 242-8244
Catalogue: $2.00

Dallas Bonsai Garden
Box 801565
Dallas, TX 75380
(800) 982-1223
Catalogue: free

Dave's Aquarium and Greenhouse
RR 1, Box 97
Kelley, IA 50134
(515) 769-2446
Catalogue: four stamps

Fujiyama™ Tool Company
Box 830384
Richardson, TX 75083
(800) 842-5523
Product: Fujiyama™ brand bonsai tools

J & J Landscaping
Bonsai International Division
Box 21683
Tampa, FL 33622
(813) 645-8777
Catalogue: $3.00

Living Sculpture Bonsai
Box 257
Princeton Junction, NJ 08550
(609) 275-9270
(800) 941-0888
Product: humidity trays
Catalogue: free

Masakuni Company USA
Box 18290

Encino, CA 91416
(818) 345-7614
Product: Masakuni brand bonsai tools
Catalogue: free

Nature's Way Nursery
1451 Pleasant Hill Road
Harrisburg, PA 17112
(717) 545-4555
Catalogue: free

Niwa Tool Company
2661 Bloomfield Court
Fairfield, CA 94533
(800) 443-5512
Catalogue: $2.00

John Palmer Bonsai
Box 29
Sudbury, MA 01776
(617) 443-5084
Catalogue: free

Raska Sales
Route 2, Box 38
Skiatook, OK 74070
(918) 396-2663
Catalogue: free

Rosade Bonsai Studio
6912 Ely Road
New Hope, PA 18938
(215) 862-5925
Catalogue: $1.00

Joshua Roth Limited
9901 SW 25th Avenue
Portland, OR 97219
(800) 624-4635
Catalogue: free

## Bonsai Containers

Bonsai by the Monastery
Box B
2625 Highway 212 SW

Conyers, GA 30208
(770) 918-9661
Catalogue: $3.00

Bonsai Northwest
5021 South 144th Street
Seattle, WA 98168
(206) 242-8244
Catalogue: $2.00

DuPont Bonsai
Box 375
Newberg, OR 97132
(503) 538-6071
Catalogue: $4.00

Flowertown Bonsai
207 East Luke Street
Summerville, SC 29483
(800) 774-0003
Catalogue: free

Little Trees
Box 41
Carlotta, CA 95528
(707) 768-3450
Product: planting stones and slabs
Catalogue: 50¢

Midwest Bonsai Pottery
8311 Racine Trail
Austin, TX 78717
Catalogue: $1.00

Oregon Outcroppings
Box 178
Trail, OR 97541
(503) 878-3313
Catalogue: $2.00

Pine Garden Bonsai Company
20331 State Route 530 NE
Arlington, WA 98223
(360) 435-5995
Catalogue: $2.00

Sara Rayner Pottery
1025 West 4th Street
Red Wing, MN 55066
Catalogue: $3.00

Sosaku Bonsai Potter
Box 520476
Salt Lake City, UT 84152
Catalogue: SASE

Tokonoma Bonsai
87 Old Trolley Road
Summerville, SC 29485
(803) 875-6567
Catalogue: free

## Other Information and Supplies

*An extensive annual directory of bonsai growers and suppliers is available from:*

Equinox, Inc.
Box 550
Nicholasville, KY 40356
(606) 887-2671
Cost: $6.00

*The Bonsai Manager database program is available from:*

Phillip Adams
140 Riverside Drive
New York, NY 10024
System requirements: DOS
Catalogue: free

*Bonsai wood-carving burrs are available from:*

Nippon Art Forms
Box 4975
Laguna Beach, CA 92652
(714) 497-5626
Catalogue: free

*Flumes (kakeki) are available from:*

I-Ten
124 Johnston Boulevard
Lexington, KY 40503
Catalogue: SASE

*Bonsai notepaper is available from:*

Jennie Popeleski
96 Greenlawn Road
Huntington, NY 11743
Catalogue: free

*Bonsai jewelry is available from:*

Lucille Lee Roberts
445 South Los Robles, Suite 207
Pasadena, CA 91101
(818) 568-8161
Catalogue: free

## Plant Sources

Allshapes Bonsai Nursery
Box 337
230 Everitts Road
Ringoes, NJ 08551
(908) 788-1938
Catalogue: SASE

Artistic Plants
608 Holly Drive
Burleson, TX 76028
(817) 295-0802
Catalogue: $1.00

Bennett's Bonsai Nursery
1816 Fairfax Avenue
Metairie, LA 70003
(504) 888-7994
Catalogue: free

Bonsai Farm
Box 130
Lavernia, TX 78121

(210) 649-2109
Catalogue: $1.00

Bonsai of Brooklyn
2443 McDonald Avenue
Brooklyn, NY 11223
(718) 339-8252
(800) 8-BONSAI
Catalogue: free

The Bonsai Shop
43 William Street
Smithtown, NY 11787
(516) 724-3055
Catalogue: $2.00

The Bonsai Tree
609 Shallowford Road
Gainesville, GA 30504
(404) 535-2991
Catalogue: free

Bonsai West
Box 1291, 100 Great Road
Littleton, MA 01460
(508) 486-3556
Catalogue: $2.00

Brussel's Bonsai Nursery
8365 Center Hill Road
Olive Branch, MS 38654
(601) 895-7457
(800) 582-2593
Catalogue: $2.00

The Cummins Garden
22 Robertsville Road
Marlboro, NJ 07746
(908) 536-2591
Catalogue: $2.00

Dallas Bonsai Garden
Box 801565
Dallas, TX 75380
(800) 982-1223
Catalogue: free

Evergreen Gardenworks
430 North Oak Street
Ukiah, CA 95482
(707) 462-8909
Catalogue: $2.00

Flowertown Bonasi
207 East Luke Street
Summerville, SC 29483
(800) 774-0003
Catalogue: free

Green Gardens Nursery
16 Burr Road
East Northport, NY 11731
(516) 499-4235
Catalogue: $1.00

Grove Way Bonsai Nursery
1239 Grove Way
Hayward, CA 94541
(510) 537-1157
Catalogue: SASE

Japan Nursery Florida, Inc.
5300 Orange Boulevard
Sanford, FL 32771
(407) 328-9793
Catalogue: $4.00

Jiu-San Bonsai
1243 Melville Road
Farmingdale, NY 11735
(516) 293-9246
Note: no mail order

Jope's Bonsai Nursery
Box 594
Wenham, MA 10984
Catalogue: $2.00

Kyodai Bonsai
5485 Riversedge
Milford, MI 48383
(800) 513-5995
Catalogue: free

Lone Pine Connection
Box 1338
Forestville, CA 95436
Catalogue: $3.00

The Maine Bonsai Gardens
Old Stage Road
Woolwich, ME 04579
(800) 532-3983
Catalogue: SASE

Marrs Tree Farm
Box 375
Puyallup, WA 98371
Catalogue: $1.00

Matsu-Momiji Nursery
Box 11414
410 Borbeck Street
Philadelphia, PA 19111
(215) 722-6286
Catalogue: $2.00

McLain's Garden Center and Bonsai
Nursery
5776 Buncomb Road
Shreveport, LA 71129
(318) 688-1640
Catalogue: $1.00

Miami Tropical Bonsai
14775 SW 232nd Street
Homestead, FL 33170
(305) 258-0865
Catalogue: free

MicroFolia Bonsai Nursery
Box 265, Camp Hill, PA 17001
(717) 691-0286
Catalogue: $1.00

Miniature Plant Kingdom
4125 Harrison Grade Road
Sebastopol, CA 95472
(707) 874-2233
Catalogue: $2.50

Mountain Maples
5901 Spyrock Road
Laytonville, CA 95454
Specialties: Japanese maple cultivars
Catalogue: $1.00

Mt. Si Bonsai
43321 SE Mt. Si Road
North Bend, WA 98045
(206) 888-0350
Catalogue: SASE

Nature's Way Nursery
1451 Pleasant Hill Road
Harrisburg, PA 17112
(717) 545-4555
Catalogue: free

New England Bonsai
914 South Main Street
Bellingham, MA 02019
(508) 883-2666
Catalogue: $1.00

Northland Gardens
315A West Mountain Road
Queensbury, NY 12804
(518) 798-4277
Catalogue: $2.00

Oriental Garden
307 Disbrow Hill Road
Perrineville, NJ 08535
(609) 490-0705
Catalogue: $2.00

Pen Y Bryn Nursery
RR 1, Box 1313, Forksville, PA 18616
(717) 924-3377
Catalogue: free

Pine Garden Bonsai Company
20331 State Route 530 NE
Arlington, WA 98223
(360) 435-5995
Catalogue: $2.00

Porterhowse Farms
41370 SE Thomas Road
Sandy, OR 97055
(503) 668-5834
Catalogue: $6.00

The Potted Forest
805 Dickens Road
Lilburn, GA 30247
(404) 564-0292
Catalogue: SASE

Rarafolia
16 Beverly Drive
Kintnersville, PA 18930
(215) 847-8208
Catalogue: $3.00

Roots 'n All Bonsai Gardens
RR 1, Box 586, Warner, NH 03278
(800) 223-3050
Catalogue: free

Royal Bonsai Garden, Inc.
1297 Park Street
Stoughton, MA 02072
(617) 344-6358
Catalogue: SASE

Shanti Bithi Nursery
3047 High Ridge Road
Stamford, CT 06903
(203) 329-0768
Catalogue: $3.00

Tom's Tiny Trees
14318 State Road
North Royalton, OH 44133
(216) 582-9411
Catalogue: free

Wildwood Gardens
14488 Rock Creek Road
Chardon, OH 44024
(216) 286-3714
Catalogue: $1.00

Wright's Nursery
1285 Southeast Township Road
Canby, OR 97013
(503) 266-8895
Catalogue: $1.00

# Butterfly Gardening

## Organizations

The Butterfly Gardeners Association
1021 North Main Street
Allentown, PA 18104

The Xerces Society
10 SW Ash Street
Portland, OR 97204
(503) 222-2788
Dues: $25.00
Publication: *Wings*
(three times annually)

## Butterfly Boxes

Old Beach
416 Brookcliff Lane
Cary, NC 27511
Catalogue: free

Treetop Designs
1117 East Webb Avenue
Burlington, NC 27215
(919) 229-9111
Catalogue: $2.00

## Butterfly Gardens

Butterfly World
Tradewinds Park South
3600 West Sample Road
Coconut Creek, FL 33063
(305) 977-4400

Butterfly World at Marine World
Marine World Parkway

Vallejo, CA 94589
(707) 644-4000

Callaway Gardens
Cecil B. Day Butterfly Center
Pine Mountain, GA 31822
(404) 663-2281

Cincinnati Zoo
3400 Vine Street
Cincinnati, OH 45220
(513) 281-4701

Des Moines Botanical Center
909 East River Drive
Des Moines, IA 50316
(515) 283-4148

Vancouver Island Butterfly World
341 West Crescent Road
Qualicum Beach, British Columbia
V0R 2T0
(604) 752-9319

*Plant Source*

Brudy's Exotics
Box 820874
HR 595
Houston, TX 77282
(800) 926-7333
Products: plants; seeds; eggs; larvae;
books
Catalogue: free

# Fragrance Gardening

*Plant Sources*

Flower Scent Gardens
14820 Moine Road
Doylestown, OH 44230
Catalogue: $2.00

The Fragrant Bower
11 Maya Loop
Santa Fe, NM 87505
(505) 983-6317
Catalogue: $5.00

The Fragrant Path
Box 328
Fort Calhoun, NE 68023
Catalogue: $1.00

Select Seeds—Antique Flowers
180 Stickney Hill Road
Union, CT 06076
(203) 684-9310
Catalogue: $2.00

# Historical Gardening

*Organizations*

Agricultural History Society
1301 New York Avenue NW, Room 1232
Washington, DC 20005
(202) 447-8183
Publication: *Agricultural History* (quarterly)

Alliance for Historic Landscape
Preservation
82 Wall Street, Suite 1105
New York, NY 10005

Association for Living Historical Farms
and Agricultural Museums
Route 14, Box 214
Santa Fe, NM 87505
(505) 471-2261
Publication: *Living Historical Farms Bulletin*
(quarterly)

Centre for Canadian Historical
Horticultural Studies
Library, Box 399
Royal Botanical Gardens
Hamilton, Ontario L8N 3H8

(416) 527-1158
Publication: *Canadian Horticultural History*

Cottage Garden Society
c/o Mrs. C. Tordorff
5 Nixon Close, Thornhill
Dewsbury, West Yorkshire WF12 0JA
England
(0924) 46-8469
Dues: $20.00
Publication: *CGS Newsletter* (quarterly)

The Garden Conservancy
Box 219
Cold Spring, NY 10516
(914) 265-2029
Dues: $35.00
Publication: newsletter

Garden History Society
Mrs. Anne Richards
5 The Knoll
Hereford HR1 1RU
England
(0432) 35-4479
Dues: £18.00
Publications: *Garden History* (semiannual);
*Newsletter* (three times annually)

Heritage Rose Foundation
1512 Gorman Street
Raleigh, NC 27606
(919) 834-2591
Publication: *Heritage Rose Foundation News*
(quarterly)

Historic Iris Preservation Society (HIPS)
Ada Godfrey
9 Bradford Street
Foxborough, MA 01035
Dues: AIS dues plus $5.00
Publication: *Roots Journal*

Historic Preservation Committee
American Society of
Landscape Architects

4401 Connecticut Ave NW
Washington, DC 20008
(202) 686-ASLA

National Association for Olmstead Parks
5010 Wisconsin Avenue NW, Suite 308
Washington, DC 20016
(202) 363-9511

New England Garden History Society
Massachusetts Horticultural Society
300 Massachusetts Avenue
Boston, MA 02115
(617) 536-9280
Dues: $25.00
Publications: *Journal* (annual);
*Belvedere* (occasional newsletter)

Pioneer Plant Society
c/o Mrs. P. A. Puryear
708 Holland Street
Navasota, TX 77868
(409) 825-3220
Dues: $7.00
Publication: *PPS Newsletter* (quarterly)

Southern Garden History Society
Old Salem, Inc.
Drawer F, Salem Station
Winston-Salem, NC 27101
(919) 724-3125
Dues: $20.00
Product: *Magnolia* (quarterly)

Texas Rose Rustlers
c/o Margaret Sharpe
9246 Kerrwood Lane
Houston, TX 77080
(713) 464-8607
Publication: *Old Texas Rose* (quarterly)

The Thomas Jefferson Center for
Historic Plants
Monticello, Box 316
Charlottesville, VA 22902
(804) 979-5283

## Publications

*The Historical Gardener*
1910 North 35th Place
Mount Vernon, WA 98273
(206) 424-3154
Frequency: quarterly
Subscription: $12.00

*Journal of Garden History*
Taylor & Francis, Inc.
1900 Frost Road, Suite 101
Bristol, PA 19007
Frequency: quarterly
Subscription: $70.00

## Plant Sources

The Thomas Jefferson Center
for Historic Plants
Monticello
Box 316
Charlottesville, VA 22902
(804) 296-4800
Catalogue: $1.00

Old House Gardens
536 3rd Street
Ann Arbor, MI 48103
(313) 995-1486
Specialties: historical bulbs
Catalogue: $1.00

Perennial Pleasures Nursery
2 Brickhouse Road
East Hardwick, VT 05836
(802) 472-5512
Specialties: plants for historical
restoration
Catalogue: $2.00

Select Seeds—Antique Flowers
180 Stickney Hill Road
Union, CT 06076
(203) 684-9310
Catalogue: $2.00

Sisters' Bulb Farm
Route 2, Box 170
Gibsland, LA 71028
(318) 843-6379
Specialties: heirloom daffodils
Catalogue: free

# Orchids

## Organizations

American Orchid Society
6000 South Olive Avenue
West Palm Beach, FL 33405
(407) 585-8666
Dues: $30.00
Publication: *Orchids* (monthly journal)

Canadian Orchid Congress
c/o Peter Root
Box 241
Goodwood, Ontario L0C 1A0
(416) 640-5643
Publication: *Canadian Orchid Journal*
(annual)

Cymbidium Society of America
533 South Woodland
Orange, CA 92669
(714) 532-4719
Dues: $25.00
Publication: *The Orchid Advocate*
 (bimonthly magazine)

Orchid Society of Great Britain
120 Crofton Road
Orpington, Kent BR6 8HZ
England

Victoria Orchid Society
Ingrid Ostrander
Box 6538, Depot 1
Victoria, British Columbia
V8P 5M4
(604) 652-6133

Dues: Canada $15.00
Publication: monthly bulletin

## Publications

*Orchid Digest*
Orchid Digest Corporation
Box 916
Carmichael, CA 95609
Frequency: quarterly
Subscription: $18.00

*The Orchid Hunter*
Terry Ferrar, Editor
RR 1, Box 62A
Adamsville, PA 16110
Frequency: monthly
Subscription: $17.00

*Orchid Information Exchange*
1230 Plum Avenue
Simi Valley, CA 93065
Frequency: monthly
Subscription: $15.00

*The Orchid Review*
The Royal Horticultural Society
80 Vincent Square
London SW1P 2PE
England
Frequency: bimonthly
Subscription: £20.00

*Phalaenopsis Fancier*
Doreen Vander Tuin, Editor
1230 Plum Avenue
Simi Valley, CA 93065
Frequency: monthly newsletter
Subscription: $15.00

## Growing Supplies

Dr. James D. Brasch
Box 354
McMaster University
Hamilton, Ontario L8S 1C0

(416) 335-1713
Product: Keikigrow plant growth
regulators
Catalogue: $2.00

Classic Stone Corporation
4044 West Lower Buckeye Road
Phoenix, AZ
(800) 644-0827
Product: media planting kits
Catalogue: free

CMI Plastics
Box 369
Cranbury, NJ 08512
(609) 395-1920
Product: Humidi-Grow® plant trays
Catalogue: free

Dyna-Gro™ Corporation
1065 Broadway
San Pablo, CA 94806
(800) DYNA-GRO
Product: liquid nutrient formula
Catalogue: free

G & B Orchid Laboratory and Nursery
2426 Cherimoya Drive
Vista, CA 92084
(619) 727-2611
(800) 786-1569
Product: propagation media
Catalogue: free

G & S Laboratories
645 Stoddard Lane
Santa Barbara, CA 93108
(805) 969-5991
Product: propagation media
Catalogue: free

M & M Orchid Supply
Box 306
Whippany, NJ 07981
(201) 515-5209
Catalogue: free

The Nova Company
Box 2192
Kearney, NE 68847
(308) 237-0971
Product: Ag-Tonic foliar feed
Catalogue: free

OFE International, Inc.
Box 161302
Miami, FL 33186
(305) 253-7080
Catalogue: $2.00

Plant Collectibles
103 Kenview Avenue
Buffalo, NY 14217
(716) 875-1221
Catalogue: $2.00

Sigma Chemical Company
Box 14508
St. Louis, MO 63178
(314) 771-5765
Product: propagation media
Catalogue: free

Stewart Orchids
Box 550
3376 Foothill Road
Carpinteria, CA 93013
(805) 684-5448
(800) 621-2450
Catalogue: $2.00

Sunshine Growers' Supply, Inc.
4760 Taylor Road
Punta Gorda, FL 33950
(800) 954-6735
Catalogue: free

Teas Nursery Company, Inc.
Box 1603
Bellaire, TX 77402
(800) 446-7723
Catalogue: $2.00

Tropical Plant Products
Box 547754
Orlando, FL 32854
(407) 293-2451
Catalogue: long SASE

Wilder Agriculture Products
Company, Inc.
4188 Bethel-Wilmington Road
New Wilmington, PA 16142
(800) 462-8102
Catalogue: free

Worm's Way, Inc.
3151 South Highway 446
Bloomington, IN 47401
(812) 331-0300
(800) 274-9676
Catalogue: free

## Tissue Culture and Other Services

Bastrop Botanical
Box 628
Bastrop, TX 78602
(512) 321-7161
Services: species flasking
Catalogue: free

Critter Creek Laboratory
400 Critter Creek Road
Lincoln, CA 95648
(916) 645-7111
Services: virus testing
Catalogue: free

G & B Orchid Laboratory and Nursery
2426 Cherimoya Drive
Vista, CA 92084
(619) 727-2611
(800) 786-1569
Services: species flasking
Catalogue: free

Halcyon Laboratories
2627 North Baldwin

Portland, OR 97217
(503) 240-1724
Services: seed flasking and tissue culture
Catalogue: free

Orchis Laboratories
4820 Mason Road
Burdett, NY 14818
(607) 546-2072
Services: tissue culture and virus testing
Catalogue: free

Stewart Orchids Micropropagation
100 Hawthorne Road
Conroe, TX 77301
(409) 760-3433
Services: seed sowing, replating,
tissue culture

## Orchid Software

Computer/Management Services
1426 Medinah Court
Arnold, MD 21012
Product: record-keeping and collection
management software
System requirements: Windows 3.1+
or DOS 6.0+
Catalogue: free

Wildcatt Database Company
5614 Valley Road
Ames, IA 50014
(515) 232-4720
Product: orchid database
System requirements: 386+,
Windows 3.1+
Catalogue: free

## Orchid-of-the-Month Clubs

Carter & Holmes Orchids
Box 668
629 Mendenhall Road
Newberry, SC 29108
(803) 276-0579

Interior Water Gardens
615 Long Beach Boulevard
Surf City, NJ 08008
(609) 494-1900
(800) 874-4937

Orchid Club
Box 463
Baldwinsville, NY 13027
(800) 822-9411

R. F. Orchids, Inc.
28100 SW 182nd Avenue
Homestead, FL 33030
(305) 245-4570

## Other Information and Services

*This nonprofit conservation organization offers
an international orchid locating and information
service, species flasking program, and orchid
inventory software:*

OrchidNet™
626 Humboldt Street
Richmond, CA 94805
(510) 235-8815

*This firm offers flasking services and a computer
bulletin-board service (BBS) for locating orchids:*

The Orchid Database, Inc.
626 Humboldt Street
Richmond, CA 94805
(510) 235-8815
Services: orchid locating
and species flasking
Catalogue: free

*Wardian cases for orchids are available from:*

Design North
1500 New Brighton Boulevard
Minneapolis, MN 55413
(612) 789-3373
Catalogue: free

*Test tubes for display, transport, and shows are available from:*

Lee's Botanical Supply
351 Buttonwood Lane
Cinnaminson, NJ 08077
(609) 829-6557
Catalogue: SASE

## Plant Sources

A & P Orchids
110 Peters Road
Swansea, MA 02777
(508) 675-1717
Specialties: paphiopedilums
and phalaenopsis
Catalogue: $5.00

Adagent Acres
2245 Floral Way
Santa Rosa, CA 95403
(707) 575-4459
Catalogue: 50¢

Adams & Foster Orchids
Box 1195
Apopka, FL 32704
(800) 884-4230
Catalogue: free

Adkins Orchids
Box 4417
Fort Lauderdale, FL 33338
(305) 563-6823
Catalogue: free

Alberts and Merkel Brothers
2210 South Federal Highway
Boynton Beach, FL 33435
(407) 732-2071
Catalogue: $1.00

Charles Alford Plants
Box 772025
Winter Garden, FL 34777

(407) 877-1007
Catalogue: free

The Angraecum House
Box 976
Grass Valley, CA 95945
(916) 273-9426
Specialties: angraecums and aeranthes
Catalogue: free

Baker & Chantry Orchids
Box 554
18611 132nd Street NE
Woodinville, WA 98072
(206) 483-0345
Specialties: hybrids
Catalogue: long SASE with two stamps

Bergstrom Orchids Nursery
Box 1502
Keaau, HI 96749
Catalogue: $1.00

Blietz-Wailea Orchids
3456 Akala Drive
Kihei, Maui, HI 96753
(808) 874-0034
Catalogue: free

Bloomfield Orchids
251 West Bloomfield Road
Pittsford, NY 14534
(716) 381-4206
Specialties: paphiopedilums
and phragmipediums
Catalogue: free

Breckinridge Orchids
6201 Summit Avenue
Brown Summit, NC 27214
(910) 656-7591
Catalogue: long SASE

Brighton Farms
Poplar & Shore Roads
Linwood, NJ 08221

(609) 927-4131
Specialties: cattleyas
Catalogue: $1.00

Cal-Orchid
1251 Orchid Drive
Santa Barbara, CA 93111
(805) 967-1312
Catalogue: $1.00

Camp Lot-A-Noise Tropicals
4084 47th Street
Sarasota, FL 34235
(813) 351-2483
(800) 351-2483
Catalogue: SASE

Carmela Orchids, Inc.
Box H
Hakalau, HI 96710
(808) 963-6189
Specialties: phalaenopsis
Catalogue: free

Carter & Holmes Orchids
Box 668
629 Mendenhall Road
Newberry, SC 29108
(803) 276-0579
Catalogue: $2.00

The Cedar Tree Nursery
2825 Allen
Kelso, WA 98626
Specialties: pleione species and hybrids
Catalogue: SASE

Chaotic Exotics
4314 West Ocean Avenue
Lompoc, CA 93436
(805) 736-0040
Specialties: laelias
Catalogue: free

Chieri Orchids
2913 9th Street North

Tacoma, WA 98406
(206) 752-5510
Catalogue: free

City Gardens
451 West Lincoln
Madison Heights, MI 48071
(313) 398-2660
Catalogue: $2.00

Clackamas Orchids
7920 South Zimmerman Road
Canby, OR 97013
(503) 651-3438
Catalogue: free

Clargreen Gardens, Ltd.
814 Southdown Road
Mississauga, Ontario L5J 2Y4
(905) 822-0992
Catalogue: $2.00

Cloud Forest Orchids
Box 370, Honokaa, HI 96727
(808) 775-9850
Catalogue: free

Coes' Orchid Acres
4647 Winding Way
Sacramento, CA 95841
(916) 482-6719
Catalogue: free

Jeff Corder
1257 Hall Road
North Fort Myers, FL 33903
(941) 997-1637
Specialties: species orchids
Catalogue: free

Creole Orchids
Box 24458
New Orleans, LA 70184
(504) 282-5191
Specialties: hybrids
Catalogue: $2.00

Drago Orchid Corporation
4601 Southwest 127th Avenue
Miami, FL 33175
(305) 554-1021
Specialties: cattleyas
Catalogue: free

Elmore Orchids
324 Watt Road
Knoxville, TN 37922
(615) 966-5294
(800) 553-3528
Specialties: phalaenopsis
Catalogue: free

Eric's Exotics
6782 Belevedere Road
West Palm Beach, FL 33413
(800) ORCHIDS
Specialties: hybrids
Catalogue: $3.00

Everglades Orchids, Inc.
1101 Tabit Road
Belle Glade, FL 33430
(407) 996-9600
Specialties: odonts and cymbidiums
Catalogue: free

John Ewing Orchids, Inc.
Box 1318
Soquel, CA 95073
(408) 684-1111
Specialties: phalaenopsis
Catalogue: free

Exotic Orchids of Maui
3141 Ua Noe Place
Haiku, HI 96708
(808) 575-2255
Catalogue: free

Fantasy Orchids, Inc.
Box 516, Louisville, CO 80027
(303) 666-5432
Catalogue: free

Fender's Flora, Inc.
4315 Plymouth Sorrento Road
Apopka, FL 32712
(407) 886-2464
Specialties: phalaenopsis
Catalogue: free

Floridel Gardens, Inc.
330 George Street
Port Stanley, Ontario N5L 1C6
(519) 782-4015
Specialties: phalaenopsis
Catalogue: $2.00

Fordyce Orchids
1330 Isabel Avenue
Livermore, CA 94550
(510) 447-7171
Specialties: miniature cattleyas
Catalogue: free

Fox Orchids, Inc.
6615 West Markham Street
Little Rock, AR 72205
(501) 663-4246
Catalogue: free

Fox Valley Orchids, Ltd.
1980 Old Willow Road
Northbrook, IL 60062
(708) 205-9660
Catalogue: free

Fuchs Orchids
26600 SW 147th Avenue
Naranja, FL 33032
(305) 258-4876
Catalogue: free

Gemstone Orchids
5750 East River Road
Minneapolis, MN 55432
(612) 571-3300
Specialties: phalaenopsis
Catalogue: free

Gold Country Orchids
390 Big Ben Road
Lincoln, CA 95648
(916) 645-8600
(800) 451-8558
Specialties: phalaenopsis
Catalogue: free

Green Plant Research
Box 735
Kaawa, HI 96730
(808) 237-8672
Catalogue: free

Green Valley Orchids
77200 Green Valley Road
Folsom, LA 70437
Specialties: phalaenopsis and cattleya
orchids
Catalogue: $1.00

H & R Nurseries
41-240 Hihimanu Street
Waimanalo, HI 96795
(808) 259-9626
Catalogue: free

Hawaiian Island Orchids, Inc.
Box 493
Waimanalo, HI 96795
(808) 259-7410
Catalogue: free

Hoosier Orchid Company
8440 West 82nd Street
Indianapolis, IN 46278
(317) 291-6269
Specialties: seed-grown species orchids
Catalogue: $1.00

Spencer M. Howard Orchid Imports
11802 Huston Street
North Hollywood, CA 91607
(818) 762-8275
Specialties: species orchids
Catalogue: long SASE with two stamps

Interior Water Gardens
615 Long Beach Boulevard
Surf City, NJ 08008
(609) 494-1900
(800) 874-4937
Catalogue: $1.00

J & L Orchids
20 Sherwood Road
Easton, CT 06612
(203) 261-3772
Specialties: species orchids
Catalogue: $1.00

J. E. M. Orchids
2595 Morikami Park Road
Delray Beach, FL 33446
(407) 498-4308
Specialties: hybrids and
lady's slippers
Catalogue: $2.00

Jungle Gems, Inc.
300 Edgewood Road
Edgewood, MD 21040
(410) 676-0672
Specialties: phalaenopsis
Catalogue: free

Kawamoto Orchid Nursery
2630 Waiomao Road
Honolulu, HI 98616
(808) 732-5808
Catalogue: $2.00

Kenner & Sons
10919 Explorer Road
La Mesa, CA 91941
(619) 660-0161
(800) 582-9933
Specialties: Australian orchids
Catalogue: free

Kensington Orchids
3301 Plyers Mill Road
Kensington, MD 20895

(301) 933-0036
Catalogue: $1.00

Khuong Orchids, Ltd.
470 Mason Road
Vista, CA 92084
(619) 941-3093
Catalogue: two stamps

Kilworth Orchids
RR 3
County Road 14
Komoka, Ontario N0L 1R0
(519) 471-9787
Catalogue: $1.00

Arnold J. Klehm Grower, Inc.
44 West 637
State Route 72
Hampshire, IL 60140
(708) 683-4761
Catalogue: free

I. N. Komoda Orchids
Box 576
Makawao, HI 96768
(808) 572-0756
Specialties: masdevallias
Catalogue: SASE

Krull-Smith Orchids
2815 Ponkan Road
Apopka, FL 32712
(407) 886-0915
Specialties: phalaenopsis and
paphiopedilums
Catalogue: free

Lauray of Salisbury
432 Undermountain Road
Salisbury, CT 06068
(203) 435-2263
Catalogue: $2.00

Lenette Greenhouses
1440 Pom Orchid Lane

Kannapolis, NC 28081
(704) 938-2042
Specialties: hybrids
Catalogue: free

Lines Orchids, Inc.
1823 Taft Highway
Signal Mountain, TN 37377
(615) 886-2111
Catalogue: free

Lion's Den Orchids
275 Olive Hill Lane
Woodside, CA 94062
(415) 851-3303
Specialties: zygo petalums
Catalogue: free

Majestic Orchids
11701 SW 80th Road
Miami, FL 33156
(305) 233-7270
Catalogue: free

Makai Farms Orchids
Box 93
Kauai, HI 96754
(808) 828-1874
Catalogue: free

Ann Mann's Orchids
9045 Ron-Den Lane
Windermere, FL 34786
(407) 876-2625
Catalogue: $1.00

Manor Hill Orchids
Box 370
Pocono Pines, PA 18350
(717) 646-4400
Specialties: rare species
Catalogue: free

James McCully Orchidculture
Box 355
Hakalau, HI 96710

(808) 963-6233
Catalogue: $1.00

Rod McLellan Company
1450 El Camino Real
South San Francisco, CA 94080
(415) 871-5655
(800) 237-4089
Catalogue: $2.00

MCM Orchids
Box 4626
Wheaton, IL 60189
(708) 668-4588
Catalogue: free

Miami Orchids
22150 SW 147th Avenue
Miami, FL 33170
(305) 258-2664
(800) 516-5348
Specialties: vanda and vadaceous hybrids
Catalogue: free

Miskimens Orchids
13420 Borden Avenue
Sylmar, CA 91342
(818) 367-8525
Specialties: phalaenopsis
Catalogue: SASE

Mohawk Valley Orchid Estate
143 East Main Street
Amsterdam, NY 12010
(518) 843-4889
Catalogue: $2.00

Motes Orchids
25000 Farmlife Road
Homestead, FL 33031
(305) 247-4398
Specialties: vandas and ascocendas
Catalogue: free

Mountain View Orchids, Inc.
Box 4235

Hilo, HI 96720
(808) 968-8029
Specialties: phalaenopsis, cattleyas, ondiciums
Catalogue: free

Oak Hill Gardens
Box 25
West Dundee, IL 60118
(708) 428-8500
Specialties: cymbidiums, cattleyas
Catalogue: $1.00

Oceanside Orchids
3015 Skyline Drive
Oceanside, CA 92054
(619) 721-5661
Specialties: phalaenopsis
Catalogue: SASE

Odom's Orchids, Inc.
1611 South Jenkins Road
Fort Pierce, FL 34947
(407) 467-1386
Specialties: phalaenopsis
Catalogue: free

Orchid Acres, Inc.
4159 120th Avenue South
Lake Worth, FL 33467
(407) 795-9190
Specialties: dendrobiums
Catalogue: free

Orchidanica
Box 13151
Oakland, CA 94661
(510) 482-0408
Catalogue: free

Orchid Art
1433 Kew Avenue
Hewlett, NY 11557
(516) 374-6426
Catalogue: free

The Orchid House
1699 Sage Avenue
Los Osos, CA 93402
(805) 528-1417
(800) 235-4139
Catalogue: free

Orchid Gardens
6700 Splithand Road
Grand Rapids, MN 55744
(218) 326-6975
Catalogue: $2.00

Orchid Magic
Box 3475
Morristown, TN 37815
(423) 581-9222
Catalogue: $1.00

Orchids by Hausermann
2N 134 Addison Road
Villa Park, IL 60181
(708) 543-6855
Catalogue: $1.00

Orchids Limited
4630 North Fernbrook Lane
Plymouth, MN 55446
(612) 559-6425
(800) 669-6006
Specialties: phragmipediums
Catalogue: free

Orchid Species Specialties
42314 Road 415
Raymond Road
Coarsegold, CA 93614
(209) 683-3239
Specialties: species orchids
Catalogue: $1.00

Orchid Thoroughbreds
731 West Siddonsburg Road
Dillsburg, PA 17019
(717) 432-8100
Catalogue: free

Orchid World International, Inc.
10885 SW 95th Street
Miami, FL 33176
(305) 271-0268
(800) 367-6720
Catalogue: free

Our Orchids
23113 SW 156th Avenue
Miami, FL 33170
(305) 852-1824
Specialties: species orchids
Catalogue: long SASE with two stamps

Owens Orchids
Box 365
Pisgah Forest, NC 18768
(704) 877-3313
Specialties: phalaenopsis
Catalogue: free

Palestine Orchids
Route 1, Box 312
Palestine, WV 26160
(304) 275-4781
Specialties: fragrant orchids
Catalogue: free

Peach State Orchids, Inc.
920 Homer Road
Woodstock, GA 30188
(404) 751-8770
Specialties: phalaenopsis
Catalogue: free

Penn Valley Orchids
239 Old Gulph Road
Wynnewood, PA 19096
(610) 642-9822
Specialties: hybrid orchids
Catalogue: $1.00

Pretty Orchids, Inc.
Box 772887, Houston, TX 77215
Specialties: phalaenopsis
Catalogue: free

R. J. Rands Orchids
421 Westlake Boulevard
Malibu, CA 90265
(818) 707-3410
Specialties: paphiopedilums
Catalogue: $1.00

Rare Orchids
Box 6332
Malibu, CA 90265
(818) 597-1389
Catalogue: free

R. F. Orchids, Inc.
28100 SW 182nd Avenue
Homestead, FL 33030
(305) 245-4570
Catalogue: free

Riverbend Orchids
14220 Lorraine Road
Biloxi, MS 39532
(601) 392-2699
Specialties: phalaenopsis
Catalogue: free

R. K. S. Orchids
RD 3, Box 56
Glen Rock, PA 17327
(717) 235-2421
(800) 206-8092
Specialties: paphiopedilums
Catalogue: free

Rolling Knolls Orchids
Route 104
Bristol, NH 03222
(603) 744-8579
Catalogue: free

Alan C. Salzman, Orchids
1806 Jackson Road
Penfield, NY 14526
(716) 377-3213
Specialties: paphiopedilums
Catalogue: free

Santa Barbara Orchid Estate
1250 Orchid Drive
Santa Barbara, CA 93111
(800) 553-3387
Specialties: cymbidium and species
orchids
Catalogue: $2.00

Seagulls Landing Orchids
Box 388
Glen Head, NY 11545
(516) 367-6336
Specialties: cattleyas
Catalogue: $2.50

George Shorter Orchids
Box 16952
Mobile, AL 36616
(205) 443-7469
Catalogue: free

South Shore Orchids
87 Pine Road
Mastic Beach, NY 11951
(516) 281-0097
Catalogue: free

Stewart Orchids, Inc.
Box 550
3376 Foothill Road
Carpinteria, CA 93013
(805) 684-5448
(800) 621-2450
Specialties: hybrids
Catalogue: $2.00

Sunset Orchids
2709 Hillside Drive
Burlingame, CA 94010
(415) 342-3092
Catalogue: SASE

Sunswept Laboratories
Box 1913
Studio City, CA 91614
(818) 506-7271

Specialties: rare and endangered species
from seed
Catalogue: free

Sweetwater Orchids, Inc.
2467 Ridgeway Drive
National City, CA 91950
(619) 472-1226
Catalogue: free

Tropical Orchid Farm
Box 354
Haiku, HI 96708
(808) 572-8569
Catalogue: free

Tropic 1 Orchids, Inc.
3710 North Orchid Drive
Haines City, FL 33844
(813) 422-4750
Specialties: phalaenopsis
Catalogue: free

Venamy Orchids
Route 22 North
Brewster, NY 10509
(800) 362-3612
Catalogue: $2.00

Venger's Orchids
1220 Pando Avenue
Colorado Springs, CO 80906
(719) 576-7686
(800) 483-6437
Catalogue: free

Wacahoota Orchids
Route 1, Box 354
County Road 320
Micanopy, FL 32667
(800) 833-3747
Catalogue: free

We-Du Nurseries
Route 5, Box 724
Marion, NC 28752

(704) 738-8300
Specialties: bletillas
Catalogue: $2.00

Ken West Orchids
Box 1332
Pahoa, HI 96778
(808) 965-9895
Specialties: cattleyas
Catalogue: free

Whippoorwill Orchids
9790 Larkin Lane
Rogers, AR 72756
(501) 925-1885
Catalogue: free

Wilk Orchid Specialties
Box 1177
45-212 Nohonani Place
Kaneohe, HI 96744
(808) 247-6733
Catalogue: free

Windsong Orchids
14N456 Factly Road
Sycamore, IL 60178
(708) 683-2139
Catalogue: free

Woodland Orchids
1816 Hart Road
Charlotte, NC 28214
(704) 394-6530
Catalogue: SASE

A World of Orchids
2501 Old Lake Wilson Road
Kissimmee, FL 34747
(407) 396-1887
Catalogue: free

Andrew Zarauskas Orchids
144 Indian Run Parkway
Union, NJ 07083
(908) 964-5763

Specialties: phaphiopedilums
and phragmipediums
Catalogue: free

Zuma Canyon Orchids
5949 Bonsall Drive
Malibu, CA 90265
(310) 457-9771
Catalogue: free

# Roses

## Organizations

American Rose Society
Box 30,000
Shreveport, LA 71130
(318) 938-5402
Dues: $32.00
Publication: *The American Rose Magazine*
(eleven times annually)
Special interest quarterlies: *Marvelous Miniatures; Rose Arranger's Bulletin; Rose Exhibitor's Forum; The Old Garden Roses and Shrubs Gazette;* all $10.00 annually

Canadian Rose Society
Anne Graber, Secretary
10 Fairfax Crescent
Scarsborough, Ontario M1L 1Z8
(416) 757-8809
Dues: Canada $18.00
Publications: *The Rosarian*
(three times annually);
*Canadian Rose Annual*

Heritage Rose Foundation
1512 Gorman Street
Raleigh, NC 27606
(919) 834-2591
Publication: *Heritage Rose Foundation* News
(quarterly)

Heritage Rose Group
Miriam Wilkins

925 Galvin Drive
El Cerrito, CA 94530
(510) 526-6960
Dues: $5.00
Publication: *Heritage Rose Letter* (quarterly)

Rose Hybridizers Association
c/o Larry D. Peterson
3245 Wheaton Road
Horseheads, NY 14845
(607) 562-8592
Dues: $7.00
Publication: quarterly newsletter

The Royal National Rose Society
The Secretary
Chiswell Green
St. Albans, Herts. AL2 3NR
England
(0727) 50-461
Dues: £13.50
Publication: *The Rose* (quarterly journal)

Texas Rose Rustlers
c/o Margaret Sharpe
9246 Kerrwood Lane
Houston, TX 77080
(713) 464-8607
Publication: *Old Texas Rose* (quarterly)

World Federation of Rose Societies
c/o Jill Bennell
46 Alexandra Road
St. Albans, Herts. AL1 3AZ
England
(0727) 833-648
Dues: £25.00
Publication: *World Rose News* (semiannual)

*All-America Rose Selections*

All-America Rose Selections is a nonprofit organization dedicated to maintaining high standards for rose introductions. AARS tests new varieties and reports the results to the public; only outstanding

new roses become selections.
Nationwide, AARS maintains twenty-four
rose test gardens and 135 public rose gardens. These public gardens serve as
showcases for AARS award winners over
the years. For more information and a
free list of AARS accredited public rose
gardens, write to:

All-America Rose Selections
221 North LaSalle Street, Suite 3900
Chicago, IL 60601
(312) 372-7090

## Tools and Growing Supplies

Harlane Company, Inc.
266 Orangeburgh Road
Old Tappan, NJ 07675
Catalogue: free

## Other Services and Supplies

Well-known rosarian Bev Dobson pub-
lishes an invaluable newsletter for the
rose lover; she also puts out an annual
source guide to help you find any rose
variety available in North America and
abroad. For information, write to:

Bev Dobson's Rose Letter/The Combined
Rose List
Beverly Dobson
215 Harriman Road
Irvington, NY 10533
Subscription: $12.00
Frequency: bimonthly

*Rose database software is available from:*

Mach Rose Farm
27646 13th Avenue
Aldergrove, British Columbia V4W 2S4
(604) 856-2631
Catalogue: free

Rosebud
3707 SW Coronado Street
Portland, OR 97219
(503) 245-0546
Catalogue: free

*Gifts and collectibles featuring roses are
available from:*

Everything Roses
189 Berdan Avenue
Wayne, NJ 07474
(800) 787-6739
Catalogue: free

## Plant Sources

The Antique Rose Emporium
Route 5, Box 143
Brenham, TX 77833
(409) 836-9051
(800) 441-0002
Specialties: old roses
Catalogue: $5.00

Arena Rose Company
536 West Cambridge Avenue
Phoenix, AZ 85003
(602) 266-2223
Specialties: old roses for hot climates
Catalogue: free

Blossoms & Bloomers
11415 East Krueger Lane
Spokane, WA 99207
(509) 922-1344
Specialties: hardy old roses
Catalogue: $1.00

Bridges Roses
2734 Toney Road
Lawndale, NC 28090
(704) 538-9412
Specialties: miniature roses
Catalogue: free

Butner's Old Mill Nursery
806 South Belt Highway
St. Joseph, MO 64507
(816) 279-7434
Catalogue: free

Carlton Rose Nurseries
Box 366
Carlton, OR 97111
(503) 852-7135
Specialties: modern roses
Catalogue: free

Carroll Gardens
Box 310
Westminster, MD 21157
(800) 638-6334
Catalogue: $3.00

Chamblee's Rose Nursery
10926 US Highway 69 North
Tyler, TX 75706
(800) 256-7673
Specialties: old and miniature roses
Catalogue: free

Conard-Pyle Company
372 Rose Hill Road
West Grove, PA 19390
(800) 458-6559
Catalogue: $1.00

Corn Hill Nursery, Ltd.
RR 5
Petitcodiac, New Brunswick E0A 2H0
(506) 756-3635
Catalogue: free

Country Bloomers Nursery
Route 2, Box 33
Udall, KS 67146
(316) 986-5518
Specialties: old and miniature roses
Catalogue: free

Donovan's Roses
Box 37800
Shreveport, LA 71133
(318) 861-6693
Catalogue: long SASE

Edmunds' Roses
6235 SW Kahle Road
Wilsonville, OR 97070
(503) 682-1476
Specialties: modern roses
Catalogue: free

Forestfarm
990 Tetherow Road
Williams, OR 97544
(503) 846-7269
Specialties: antique roses
Catalogue: $3.00

Forevergreen Farm
70 New Gloucester Road
North Yarmouth, ME 04097
(207) 829-5830
Catalogue: $1.00

Garden Valley Nursery
Box 750953
498 Pepper Road
Petaluma, CA 94975
(707) 795-5266
Catalogue: $1.00

Giles' Ramblin' Roses
2968 State Road 710
Okeechobee, FL 34974
(813) 763-6611
Catalogue: SASE

Gloria Dei Nursery
36 East Road
High Falls, NY 12440
(914) 687-9981
Specialties: miniature roses
Catalogue: free

Greenmantle Nursery
3010 Ettersburg Road
Garberville, CA 95442
(707) 986-7504
Catalogue: long SASE

Hardy Roses for the North
Box 273, Danville, WA 99121
(604) 442-8442
(800) 442-8122
Specialties: hardy roses
Catalogue: $2.00

Heirloom Old Garden Roses
24062 North Riverside
St. Paul, OR 97137
(503) 538-1576
Specialties: old roses
Catalogue: $5.00

Heritage Rosarium
211 Haviland Mill Road
Brookeville, MD 20833
(301) 774-2806
Specialties: old roses
Catalogue: $1.00

Heritage Rose Gardens
16831 Mitchell Creek Drive
Fort Bragg, CA 95437
(707) 984-6959
Specialties: old roses
Catalogue: $1.50

Hidden Garden Nursery, Inc.
13515 SE Briggs
Milwaukie, OR 97222
Specialties: miniature roses
Catalogue: long SASE

High Country Rosarium
1717 Downing Street
Denver, CO 80218
(303) 832-4026
Specialties: old and hardy roses
Catalogue: free

Historical Roses
1657 West Jackson Street
Painesville, OH 44077
(216) 357-7270
Specialties: old roses
Catalogue: long SASE

Hortico, Inc.
RR 1
723 Robson Road
Waterdown, Ontario L0R 2H1
(905) 689-3002
Catalogue: $3.00

Howertown Rose Nursery
1657 Weaversville Road
Northampton, PA 18067
Catalogue: free

Ingraham's Cottage Garden Roses
Box 126
Scotts Mills, OR 97375
(503) 873-8610
Specialties: old and modern roses
Catalogue: $1.00

Jackson & Perkins Company
1 Rose Lane
Medford, OR 97501
(503) 776-2000
(800) USA-ROSE
Catalogue: free

Justice Miniature Roses
5947 SW Kahle Road
Wilsonville, OR 97070
(503) 682-2370
Specialties: miniature roses
Catalogue: free

Kimbrew-Walter Roses
Route 2, Box 172
Grand Saline, TX 75140
Catalogue: free

V. Kraus Nurseries
Box 180
1380 Centre Road
Carlisle, Ontario L0R 1H0
(416) 689-4022
Catalogue: $1.00

Lowe's Own-Root Roses
6 Sheffield Road
Nashua, NH 03062
(603) 888-2214
Specialties: old roses
Catalogue: $2.00

Magic Moment Miniatures
Box 499
Rockville Centre, NY 11571
Specialities: miniature roses
Catalogue: free

McDaniel's Miniature Roses
7323 Zemco Street
Lemon Grove, CA 91945
(619) 469-4669
Specialties: miniature roses
Catalogue: free

Mendocino Heirloom Roses
Box 670
Mendocino, CA 95460
(707) 877-1888
Specialties: old roses
Catalogue: $1.00

Michigan Miniature Roses
45951 Hull Road
Belleville, MI 48111
Specialties: miniature roses
Catalogue: free

Milaeger's Gardens
4838 Douglas Avenue
Racine, WI 53402
(414) 639-2371
Catalogue: $1.00

Miniature Plant Kingdom
4125 Harrison Grade Road
Sebastopol, CA 95472
(707) 874-2233
Specialties: miniature roses
Catalogue: $2.50

The Mini-Rose Garden
Box 203
Cross Hill, SC 29332
(864) 998-4331
Specialties: miniature roses
Catalogue: free

Nor'East Miniature Roses, Inc.
Box A
Rowley, MA 01969
(508) 948-7964
Specialties: miniature roses
Catalogue: free

Oregon Miniature Roses, Inc.
8285 SW 185th Avenue
Beaverton, OR 97007
(503) 649-4482
Specialties: miniature roses
Catalogue: free

Richard Owen Nursery
2300 East Lincoln Street
Bloomington, IL 61701
Catalogue: $2.00

Carl Pallek & Son Nurseries
Box 137
Virgil, Ontario L0S 1T0
Specialties: tea roses
Catalogue: free

Petaluma Rose Company
Box 750953
581 Gossage Avenue
Petaluma, CA 94975
(707) 769-8862
Catalogue: free

Pickering Nurseries, Inc.
670 Kingston Road
Pickering, Ontario L1V 1A6
(905) 839-2111
Catalogue: $3.00

Pixie Treasures Miniature Roses
4121 Prospect Avenue
Yorba Linda, CA 92686
(714) 993-6780
Specialties: miniature roses
Catalogue: $1.00

Rabbit Shadow Farm
2880 East Highway 402
Loveland, CO 80538
(303) 667-5531
Catalogue: $1.00

Rennie Roses International
RR 2
Elora, Ontario N0B 1SO
(519) 846-0329
Specialties: miniature roses
Catalogue: free

Roseberry Gardens
Box 933, Postal Station F
Thunder Bay, Ontario P7C 4X8
Catalogue: free

Rosehaven Nursery
8617 Tobacco Lane SE
Olympia, WA 98503
Catalogue: free

Rosehill Farm
Box 188
Gregg Neck Road
Galena, MD 21635
(410) 648-5538
Specialties: miniature roses
Catalogue: free

The Roseraie at Bayfields
Box R

Waldboro, ME 04572
Catalogue: $5.00

The Rose Ranch
Box 10087
240 Cooper Road
Salinas, CA 93912
(408) 758-6965
Catalogue: $3.00

Roses & Wine
6260 Fernwood Drive
Shingle Springs, CA 95682
(916) 677-9722
Specialties: old roses
Catalogue: long SASE

Roses of Yesterday and Today
802 Brown's Valley Road
Watsonville, CA 95076
(408) 724-3537
Specialties: old, rare, and new roses
Catalogue: $3.00

Roses Unlimited
Route 1, Box 587
Laurens, SC 29360
(803) 682-ROSE
Catalogue: SASE

Rozell Rose Nursery & Violet Boutique
12206 Highway 31 West
Tyler, TX 75709
(903) 595-5137
Catalogue: $1.00

Royall River Roses
70 New Gloucester Road
North Yarmouth, ME 04097
(207) 829-5830
Catalogue: $1.00

Schumacher's Hill Country Gardens
588 FM Highway 1863
New Braunfels, TX 78132
Catalogue: $1.00

Sequoia Nursery/
Moore Miniature Roses
2519 East Noble Avenue
Visalia, CA 93277
(209) 732-0190
Specialties: miniature roses
Catalogue: $1.00

Spring Hill Nursery
Box 1758
Peoria, IL 61632
(309) 689-3849
Catalogue: $1.00

Stanek's Garden Center
2929 27th Avenue East
Spokane, WA 99223
(509) 535-2939
Specialties: hybrid roses
Catalogue: free

Tate Rose Nursery
10306 FM Road 2767
Tyler, TX 75708
(903) 593-1020
Specialties: hybrid roses
Catalogue: free

Taylor's Roses
Box 11272
Chicasaw, AL 36671
Specialties: miniature roses
Catalogue: free

Texas Mini Roses
Box 267
Denton, TX 76202
(817) 566-3034
Catalogue: $1.00

Thomasville Nurseries
Box 7
1842 Smith Avenue
Thomasville, GA 31792

(912) 226-5568
Specialties: modern roses
Catalogue: free

Tiny Petals Miniature Rose Nursery
489 Minot Avenue
Chula Vista, CA 91910
(619) 422-0385
Specialties: miniature roses
Catalogue: free

Vintage Gardens
2227 Gravenstein Highway South
Sebastopol, CA 95472
(707) 829-2035
Specialties: old roses
Catalogue: $4.00

Witherspoon's Roses
Box 51655
Durham, NC 27717
Catalogue: $3.00

Wayside Gardens
One Garden Lane
Hodges, SC 29695
(800) 845-1124
Catalogue: free

A World of Roses
Box 90332
Gainesville, FL 32607
Catalogue: $1.00

York Hill Farm
271 North Haverhill Road
Kensington, NH 03833
(603) 772-8567
Catalogue: $1.00

Young's American Rose Nursery
Route 2, Box 112
Elsberry, MO 63343
Catalogue: $3.00

# Seed Exchanges

## Organizations

Heritage Seed Program
RR 3
Uxbridge, Ontario L0C 1K0
(416) 852-7965
Dues: $18.00
Publication: *Heritage Seed Program*
(three times annually)

Seed Savers Exchange
3076 North Winn Road
Decorah, IA 52101
(319) 382-5990
Dues: $25.00
Publications: yearbook; newsletter

## Publications

*Gardeners' Seed Swap*
703 Church Street
Scott City, KS 67871
Frequency: monthly newsletter
Subscription: $14.00

*Seed Exchange Monthly*
Peter Collier
56 Red Willow
Harlow, Essex CM19 5PD
England
Frequency: monthly
Subscription: write for information

*Seed Traders' Companion*
222 New Elizabeth Street
Wilkes-Barre, PA 18702
Frequency: monthly newsletter
Subscription: write for information

## Seed Supplies

V.L. Price Horticultural
506 Grove Avenue
Catawissa, PA 17820

Products: seed-saving supplies
Catalogue: free

Seed Saver®/KLACK Company
Box 2726
Idaho Falls, ID 83403
(208) 522-2224
Products: seed files and storage
equipment
Catalogue: free

Twinholly's
3633 NE 19th Avenue
Portland, OR 97212
Product: seed storage envelopes
Catalogue: free

## Seed Exchanges

Abundant Life Seed Foundation
Box 772
Port Townsend, WA 98368
(206) 385-5660
Catalogue: $1.00

AHS Seed Exchange Program
7931 East Boulevard Drive
Alexandria, VA 22308
Catalogue: free

Alberene Seed Foundation
Box 271
Keene, VA 22946
Catalogue: $1.00

Blue Ridge Seed Savers
Box 106
Batesville, VA 22924
Catalogue: $1.00

Central Prairie Seed Exchange
7949 SW 21st Street
Topeka, KS 66604
(913) 478-4944
Catalogue: $1.00

Dyck Arboretum of the Plains
Seed Exchange
Hesston College
Box 3000
Hesston, KS 67062
(316) 327-8127
Specialties: prairie plants
Catalogue: long SASE

Kusa Research Foundation
Box 761
Ojai, CA 93023
Catalogue: $1.00

Liberty Seed Company
Box 806
New Philadelphia, OH 44663
(216) 364-1611
Catalogue: $1.00

National Heirloom Flower Seed
Exchange
136 Irving Street
Cambridge, MA 02138
(617) 576-5065
Catalogue: $1.00

Native Seeds/SEARCH
2509 North Campbell Avenue
Tucson, AZ 85719
(602) 327-9123
Catalogue: $1.00

Peace Seeds
2385 SE Thompson Street
Corvallis, OR 97333
Catalogue: $1.00

Seed Savers Exchange
Kent Wheatly
RR 3, Box 239
Decorah, IA 52101
Catalogue: $1.00

Southern Exposure Seed Exchange
Box 158

North Garden, VA 22959
(804) 973-4703
Catalogue: $3.00

Seeds Blüm
Idaho City Stage
Boise, ID 83707
Catalogue: $2.00

# Water Gardening

## Organizations

Aquatic Gardeners Association
c/o Dorothy Reimer, Membership
83 Cathcart Street
London, Ontario N6C 3L9
Dues: $15.00
Publication: *The Aquatic Gardener*
(bimonthly journal)

International Water Lily Society
c/o Dr. Edward Schneider
Santa Barbara Botanic Gardens
Santa Barbara, CA 93105
(805) 682-4726
Dues: $18.00
Publication: *Water Garden Journal*
(quarterly)

## Publications

*Pondscapes*
National Pond Society
Box 449
Acworth, GA 30101
(800) 742-4701
Frequency: ten times annually
Subscription: $24.00

*The Practical Pondkeeper*
1670 South 900 East
Zionsville, IN 46077
Frequency: ten times annually
Subscription: $20.00

*The Water Gardener*
East-West Specialties
Box 6004, Norfolk, VA 23508
(804) 461-0665
Frequency: bimonthly newsletter
Subscription: $15.00

## Pond Supplies—General

Cherryhill Aquatics, Inc.
2627 North County Line Road
Sunbury, OH 43074
(614) 965-2798
Catalogue: free

Discount Pond Supplies
Box 423371
Kissimmee, FL 34742
(407) 847-7937
Catalogue: free

Hardwicke Gardens
254A Boston Turnpike Road
Westboro, MA 01581
Catalogue: $2.00

Henri Water Gardening
Wauconda, IL 60084
(800) 92-HENRI
Catalogue: free

Lilypons Water Gardens
6800 Lilypons Road
Buckeystown, MD 21717
(301) 428-0686
(800) 723-7667
Catalogue: $5.00

Paradise Water Gardens
14 May Street
Whitman, MA 02382
(617) 447-4711
Catalogue: $3.00

Patio Garden Ponds
7919 South Shields

Oklahoma City, OK 73149
(800) 487-LILY
Catalogue: free

Perry's Water Gardens
191 Leatherman Gap Road
Franklin, NC 28734
(704) 524-3264
Catalogue: free

Pets Unlimited
1888 Drew
Clearwater, FL 34625
(813) 442-2197
Catalogue: $2.00

S. Scherer & Sons
104 Waterside Road
Northport, NY 11768
(516) 261-7432
Catalogue: $1.00

Slocum Water Gardens
1101 Cypress Gardens Boulevard
Winter Haven, FL 33880
(813) 293-7151
Catalogue: $3.00

Stigall Water Gardens
7306 Main Street
Kansas City, MO 64114
(816) 822-1256
Catalogue: $1.00

Tetra Pond
3001 Commerce Street
Blacksburg, VA 20460
(703) 951-5400
Catalogue: free

William Tricker, Inc.
7125 Tanglewood Drive
Independence, OH 44131
(800) 524-3492
Catalogue: $3.50

West Kentucky Ornamental Water
Gardens
(800) 705-5509
Catalogue: free

Al Zimmer Ponds & Supplies
(215) 582-9714
(800) 722-8877
Catalogue: free

## Pond Supplies—Products

Adams & Adkins, Inc.
104 South Early Street
Alexandria, VA 22304
(703) 823-3404
(800) 928-3588
Product: Water Flute$^{TM}$ fountain pond
Catalogue: free

Aquarium Pharmaceuticals, Inc.
50 East Hamilton Street
Chalfont, PA 18914
(215) 822-8181
Product: pond maintenance supplies
Catalogue: $1.00

Aquarium Products, Inc.
180-L Penrod Court
Glen Burnie, MD 21061
(410) 761-2100
Product: pond maintenance supplies
Catalogue: free

Beckett Corporation
2521 Willowbrook Road
Dallas, TX 75220
Product: pumps
Catalogue: free

E. G. Danner Manufacturing, Inc.
160 Oval Drive
Central Islip, NY 11722
(516) 234-5261
Product: pumps
Catalogue: free

Hermitage Gardens
Box 361
Canastoga, NY 13032
(315) 697-9093
Products: pumps; submersible lighting
Catalogue: $1.00

Little Giant Pump Company
Box 12010
Oklahoma City, OK 73157
(405) 947-2511
Products: pumps; submersible lighting
Catalogue: free

Northwest Landscape Supply, Inc.
12500 132nd Avenue NE
Kirkland, WA 98034
(206) 820-9325
Product: pond liners
Catalogue: free

Plantabbs Products
Box 397
Timonium, MD 21093
(800) 227-4340
Product: aquatic plant food
Catalogue: free

Pondfiltration, Inc.
501 West Travelers Trail
Burnsville, MN 55337
(800) 882-5327
Product: filters
Catalogue: free

Remanoid Lawn Ponds
3001 Rouse Avenue
Pittsburg, KS 66762
(316) 232-2400
Product: pond maintenance supplies
Catalogue: free

Resource Conservation Technology
2633 North Calvert Street
Baltimore, MD 21218
(410) 366-1146

Product: pond liners
Catalogue: free

SeaChem
1939 C Parker Court
Stone Mountain, GA 30087
(404) 972-5999
Product: pond maintenance supplies
Catalogue: free

Unit Liner Company
(800) 633-4603
Product: pond liners
Catalogue: free

Waterscapes
155 Washington
Kingston, NY 12401
(914) 339-8382
Product: custom pond kits
Catalogue: free

Winston Company, Inc.
Box 636
Bixby, OK 74008
(800) 331-9099
Product: water treatment products
Catalogue: free

*Aquatic, Pond, and Bog Plants*

Aquatics and Exotics
Box 693
Indian Rocks Beach, FL 34635
(813) 595-3075
Catalogue: free

Bee Fork Water Gardens
Box 440037
Brentwood, MO 63144
(314) 962-1583
Specialties: water lilies
Catalogue: $1.00

Country Wetlands Nursery
South 75 West 20755
Field Drive
Muskego, WI 53150
(414) 679-1268
Specialties: wetland plants
Catalogue: $2.00

Crystal Palace Perennials
Box 154
St. John, IN 46373
(219) 374-9419
Specialties: water plants
Catalogue: free

Hemlock Hollow Nursery
Box 125
Sandy Hook, KY 41171
(606) 738-6285
Specialties: water lilies and lotus
Catalogue: free

J's Custom Koi Ponds
14050 FM Road 848
Whitehouse, TX 75791
Catalogue: $3.00

Green & Hagstrom, Inc.
Box 658
Fairview, TN 37062
(615) 799-0708
Catalogue: free

Japonica
36484 Camp Creek Road
Springfield, OR 97478
Catalogue: SASE

Lilyblooms Water Gardens
(800) 921-0005
Specialties: water lilies
Catalogue: free

Lilypons Water Gardens
6800 Lilypons Road
Buckeystown, MD 21717

(301) 428-0686
(800) 723-7667
Catalogue: $5.00

Maryland Aquatic Nurseries
3427 North Furnace Road
Jarrettsville, MD 21084
(410) 557-7615
Catalogue: $5.00

Miami Water Lilies
22150 SW 147th Avenue
Miami, FL 33170
(305) 258-2664
Specialties: water lilies
Catalogue: free

Moore Water Gardens
Box 70
Port Stanley, Ontario N5L 1J4
(519) 782-4052
Catalogue: free

Perry's Water Gardens
191 Leatherman Gap Road
Franklin, NC 28734
(704) 524-3264
Catalogue: free

Picov Greenhouses
380 Kingston Road East
Ajax, Ontario L1S 4S7
(416) 686-2151
(800) 663-0300
Catalogue: free

Pond Doctor
HC 65, Box 265
Kingston, AR 72742
(501) 665-2232
Catalogue: $2.00

Reed Water Lilies
Box 9154
College Station, TX 77842
(409) 361-2378

Specialties: water lilies
Catalogue: free

Renrick's
Box 1383
Chickasha, OK 7303
Specialties: water lilies
Catalogue: SASE

Santa Barbara Water Gardens
160 East Mountain Drive
Santa Barbara, CA 93108
(805) 969-5129
Catalogue: $2.00

S. Scherer & Sons
104 Waterside Road
Northport, NY 11768
(516) 261-7432
Catalogue: $1.00

Scottsdale Fishponds
6915 East Oak Street
Scottsdale, AZ 85257
(602) 946-8025
Catalogue: $2.00

Slocum Water Gardens
1101 Cypress Gardens Boulevard
Winter Haven, FL 33880
(813) 293-7151
Specialties: water lilies
Catalogue: $3.00

Stigall Water Gardens
7306 Main Street
Kansas City, MO 64114
(816) 822-1256
Catalogue: $1.00

Tilley's Nursery/The WaterWorks
111 East Fairmount Street
Coopersburg, PA 18036
(215) 282-4784
Catalogue: $2.00

Trees by Touliatos
202 Brooks Road
Memphis, TN 38116
(901) 345-7361
Catalogue: long SASE

William Tricker, Inc.
7125 Tanglewood Drive
Independence, OH 44131
(800) 524-3492
Specialties: water lilies
Catalogue: $3.50

Tropical Pond and Garden
17888 61st Place North
Loxahutchee, FL 33470
Specialties: water lilies
Catalogue: free

Van Ness Water Gardens
2460 North Euclid Avenue
Upland, CA 91786
(909) 982-2425
Catalogue: $4.00

Waterford Gardens
74 East Allendale Road
Saddle River, NJ 07458
(201) 327-0721
Catalogue: $5.00

Water's Edge
2775 Hardin Road
Choctaw, OK 73020
Catalogue: free

Water Ways Nursery
Route 2, Box 247
Lovettsville, VA 22080
(703) 822-5994
Catalogue: $2.00

Wicklein's Water Gardens
Box 9780
Baldwin, MD 21013
(410) 823-1335
Catalogue: $2.00

Wildlife Nurseries, Inc.
Box 2724
Oshkosh, WI 54903
(414) 231-3780
Catalogue: $3.00

Windy Oaks Daylilies & Aquatics
West 377 South 10677
Betts Road
Eagle, WI 53119
(414) 594-2803
Catalogue: free

# Indoor Gardening

INDOOR GARDENING can go far, far beyond a few potted plants on a windowsill. This section lists organizations, publications, and manufacturers of home greenhouses and solariums, along with retailers of greenhouse and propagation supplies, grow lights, and other indoor essentials. Many of the manufacturers listed here will sell directly to home gardeners. In many cases, however, the manufacturer will provide descriptive catalogues, brochures, and the like, and refer you to a dealer in your area to make your purchase.

## Organizations

Hobby Greenhouse Association
18517 Kingshill Road
Germantown, MD 20874
(410) 275-0377
Dues: $15.00
Publications: *Hobby Greenhouse*
(quarterly magazine);
*HGA News* (quarterly); annual directory
of greenhouse manufacturers

Hydroponic Society of America
2819 Crow Canyon Road, Suite 218
San Ramon, CA 94583
(510) 743-9605
Dues: $30.00
Publication: *Soilless Grower*
(bimonthly)

Indoor Gardening Society of America
Sharon Zentz, Membership Secretary
944 South Munro Road
Tallmadge, OH 44278
(216) 733-8414

Dues: $20.00
Publication: *The Indoor Garden*
(bimonthly)

International Society of Greenhouse
Gardeners
Box 7567
Olympia, WA 98507
Publication: newsletter

## Publications

*The Growing EDGE Magazine*
New Moon Publishing
Box 1027
Corvallis, OR 97339
(800) 888-6785
Frequency: quarterly
Subscription: $18.00

*The Twenty-First Century Gardener*
Growers Press, Inc.
Box 189
Princeton, British Columbia V0X 1W0

Frequency: bimonthly
Subscription: Canada $26.00

# Greenhouses

Amdega Machin Conservatories
Box 7, Glenview, IL 60025
(800) 922-0110
Catalogue: $10.00

Charley's Greenhouse Supply
1569 Memorial Highway
Mount Vernon, WA 98273
(800) 322-4707
Product: traditional English greenhouses
Catalogue: free

Everlite Greenhouses, Inc.
9515 Gerwig Lane, Suite 115
Columbia, MD 20146
(301) 381-3881
Products: greenhouses and conservatories
Catalogue: free

Farm Wholesale, Inc.
2396 Perkins Street NE
Salem, OR 97303
(503) 393-3973
(800) 825-1925
Product: stretch Quonset greenhouses
Catalogue: free

Four Seasons Solar Products
5005 Veterans Highway
Holbrook, NY 11741
(516) 694-4400
(800) FOURSEA
Catalogue: free

Fox Hill Farm
1358 Bridge Street
South Yarmouth, MA 02664
(800) 760-5192
Product: Hoop House greenhouses
Catalogue: $1.00

Gardener's Supply Company
128 Intervale Road
Burlington, VT 05401
(800) 863-1700
Catalogue: free

GardenStyles
Box 50670
Minneapolis, MN 55405
(800) 356-8890
Product: Juliana greenhouses
Catalogue: free

Garden Trends, Inc.
Box 22960
Rochester, NY 114692
(800) 514-4441
Product: Elite greenhouses
Catalogue: free

Gothic Arch Greenhouses
Box 1564
Mobile, AL 36633
(205) 432-7529
(800) 628-4974
Catalogue: $5.00

Hobby Gardens
Box 83
Grand Isle, VT 05458
(802) 372-4041
Catalogue: free

Janco Greenhouses
9390 Davis Avenue
Laurel, MD 20723
(301) 498-5700
(800) 323-6933
Catalogue: free

National Greenhouses
400 East Main Street
Pana, IL 62557
(800) 826-9314
Product: residential greenhouses
Catalogue: free

Northwest Eden Sales, Inc.
15103 NE 68th Street
Redmond, WA 98052
(800) 545-3336
Catalogue: free

Pacific Coast Greenhouse
Manufacturing Company
Box 2130
Petaluma, CA 94953
(800) 227-7061
Product: redwood greenhouses
Catalogue: $2.00

Pacific Greenhouse
25550 Rio Vista Drive
Carmel, CA 93923
(408) 622-9233
Product: redwood greenhouse kits
Catalogue: free

Powell & Powell Supply Company
1206 Broad Street
Fuquay-Varina, NC 27526
(919) 552-9708
Product: The Little Greenhouse
Catalogue: free

Progressive Building Products
Box 453
Exeter, NH 03833
(603) 679-1208
(800) 776-2534
Catalogue: free

Santa Barbara Greenhouses
721 Richmond Avenue
Oxnard, CA 93030
(805) 483-4288
(800) 544-5276
Product: redwood greenhouses
Catalogue: free

Simpson Strong-Tie Company
4637 Chabot Drive
Pleasanton, CA 94588

(800) 999-5099
Product: GardenHouse kits
Catalogue: free

Solar Components Corporation
121 Valley Street
Manchester, NH 03103
(603) 668-8186
Products: greenhouses and greenhouse
kits
Catalogue: $2.00

Solar Prism Manufacturing Inc.
Box 29
McMinnville, OR 97128
(503) 472-1285
Catalogue: free

Sturdi-Built Greenhouse
Manufacturing Company
11304 SW Boones Ferry Road
Portland, OR 97219
(503) 244-4100
(800) 722-4115
Product: redwood greenhouses
Catalogue: free

Sundance Greenhouses
1813 Cedar Street
Berkeley, CA 94703
Catalogue: $2.00

Sunglo Solar Greenhouses
4441 26th Avenue West
Seattle, WA 98199
(206) 284-8900
(800) 647-0606
Product: kit greenhouses
Catalogue: free

Sun 'N Rain Greenhouses
45 Dixon Avenue
Amityville, NY 11701
(800) 999-9459
Product: Clicker 2000
Catalogue: free

Sunspot, Inc.
5030 40th Avenue
Hudsonville, MI 49426
(616) 669-9400
(800) 635-4786
Catalogue: free

Turner Greenhouses
Box 1260
Goldsboro, NC 27533
(800) 672-4770
Products: greenhouses and accessories
Catalogue: free

Under Glass Manufacturing Corporation
Box 323
Wappingers Falls, NY 12590
(914) 298-0645
Products: greenhouses and solariums
Catalogue: $3.00

## Solariums and Conservatories

Amdega Machin Conservatories
Box 7
Glenview, IL 60025
(800) 922-0110
Products: conservatories and garden
buildings
Catalogue: $10.00

Pella
Box 308
Moline, IL 61265
(800) 524-3700
Product: solariums
Catalogue: $2.00

Sun-Porch
Vegetable Factory, Inc.
Box 1353
Stamford, CT 06904
Product: solariums
Catalogue: $2.00

Sun Room Company, Inc.
322 East Main Street
Leola, PA 17540
(800) 426-2737
Product: solariums
Catalogue: free

Sunspot, Inc.
5030 40th Avenue
Hudsonville, MI 49426
(616) 669-9400
(800) 635-4786
Product: solariums
Catalogue: free

Tanglewood Conservatories
Silver Spring, MD
(800) 229-2925
Product: period glasshouses
Catalogue: $1.00

Texas Greenhouse Company
2524 White Settlement Road
Fort Worth, TX 76107
(800) 227-5447
Catalogue: $4.00

Turner Greenhouses
Box 1260
Goldsboro, NC 27533
(800) 672-4770
Catalogue: free

Under Glass Manufacturing Corporation
Box 323
Wappingers Falls, NY 12590
(914) 298-0645
Products: greenhouses and solariums
Catalogue: $3.00

Victory Garden Supply Company
1428 East High Street
Charlottesville, VA 22902
(804) 293-2298
Product: aluminum greenhouses
Catalogue: free

## Minigreenhouses, Cold Frames, and Plant Stands

Day-Dex Company
4725 NW 36th Avenue
Miami, FL 33142
(305) 635-5241
Product: galvanized steel tiered benches
Catalogue: free

Floralight Gardens
6-620 Supertest Road
North York, Ontario M3J 2M5
(416) 665-4000
(800) 665-4000
Product: plant stands
Catalogue: free

Florist Products, Inc.
2242 North Palmer Drive
Schaumburg, IL 60173
(312) 885-2242
Product: Wonder Garden lighted plant stand
Catalogue: free

Green Thumb Industries
2400 Easy Street
San Leandro, CA 94578
(510) 276-0252
Product: English RollHouse cold frames
Catalogue: free

Home Gardener Manufacturing Company
30 Wright Avenue
Lititz, PA 17543
(800) 880-2345
Product: RotoGro growing shelves
Catalogue: free

Humbug Manufacturing Company
Box 541
North Hampton, NH 03862
(603) 964-1115
Product: minigreenhouses
Catalogue: free

Mason-Kemp Associates, Inc.
Box 1371
Madison, CT 06443
(203) 245-2734
Product: Gro Mate minigreenhouses
Catalogue: free

Northern Tier
Box 5083, Sheridan, WY 82801
(800) 443-7467
Product: Window Shelter minigreen houses
Catalogue: free

Radco
120 Plant Avenue
Wayne, PA 19087
(610) 688-8989
Products: plant shelves
Catalogue: free

Silver Creek Supply
RR 1, Box 70
Port Trevorton, PA 17864
(717) 374-8010
Products: Hot Kaps cold frames
Catalogue: free

Volkmann Brothers Greenhouses
2714 Minert Street
Dallas, TX 75219
(214) 526-3484
Product: plant stands
Catalogue: $1.00

## Greenhouse and Propagation Supplies

### General Supplies

Alternative Garden Supply, Inc.
297 North Barrington Road
Streamwood, IL 60107
(708) 885-8282
(800) 444-2837
Catalogue: free

American Hydroponics
186 South G Street
Arcata, CA 95521
(800) 458-6543
Catalogue: $1.00

Aqua Culture, Inc.
700 West 1st Street
Tempe, AZ 85281
(800) 633-2137
Catalogue: free

Aquaducts Hydroponics Systems
Box 99
Mill Valley, CA 94942
(415) 388-0838
Catalogue: free

Aqua-Ponics International
121A North Harbor Boulevard
Fullerton, CA 92632
(800) 426-1261
Catalogue: free

Brighton By-Products Company, Inc.
Box 23, New Brighton, PA 15066
(800) 245-3502
Catalogue: free

Cascade Greenhouse Supply
4441 26th Avenue West
Seattle, WA 98199
(206) 428-2626
Catalogue: $2.00

Charley's Greenhouse Supply
1569 Memorial Road
Mount Vernon, WA 98273
(800) 322-4707
Catalogue: free

Chicago Indoor Garden Supply
297 North Barrington Road
Streamwood, IL 60107
(708) 885-8282
Catalogue: free

CropKing, Inc.
Box 310
Medina, OH 44258
(216) 725-5656
(800) 321-5211
Catalogue: free

Eco Enterprises
1240 NE 175th Street
Seattle, WA 98155
(800) 426-6937
Catalogue: free

Foothill Hydroponics
10705 Burbank Boulevard
North Hollywood, CA 91601
(801) 760-0688
Catalogue: free

Garden District
5160 Commerce Drive
Baldwin Park, CA 91706
(800) 677-9977
Catalogue: free

E. C. Geiger, Inc.
Box 285
Harleysville, PA 19438
(800) 443-4437
Catalogue: free

Greentrees Hydroponics
2244 South Santa Fe Avenue
Vista, CA 92084
(619) 598-7551
(800) 772-1997
Catalogue: free

The Growing Experience
1901 NW 18th Street
Pompano Beach, FL 33069
(305) 960-0822
(800) 273-6092
Catalogue: free

Hamilton Technology Corporation
14902 South Figueroa Drive
Gardena, CA 90248
(800) 458-7474
Catalogue: free

Heartland Hydroponics
115 Townline Road
Vernon Hills, IL 60061
(701) 816-4769
Catalogue: free

Hollister's Hydroponics
Box 16601
Irvine, CA 92713
(714) 551-3822
Catalogue: $1.00

Home Harvest Garden Supply, Inc.
13426 Occoquan Road
Woodbridge, VA 22191
(800) 348-4769
Catalogue: free

Hydrofarm Gardening Products
3135 Kerner Boulevard
San Rafael, CA 94901
(800) 634-9999
Catalogue: free

Hydro-Gardens, Inc.
Box 25845
Colorado Springs, CO 80936
(800) 634-6362
Catalogue: free

Indoor Garden Supplies
914 164th Street SE
Mill Creek, WA 98012
(800) 335-4707
Catalogue: free

Indoor Gardening Supplies
Box 40567, Detroit, MI 48240
(313) 426-9080
Catalogue: free

M. A. H.
115 Commerce Drive
Hauppauge, NY 11788
(516) 434-6872
Catalogue: free

New Earth Indoor Garden Center
3623 East Highway 44
Shepherdsville, KY 40165
(800) 462-5953
Catalogue: free

Northwest Agriculture
12414 Highway 99 South
Everett, WA 98204
(800) 335-4707
Catalogue: free

Plant Collectibles
103 Kenview Avenue
Buffalo, NY 14217
(716) 875-1221
Catalogue: $2.00

Rain or Shine
13126 NE Airport Way
Portland, OR 97230
(800) 248-1981
Catalogue: free

Season Extenders
Box 312
971 Nichols Avenue
Stratford, CT 06497
(203) 375-1317
Catalogue: free

Smith Greenhouse & Supply
Box 618
603 14th Street
Mendota, IL 61342
(800) 255-4906
Catalogue: free

Texas Greenhouse Company
2524 White Settlement Road

Fort Worth, TX 76107
(800) 227-5447
Catalogue: $4.00

Worm's Way, Inc.
3151 South Highway 446
Bloomington, IN 47401
(812) 331-0300
(800) 274-9676
Catalogue: free

## Specialized Supplies and Products

Aquamonitor
Box 327
Huntington, NY 11743
(516) 427-5664
Product: greenhouse mist
irrigation systems
Catalogue: free

Back To Nature Filtration
3837 Cedarbend Drive
Glendale, CA 91214
(818) 248-7133
Product: reverse osmosis
water purification systems
Catalogue: free

BioTherm Hydronic, Inc.
Box 750967
Petaluma, CA 94975
(800) GET-HEAT
Product: greenhouse heating systems
Catalogue: $2.00

Bramen Company, Inc.
Box 70
Salem, MA 01970
(508) 745-7765
Product: window ventilation controllers
Catalogue: free

Discus Haven Ultra Pure Water Systems
539 Diana Avenue
Morgan Hills, CA 95037

(408) 779-8482
(800) 407-8734
Product: reverse osmosis
water purification systems
Catalogue: free

Eco Enterprises
1240 NE 175th Street
Seattle, WA 98155
(800) 426-6937
Product: liquid nutrient formulas
Catalogue: free

Environmental Concepts
710 SW 57th Street
Fort Lauderdale, FL 33309
(305) 491-4490
Product: greenhouse meters
Catalogue: free

EZ Soil Company
Route 3, Box 176
Idabel, OK 74745
(405) 286-9447
(800) 441-3672
Product: compressed potting mixes
Catalogue: free

Florist Products, Inc.
2242 North Palmer Drive
Schaumburg, IL 60173
(312) 885-2242
Product: Wonder Garden
lighted plant stand
Catalogue: free

GreenTech Environmental Systems
(800) 844-3665
Product: computerized
greenhouse controls
Catalogue: free

Jaybird Manufacturing, Inc.
RD 1, Box 489A
Center Hall, PA 16828
(814) 364-1810

Products: environmental and humidity control systems
Catalogue: free

Malley Supply
7439 La Palma Avenue, Suite 514
Buena Park, CA 90620
Products: plastic pots and growing containers
Catalogue: $1.00

Ann Mann's Orchids
9045 Ron-Den Lane
Windermere, FL 34786
(407) 876-2625
Product: micro-foggers
Catalogue: $1.00

Dan Mattern
267 Filbert Street
San Francisco, CA 94133
(415) 781-6066
Product: HERRmidifier greenhouse humidifiers
Catalogue: free

Northern Greenhouse Sales
Box 42
Neche, ND 58265
(204) 327-5540
Product: polyethylene for greenhouses
Catalogue: $1.00

Plastic Specialties, Ltd.
Box 168
Ventura, IA 50482
(515) 829-4464
Product: plastic trellises for potted plants
Catalogue: free

Retrac Gifts and Collectables
6305 Hoovers Gap Road
Christiana, TN 37037
(615) 896-8449
Product: moisture meter
Catalogue: free

Rodco Products Company, Inc.
2565 16th Avenue
Columbus, NE 68601
(800) 323-2799
Product: temperature monitors
Catalogue: free

Southern Burner Company
Box 885
Chickasha, OK 73023
(405) 224-5000
(800) 375-5001
Product: vented greenhouse heaters
Catalogue: free

Spiral Filtration, Inc.
747 North Twin Oaks Valley Road
San Marcos, CA 92069
(619) 744-3012
Product: reverse osmosis water purification systems
Catalogue: free

Superior Autovents
17422 La Mesa Lane
Huntington Beach, CA 92647
Product: automatic vent openers
Catalogue: free

Tamarack Technologies, Inc.
Box 490
West Wareham, MA 02576
(800) 222-5932
Products: The Turbulator$^{TM}$ air circulator
Catalogue: free

Yonah Manufacturing Company
Box 280
Cornelia, GA 30531
(800) 972-8057
Product: shade cloth
Catalogue: free

# Grow Lights

Diamond Lights
628 Lindaro Street
San Rafael, CA 94901
(800) 331-3994
Catalogue: free

Duro-Lite Lamps, Inc.
9 Law Drive
Fairfield, NJ 07004
(800) 526-7193
Catalogue: free

Energy Technics
3925 Ridgewood Road
York, PA 17402
(717) 755-5642
Catalogue: free

Environmental Lighting Concepts, Inc.
3923 Coconut Palm Drive
Tampa, FL 33619
(800) 842-8848
Product: OTT-Lite®
Catalogue: free

Floralight Gardens
6-620 Supertest Road
North York, Ontario M3J 2M5
(416) 665-4000
(800) 665-4000
Catalogue: free

Full Spectrum Lighting
27 Clover Lane
Burlington, VT 05401
(800) 261-3101
Product: Wonderlite®
Catalogue: free

GTE Sylvania
100 Endicott Street
Danvers, MA 01923
(800) 544-4828
Catalogue: free

Hamilton Technology Corporation
14902 South Figueroa Street
Gardena, CA 90248
(800) 458-7474
Products: metal halide and HPS lights
Catalogue: free

Light Manufacturing Company
1634 SE Brooklyn Street
Portland, OR 97202
(800) NOW-LITE
Catalogue: $3.00

Lumenarc Lighting USA
37 Fairfield Place
West Caldwell, NJ 07006
(800) 845-4815
(800) 8-SODIUM
Products: Super Agro lamp
and other lights
Catalogue: free

Phillips Lighting
Box 200
Somerset, NJ 08875
(201) 563-3000
Products: Son Agro lamps
and other lights
Catalogue: free

Public Service Lamp Corporation
410 West 16th Street
New York, NY 10011
(800) 221-4392
Product: Wonderlite®
Catalogue: free

Verilux, Inc.
Box 2937
Stamford, CT 06906
(203) 921-2430
(800) 786-6850
Product: Verilux® lights
Catalogue: free

Voight Lighting Industries, Inc.
135 Fort Lee Road
Leonia, NJ 07605
(201) 461-2493
Product: lighting fixtures
Catalogue: free

# Tools for Gardeners

T HE RIGHT TOOL MAKES any gardening job easier. Most local garden centers carry a reasonably good selection of gardening tools, but the mail-order tool suppliers listed below offer extensive selections that often include hard-to-find specialty items. Also listed are manufacturers and retailers of watering equipment, garden carts, and gardening gloves and clothing.

The decision to purchase a large, expensive item such as a lawn tractor, chipper, or tiller should not be made lightly. The manufacturers listed below will gladly help you make an informed choice by sending you catalogues, brochures, and other information about their products. They will usually refer you to a local dealer for making your purchase.

## Hand Tools

### Tool Emporiums

Alsto's Handy Helpers
Box 1267
Galesburg, IL 61401
(309) 343-6181
(800) 447-0048
Catalogue: free

American Arborist Supplies, Inc.
882 South Matlack Street
West Chester, PA 19382
(610) 430-1214
(800) 352-3458
Catalogue: $4.00

Berry Hill Limited
75 Burwell Road
St. Thomas, Ontario N5P 3R5
(519) 631-0480
Catalogue: free

Brookstone Hard-to-Find Tools
1655 Bassford Drive
Mexico, MO 65265
(800) 926-7000
Catalogue: free

Denman & Company
187 West Orangethorpe Avenue
Placentia, CA 92670
(714) 524-0668
Catalogue: free

de Van Koek Dutch Traders, Ltd.
9400 Business Drive
Austin, TX 78758
(800) 992-1220
Catalogue: free

The English Garden Emporium
Box 222, Manchester, VT 05254
(800) 347-8130
Catalogue: free

Gardener's Supply Company
128 Intervale Road
Burlington, VT 05401
(800) 863-1700
Catalogue: free

The Garden Pantry
Box 1145
Folsom, CA 95673
(800) 916-3332
Catalogue: free

Gates English Garden Tools
Box 24196
Ventura, CA 93002
(805) 645-5439
Catalogue: free

Harmony Farm Supply
Box 460
3244 Highway 116 North
Graton, CA 95444
(707) 823-9125
Catalogue: $2.00

Kinsman Company, Inc.
River Road
Point Pleasant, PA 18950
(800) 733-4146
Catalogue: free

Langenbach Fine Garden Tools
Box 1140
El Segundo, CA 90245
(800) 362-1991
Catalogue: free

Lee Valley Tools, Ltd.
Box 1780
Ogdensburg, NY 13669
(800) 871-8158
Catalogue: free

Lehman Hardware & Appliances
Box 41
Kidron, OH 44636

(216) 857-5441
Catalogue: $2.00

A. M. Leonard, Inc.
Box 816, Piqua, OH 45356
(513) 773-2694
(800) 543-8955
Catalogue: $1.00

MacKenzie Nursery Supply, Inc.
Box 322
Perry, OH 44081
(216) 259-3004
(800) 777-5030
Catalogue: free

Milestone-Windsor, Ltd.
446 Ellis Place
Wyckoff, NJ 07481
(800) 262-3334
Catalogue: free

MNS, Inc.
3891 Shepard Road
Perry, OH 44081
(800) 777-5030
Catalogue: free

The Natural Gardening Company
217 San Anselmo Avenue
San Anselmo, CA 94960
(415) 456-5060
Catalogue: free

Walt Nicke Company
36 McLeod Lane
Topsfield, MA 01983
(508) 887-3388
(800) 822-4114
Catalogue: free

Niwa Tool Company
2661 Bloomfield Court
Fairfield, CA 94533
(800) 443-5512
Catalogue: $2.00

Peaceful Valley Farm Supply
Box 2209
Grass Valley, CA 95945
(916) 272-4769
Catalogue: free

Seasons Change
19–21 Aubrey Terrace
Malden, MA 02148
(800) 222-0606
Catalogue: free

Smith & Hawken
117 East Strawberry Drive
Mill Valley, CA 94941
(800) 776-3336
Catalogue: free

Vermont Garden Shed
RR 2, Box 180
Wallingford, VT 05773
(800) 288-SHED
Catalogue: free

## Specialized Hand Tools

American Standard Company
157 Water Street
Southington, CT 06489
(800) 275-3618
Product: Florian Ratchet-Cut™ pruning
tools
Catalogue: free

Beaco, Inc.
Box 1168, Glenside, PA 19038
Product: Cutly shears
Catalogue: free

Corona Clipper Company
1540 East 6th Street
Corona, CA 91719
(714) 737-6515
(800) 234-CLIP
Product: edged hand tools
Catalogue: free

Craftech Industries
Box 636
Hudson, NY 12534
Product: dibbles
Catalogue: free

Creative Enterprises
Box 3452
Idaho Falls, ID 83403
(800) 388-4539
Product: Wing Weeder tools
Catalogue: free

Edge-a-Lawn Tool Company
Box 7028
Jacksonville, NC 28540
(910) 347-6292
(800) 533-7027
Product: edgers
Catalogue: free

Fiskars®
(800) 500-4849
Products: Softouch™ and Power-Lever®
pruning tools
Catalogue: free

Genuine Ratchet Cut
674 Meriden-Waterbury Road
Southington, CT 06489
(203) 621-2004
Product: ratchet-action pruning tools
Catalogue: free

Handy Forks
6223 Knollwood Road
Springfield, OH 45502
(800) 467-3398
Product: Handy Forks pickup tools
Catalogue: free

Hilltop Enterprises
4 Lisa Court
Red Hook, NY 12571
Product: ratchet-action garden shears
Catalogue: free

Marugg Company
Box 1418
Tracy City, TN 37387
Products: Austrian scythes and cutting
tools
Catalogue: free

MTP
Box 1049
Chino, CA 91710
Product: Handy Rakes pickup tools
Catalogue: free

RMN Sales
Box 666
Jacksonville, OR 97530
(503) 899-7117
Product: Weed Twist weeders
Catalogue: free

Rudon International Trading Company
Box 331104
Fort Worth, TX 76163
(817) 292-8485
Product: EZ-Diggers
Catalogue: free

Snow & Nealley
Bangor, ME 04401
(207) 947-6642
Catalogue: free

Sonoran Horticultural
6049 West Grandview
Glendale, AZ 83506
(602) 843-0027
Product: Shark Saw pruning tools
Catalogue: free

UnionTools
500 Dublin Avenue
Columbus, OH 43216
(614) 222-4400
Product: long-handled tools
Catalogue: free

Valley Oak Tool Company
448 West 2nd Avenue
Chico, CA 95926
(916) 342-6188
Products: wheel hoes; cultivators
Catalogue: free

Wonder Hoe
Box 11618
Prescott, AZ 86304
Product: Wonder Hoe multipurpose tools
Catalogue: free

## Power Tillers

Ariens Company
655 West Ryan Street
Brillon, WI 54110
(414) 756-2141
(800) 678-5443
Catalogue: free

BCS America, Inc.
Box 7162
Charlotte, NC 28241
(800) 227-8791
Catalogue: free

Echo, Inc.
400 Oakwood Road
Lake Zurich, IL 60047
(708) 540-8400
(800) 432-3246
Catalogue: free

Hoffco®, Inc.
358 NW F Street
Richmond, IN 47374
(800) 999-8161
Product: Li'L Hoes
Catalogue: free

Homelite
14401 Carowinds Boulevard
Charlotte, NC 28241

(704) 588-3200
Catalogue: free

Honda Power Equipment
4475 River Green Parkway
Duluth, GA 30136
(404) 497-6000
Catalogue: free

Husqvarna Forest and Garden Company
9006 Perimeter Woods Drive
Charlotte, NC 28216
(800) 438-7297
Catalogue: free

Kubota Tractor Corporation
550 West Artesia Boulevard
Compton, CA 90220
(213) 537-2531
Catalogue: free

MacKissic, Inc.
Box 111
Parker Ford, PA 19457
(610) 495-7181
Catalogue: free

Mainline Tillers
Box 526
London, OH 43140
(614) 852-9733
(800) 837-2097
Catalogue: free

Mantis
1028 Street Road
Southampton, PA 18966
(800) 366-6268
Catalogue: free

MTD Yard Machine
Box 368022
Cleveland, OH 44136
(800) 800-7310
Catalogue: free

Poulan Pro
5020 Flournoy-Lucas Road
Shreveport, LA 71129
(318) 687-0100
(800) 554-6723
Catalogue: free

Ryobi America Corporation
5201 Pearman Dairy Road
Anderson, SC 29625
(800) 525-2579
Catalogue: free

Snapper Power Equipment
535 Macon Highway
McDonough, GA 30253
(404) 954-2500
Catalogue: free

Troy-Bilt Manufacturing Company
102nd Street and 9th Avenue
Troy, NY 12180
(800) 828-5500
Catalogue: free

## Shredders and Chippers

Atlas Power Equipment Company
Box 70
Harvard, IL 60033
(815) 943-7417
Catalogue: free

Baker™ Corporation
500 North Spring Street
Port Washington, WI 53074
(414) 284-8669
(800) 945-0235
Catalogue: free

BCS America, Inc.
Box 7162
Charlotte, NC 28241
(800) 227-8791
Catalogue: free

Billy Goat Industries, Inc.
Box 308
Lees Summit, MO 64063
(816) 524-9666
Product: The Termite
Catalogue: free

Crary Company
Box 849
West Fargo, ND 58078
(701) 282-5520
(800) 247-7335
Products: Bear Cat™ line
Catalogue: free

Cub Cadet Power Equipment
Box 368023
Cleveland, OH 44136
(216) 273-9723
Catalogue: free

John Deere
Box 29533, Raleigh, NC 27626
(800) 537-8233
Catalogue: free

Easy Rake
1001 South Ransdell Road
Lebanon, IN 46052
(800) 777-6074
Catalogue: free

Echo, Inc.
400 Oakwood Road
Lake Zurich, IL 60047
(708) 540-8400
(800) 432-3246
Catalogue: free

Flowtron Outdoor Products
2 Main Street
Melrose, MA 02176
(617) 321-2300
(800) 343-3280
Product: Leafeater mulcher
Catalogue: free

Goossen Industries
Box 705
Beatrice, NE 68310
(800) 228-6542
Catalogue: free

Ingersoll Equipment Company
Box 5001
Winneconne, WI 54986
(414) 582-5021
Catalogue: free

Kemp Company
160 Koser Road
Lititz, PA 17543
(717) 627-7979
(800) 441-5367
Catalogue: free

Lambert Corporation
117 South 3rd Street
Ansonia, OH 45303
(513) 337-3641
Catalogue: free

Little Wonder
Box 38
Southampton, PA 18966
(215) 357-5110
Catalogue: free

MacKissic, Inc.
Box 111
Parker Ford, PA 19457
(610) 495-7181
Product: Might Mac chippers
Catalogue: free

The Patriot Company
944 North 45th Street
Milwaukee, WI 53208
(800) 798-2447
Catalogue: free

Parker Sweeper Company
Box 1758

Springfield, OH 45501
(513) 323-9420
Products: Minuteman line
Catalogue: free

Roto-Hoe
345 15th Street NW
Barberton, OH 44203
(216) 753-2320
Catalogue: free

Ryobi America Corporation
5201 Pearman Dairy Road
Anderson, SC 29625
(800) 525-2579
Catalogue: free

Salsco, Inc.
105 School House Road
Cheshire, CT 06410
(800) 8-SALSCO
Catalogue: free

Simplicity Manufacturing, Inc.
Box 997
Port Washington, WI 53074
(414) 284-8789
Catalogue: free

Steiner Turf Equipment, Inc.
289 North Kurzen Road
Dalton, OH 44618
(216) 828-0200
Catalogue: free

Tilton Equipment Company
Box 68
Rye, NH 03870
(800) 447-1152
Catalogue: free

Trim-Rite, Inc.
Box 1506
Weatherford, TX 76086
(800) 553-2100
Catalogue: free

Troy-Bilt Manufacturing Company
102nd Street and 9th Avenue
Troy, NY 12180
(800) 828-5500
Catalogue: free

White Outdoor Products Company
Box 361131
Cleveland, OH 44136
(216) 273-7786
(800) 94-WHITE
Catalogue: free

## Mowers and Lawn Tractors

*Push Mowers*

Agri-Fab, Inc.
303 West Raymond Street
Sullivan, IL 61951
(217) 728-8388
Catalogue: free

American Lawn Mower Company/Great
States Corporation
830 Webster Street
Shelbyville, IN 46176
(317) 392-3615
Catalogue: free

McLane Manufacturing, Inc.
7110 East Rosecrans Avenue
Paramount, CA 90723
(213) 633-8158
Catalogue: free

C. K. Petty & Company
203 Wildemere Drive
South Bend, IN 46615
(219) 232-4095
Catalogue: free

## Power Mowers and Lawn Tractors

Ariens Company
655 West Ryan Street
Brillon, WI 54110
(414) 756-2141
(800) 678-5443
Catalogue: free

Cub Cadet Power Equipment
Box 368023
Cleveland, OH 44136
(216) 273-9723
Catalogue: free

John Deere
Box 29533
Raleigh, NC 27626
(800) 537-8233
Catalogue: free

The Grasshopper Company
Box 637
Moundridge, KS 67107
(316) 345-8621
Catalogue: free

Gravely International, Inc.
1 Gravely Lane
Clemmons, NC 27012
(919) 766-4721
Catalogue: free

Honda Power Equipment
4475 River Green Parkway
Duluth, GA 30136
(404) 497-6000
Catalogue: free

Husqvarna Forest and Garden Company
9006 Perimeter Woods Drive
Charlotte, NC 28216
(800) 438-7297
Catalogue: free

Ingersoll Equipment Company
Box 5001
Winneconne, WI 54986
(414) 582-5021
Catalogue: free

Kubota Tractor Corporation
550 West Artesia Boulevard
Compton, CA 90220
(213) 537-2531
Catalogue: free

Poulan Pro
5020 Flournoy-Lucas Road
Shreveport, LA 71129
(318) 687-0100
(800) 554-6723
Catalogue: free

Power King Products Company
1100 Green Valley Road
Beaver Dam, WI 53916
(800) 262-1191
Catalogue: free

Simplicity Manufacturing, Inc.
Box 997
Port Washington, WI 53074
(414) 284-8789
Catalogue: free

Snapper Power Equipment
535 Macon Highway
McDonough, GA 30253
(404) 954-2500
Catalogue: free

Steiner Turf Equipment, Inc.
289 North Kurzen Road
Dalton, OH 44618
(216) 828-0200
Catalogue: free

The Toro Company
8111 Lyndale Avenue South
Minneapolis, MN 55420

(612) 888-8801
(800) 321-TORO
Catalogue: free

Walker Manufacturing Company
5925 East Harmony Road
Fort Collins, CO 80525
(303) 221-5614
Catalogue: free

White Outdoor Products Company
Box 361131
Cleveland, OH 44136
(216) 273-7786
(800) 94-WHITE
Catalogue: free

Yard-Man Outdoor Power Products
Box 360940
Cleveland, OH 44136
(216) 273-3600
Catalogue: free

Yazoo Manufacturing Company
3650 Bay Street
Jackson, MS 39206
(800) 354-6562
Catalogue: free

# Sprayers

Dramm Corporation
Box 1960
Manitowoc, WI 54221
(414) 684-0227
(800) 258-0808
Catalogue: free

K & G Manufacturing, Inc.
Box 350
Duke, OK 73532
(405) 679-3955
Product: Spray Boss
Catalogue: free

PeCo, Inc.
100 Airport Road
Arden, NC 28704
(704) 684-1234
(800) 438-5823
Catalogue: free

# Wheelbarrows and Garden Carts

Carts Vermont
1890 Airport Parkway
South Burlington, VT 05403
(802) 862-6304
Product: garden carts
Catalogue: free

Cart Warehouse
Box 3
Point Arena, CA 95468
(800) 852-2588
Product: garden carts
Catalogue: free

Catamount Cart
Box 365
Shelburne Falls, MA 01370
(413) 625-0284
(800) 444-0056
Product: Catamount garden carts
Catalogue: free

Country Home Products
Box 89
Ferry Road
Charlotte, VT 05445
(800) 641-8008
Product: DR® Powerwagon™
Catalogue: free

DuCART
(800) 360-2278
Product: utility carts
Catalogue: free

Homestead Carts
2396 Perkins Street NE
Salem, OR 97303
(503) 393-3973
(800) 825-1925
Product: Homestead carts
Catalogue: free

Kadco USA
27 Jumel Place
Saratoga Springs, NY 12866
(518) 587-2224
(800) 448-5503
Product: Carry-It garden carts
Catalogue: free

Norway Industries
41 East 9237 Highway O
Sauk City, WI 53583
(608) 544-5000
Product: Carry-All carts
Catalogue: free

Roll'Erg North America, Inc.
970 Golden Hills Road
Colorado Springs, CO 80919
(719) 598-5274
Product: Roll'Erg™ wheelbarrow

S.A.N. Associates, Inc.
Box 88
Greendell, NJ 07839
(908) 852-4612
Product: Big Daddy™ garden caddy
Catalogue: free

Scenic Road Manufacturing
3539 Scenic Road
Gordonville, PA 17529
(717) 768-3364
Product: wheelbarrows
Catalogue: free

True Engineering, Inc.
999 Roosevelt Trail
Windham, ME 04062

(207) 892-0200
Product: Muller's Smart Carts
Catalogue: free

WheelAround Corporation
241 Grandview Avenue
Bellevue, KY 41073
(800) 335-CART
Product: WheelAround® carts
Catalogue: free

Wisconsin Wagon Co.
507 Laurel Avenue
Janesville, WI 53545
(608) 754-0026
Products: wagons and wheelbarrows
Catalogue: free

# Watering Supplies

Ames
Box 1774
Parkersburg, WV 26102
(304) 424-3000
(800) 624-2654
Products: hoses and hose reels
Catalogue: fee

Aquapore Moisture Systems
610 South 80th Avenue
Phoenix, AZ 85043
(800) 635-8379
Product: Moisture Master™ soaker hoses
Catalogue: free

D. I. G. Corporation
130 Bosstick Boulevard
San Marcos, CA 92082
(619) 727-0914
(800) 322-9146
Product: drip irrigation supplies
Catalogue: free

Dramm Corporation
Box 1960

Manitowoc, WI 54221
(414) 684-0227
(800) 258-0808
Products: Dramm Water Breaker
nozzles; watering cans
Catalogue: free

Dripworks-Everliner
380 Maple Street
Willits, CA 95490
(707) 459-6323
(800) 522-3747
Product: drip irrigation systems
Catalogue: free

Environmental Concepts, Inc.
710 NW 57th Street
Fort Lauderdale, FL 33309
(305) 491-4490
Product: moisture meters
Catalogue: free

Gardener's Supply Company
128 Intervale Road
Burlington, VT 05401
(800) 863-1700
Product: drip irrigation supplies
Catalogue: free

Gilmour Manufacturing Company
Box 838
Somerset, PA 15501
(814) 443-4802
(800) 458-0107
Product: Flexogen hoses
Catalogue: free

The Great American Rain Barrel
Company, Inc.
295 Maverick Street
East Boston, MA 02120
(617) 569-3690
(800) 251-2352
Product: plastic rain barrels
Catalogue: free

Grosoke, Inc.
7415 Whitehall Street
Fort Worth, TX 76118
(817) 284-0696
(800) 522-0696
Product: Agrosoke hydrogels
Catalogue: free

Harmony Farm Supply
3244 Highway 116 North
Graton, CA 95444
(707) 823-9125
Product: drip irrigation supplies
Catalogue: $2.00

International Irrigation Systems
Box 360
Niagara Falls, NY 14304
(905) 688-4090
Product: IRRIGRO® drip
irrigation systems
Catalogue: free

Janziker
Box 957
Davis, CA 95617
Product: SuperSorb water-absorbing
crystals
Catalogue: free

Jasco Distributing
Box 520
Lancaster, NH 03584
(603) 788-4744
Product: Aqua Spike slow-release
watering reservoirs
Catalogue: free

Magnalawn 2000
2935 Bayberry Road
Hatboro, PA 19040
(800) 699-1102
Product: Magnalawn 2000®
water purification devices
Catalogue: free

Multiple Concepts
Box 4248
Chattanooga, TN 37405
(615) 266-3967
Product: Moisture Mizer hydrogels
Catalogue: long SASE with two stamps

Northern Tier
Box 5083
Sheridan, WY 82801
(800) 443-7467
Product: Big Dripper™ tank drip
irrigation systems
Catalogue: free

Plant Collectibles
103 Kenview Avenue
Buffalo, NY 14217
(716) 875-1221
Products: Aquamatic hose waterers;
nozzles
Catalogue: $2.00

Plastic Plumbing Products, Inc.
Box 186
Grover, MO 63040
(314) 458-2226
Product: drip irrigation supplies
Catalogue: $1.00

Rain Control
Box 662
Adrian, MI 49221
(517) 263-5226
Product: Irri-Gator drip irrigation systems
Catalogue: free

Raindrip, Inc.
2250 Agate Court
Simi Valley, CA 93065
(800) 367-3747
(800) 544-3747
Product: drip irrigation systems
Catalogue: free

Submatic Irrigation Systems
Box 246
Lubbock, TX 79408
(800) 692-4100
Product: drip irrigation supplies
Catalogue: free

Swan Garden Hose
Box 509
Worthington, OH 43085
(614) 548-6511
Product: Perfect Gardener hoses
Catalogue: free

Teknor Apex Company
Pawtucket, RI 02861
(800) 556-3864
Product: garden hoses
Catalogue: free

TFS Injector Systems
211 West Maple Avenue
Monrovia, CA 91016
(818) 358-5507
Product: drip irrigation supplies
Catalogue: long SASE

Universal Products
Box 4293, Reading, PA 19606
Product: garden hose guides
Catalogue: free

The Urban Farmer Store
2833 Vicente Street
San Francisco, CA 94116
(415) 661-2204
Product: drip irrigation systems
Catalogue: $1.00

Wade Manufacturing Company
Box 23666
Portland, OR 97281
(800) 222-7246
Product: Acu-Drip® System EZ
drip irrigation systems
Catalogue: free

Waterboy Garden Trellis
23 McKinley Street
Uniontown, PA 15401
Product: self-watering garden trellises
Catalogue: free

Watermiser Drip Irrigation
Box 18157
Reno, NV 89511
(800) 332-1570
Product: drip irrigation supplies
Catalogue: free

Witherspoon-Pike Enterprises, Inc.
Box 51655
Durham, NC 27717
(800) 643-0315
Product: Shur-Flo™ water savers
Catalogue: free

# Clothing and Gloves

Calo Enterprises
4625 Broadway
Union City, NJ 07087
Product: gloves
Catalogue: free

Carolina Glove Company
Drawer 820
Newton, NC 28658
(704) 464-1132
(800) 438-6888
Product: gardening gloves
Catalogue: free

Clothcrafters, Inc.
Box 176
Elkhart Lake, WI 53020
(414) 876-2112
Products: gloves; aprons
Catalogue: free

Denman & Company
187 West Orangethorpe Avenue
Placentia, CA 92670
(714) 524-0668
Product: Greenknee™ gardening trousers
Catalogue: free

Little's Good Gloves
Box 808
Johnstown, NY 12095
(518) 736-5014
Product: gardening gloves
Catalogue: free

MN Productions
Box 577
Freeland, WA 98249
(206) 331-7995
Product: Iron-Neezers™
gardening trousers
Catalogue: free

Womanswork
Box 543
York, ME 03909
(207) 363-0804
Product: gardening gloves
Catalogue: free

# Composting, Fertilizers, and Soil Care

$T$AKING GOOD CARE *of your garden soil pays off handsomely in stronger, healthier plants with better blooms. Adding compost to your soil is an inexpensive, ecologically sound way to add nutrients and improve the tilth. The retailers and manufacturers below sell composters, composting supplies, organic fertilizers, and other organic supplies. For the sake of completeness, some manufacturers of chemical fertilizers and plant foods are also listed. Soil-testing laboratories, which can provide detailed information about your soil, end the listings.*

## Organic Supplies Emporiums

Bozeman Bio-Tech, Inc.
Box 3146
Bozeman, MT 59772
(800) 289-6656
Catalogue: free

Charley's Greenhouse Supply
1569 Memorial Highway
Mount Vernon, WA 98273
(800) 322-4707
Catalogue: free

Gardener's Supply Company
128 Intervale Road
Burlington, VT 05401
(800) 863-1700
Catalogue: free

Garden-Ville of Austin
8648 Old Bee Cave Road

Austin, TX 78735
(512) 288-6115
(800) 320-0724
Catalogue: free

Harmony Farm Supply
Box 460, 3244 Highway 116 North
Graton, CA 95444
(707) 823-9125
Catalogue: $2.00

Peaceful Valley Farm Supply
Box 2209
Grass Valley, CA 95945
(916) 272-4769
Catalogue: free

Richters
357 Highway 47
Goodwood, Ontario L0C 1A0
(416) 640-6677
Catalogue: $2.00

Worm's Way, Inc.
3151 South Highway 446
Bloomington, IN 47401
(812) 331-0300
(800) 274-9676
Catalogue: free

## Composters

A & N Enterprises
Box 537
Bethany, OK 73008
Product: composter construction plans
Catalogue: free

Blue Planet, Ltd.
Box 1500
Princeton, NJ 08542
(800) 777-9201
Product: Composift composters
Catalogue: free

Compost and Recycling Systems
Box 265
Fox River Grove, IL 60021
(800) 848-3829
Product: The Composter
Catalogue: free

Gardner Equipment Company
(800) 393-0333
Product: No-Turn™ composters
Catalogue: free

Gear Up Technologies Corporation
12900 Eckel Junction Road
Perrysburg, OH 43551
Product: The Compost Corral™
composters
Catalogue: free

Home Gardener Manufacturing
Company
30 Wright Avenue
Lititz, PA 17543

(800) 880-2345
Product: ComposTumbler® composters
Catalogue: free

Kemp Company
160 Koser Road
Lititz, PA 17543
(717) 627-7979
(800) 441-5367
Product: compost tumblers
Catalogue: free

Master Garden Products, Inc.
(800) 949-6620
Product: Mulch Master® composters
Catalogue: free

Morco Products
Box 160
Dundas, MN 55019
(507) 645-4277
Product: Turn Easy composters
Catalogue: free

Nature's Backyard, Inc.
126 Duchaine Boulevard
New Bedford, MA 02745
(800) 853-2525
Product: Brave New Composter
Catalogue: free

Northwest Toolbox
12808 North Point Lane
Laurel, MD 20708
(301) 604-0090
Product: aerobic composting systems
Catalogue: free

Palmor Products
Box 38
Thorntown, IN 46071
(800) 872-2822
Product: rotary composters
Catalogue: free

Rivendell Company
Box 174
Old Saybrook, CT 06475
(800) 690-0899
Product: The Best Little Composter in
America®
Catalogue: free

Solarcone, Inc.
Box 67
Seward, IL 61077
(815) 247-8454
(800) 80-SOLAR
Product: The Green Keeper™
composters
Catalogue: free

The Toro Company
8111 Lyndale Avenue South
Minneapolis, MN 55420
(612) 888-8801
(800) 321-TORO
Product: YardCycler™ composters
Catalogue: free

Tumblebug
2029 North 23rd Street
Boise, ID 83702
(800) 531-0102
Product: Tumblebug® rolling composters
Catalogue: free

## Composting Supplies

Bronwood Worm Gardens
Box 28
Bronwood, GA 31726
(912) 995-5994
Product: redworms
Catalogue: long SASE

Cape Cod Worm Farm
30 Center Avenue
Buzzards Bay, MA 02532
(508) 759-5664

Product: redworms
Catalogue: free

The Crafter's Garden
Box 3194
Peabody, MA 01961
(508) 535-1142
Product: composting supplies
Catalogue: free

Morning Mist Worm Farm
Box 1155
Davis, CA 95617
(707) 448-6836
Product: redworms
Catalogue: free

Ratskee Worm Farm
Box 764
Bolinas, CA 94924
(415) 868-9556
Product: redworms
Catalogue: free

Smith Worms
Boston, GA 31626
(912) 498-1605
Product: redworms
Catalogue: free

The Worm Czar
Amherst Junction, WI 54407
(715) 824-3868
Product: redworms
Catalogue: long SASE with two stamps

## Organic Fertilizers

Age-Old Organics
Box 1556
Boulder, CO 80306
(303) 499-0201
Catalogue: free

A Natural Way to Grow
39 East Main Street
Sykesville, PA 15865
(800) 685-4769
Catalogue: free

Arbico, Inc.
Box 4247
Tucson, AZ 85712
(602) 825-9785
(800) 827-2847
Catalogue: free

Astoria-Pacific, Inc.
Box 830
Clackamas, OR 97015
(800) 536-3111
Product: Dip 'n Grow® rooting
hormones
Catalogue: free

Avant Horticultural Products
5755 Balfrey Drive
West Palm Beach, FL 33414
(800) 334-7979
Product: reacted liquid plant foods
Catalogue: free

Bio-Gard Agronomics
Box 4477
Falls Church, VA 22044
(800) 673-8502
Product: foliar fertilizers
Catalogue: free

BioResource Recovery Systems, Inc.
Box 255
Lone Tree, IA 52755
(319) 629-4407
(800) 299-1898
Catalogue: free

Cape Cod Worm Farm
30 Center Avenue
Buzzards Bay, MA 02532
(508) 759-5664

Product: worm castings
Catalogue: free

Cotton, Inc.
Box 30067
Raleigh, NC 27622
Product: cottonseed meal
Catalogue: free

Dirt Cheap Organics
5645 Paradise Drive
Corte Madera, CA 94925
(415) 924-0369
Catalogue: free

Earlee, Inc.
2002 Highway 62
Jeffersonville, IN 47130
(812) 282-9134
Catalogue: free

Elgin Landscape and Garden Center
1881 Larkin Avenue
Elgin, IL 60123
(708) 697-8733
Catalogue: $2.00

EnP, Inc.
Box 618
Mendota, IL 61342
(800) 255-4906
Catalogue: free

Erth-Rite, Inc.
RD 1, Box 243
Gap, PA 17527
(717) 442-4171
Catalogue: free

Gardens Alive!
5100 Schenley Place
Lawrenceburg, IN 47025
(812) 537-8650
Catalogue: free

Green Growers Supply
Box 3168
Framingham, MA 01701
Product: liquid fish fertilizers
Catalogue: free

Guano Company International, Inc.
3562 East 80th Street
Cleveland, OH 44105
(216) 641-1200
(800) 424-8266
Product: seabird guano
Catalogue: free

Integrated Fertility Management
333 Ohme Gardens Road
Wenatchee, WA 98801
(509) 662-3179
(800) 332-3179
Catalogue: free

Johnny's Selected Seeds
Foss Hill Road
Albion, ME 04910
(207) 437-9294
Catalogue: free

Liquid Fish, Inc.
Box 99
Bonduel, WI 54107
(715) 758-2280
(800) 448-2280
Catalogue: free

Maestro-Gro
Box 6670
Springdale, AR 72766
(501) 361-9155
Catalogue: free

Milorganite
Box 3049
Milwaukee, WI 53201
(414) 225-2222
Catalogue: free

Mother Nature's Worm Castings
Box 1055
Avon, CT 06001
(203) 673-3029
Product: worm castings
Catalogue: long SASE

Natural Products, Inc.
1000 Oak Street
Grinnell, IA 50112
(800) 238-4634
Product: alfalfa meal
Catalogue: free

The Necessary Trading Company
1 Natures Way
New Castle, VA 24127
(703) 864-5103
Product: CONCERN® plant foods
Catalogue: free

New Earth
3623 East Highway 44
Shepherdsville, KY 40165
(800) 462-5953
Catalogue: free

Nitron Industries, Inc.
Box 1447
Fayetteville, AR 72702
(800) 835-0123
Catalogue: $1.00

North American Kelp
Box 279A
Waldoboro, ME 04572
(207) 832-7506
Product: seaweed fertilizers
Catalogue: free

Ohio Earth Food, Inc.
5488 Swamp Street NE
Hartville, OH 44632
(216) 877-9356
Catalogue: free

Primary Products
100E Tower Office Park
Woburn, MA 01801
(617) 932-8509
Product: MegaBoost™ growth stimulants
Catalgue: free

Rainbow Red Worms
Box 278
Lake Elsinor, CA 92531
(909) 674-7041
Product: worm castings
Catalogue: free

Saltwater Farms
102 South Freeport Road
Freeport, ME 04032
(207) 865-9066
(800) 293-KELP
Product: seaweed fertilizers
Catalogue: free

Sea Born/Lane, Inc.
Box 204
Charles City, IA 50616
(800) 457-5013
Product: seaweed fertilizers
Catalogue: free

Spray-N-Grow, Inc.
20 Highway 35 South
Rockport, TX 78382
(512) 790-9033
Product: Spray-N-Grow growth stimulants
Catalogue: free

Territorial Seed Company
Box 157
Cottage Grove, OR 97424
(503) 942-9547
Catalogue: free

# Chemical Fertilizers

Crystal Company
Box 220055
St. Louis, MO 63122
(314) 966-5999
(800) 845-4777
Product: Throw & Grow™ plant foods
Catalogue: free

Dyna-Gro™ Corporation
1065 Broadway
San Pablo, CA 94806
(800) DYNA-GRO
Product: Dyna-Gro™ nutrient formulas
Catalogue: free

JRP International, Inc.
17 Forest Avenue
fond du Lac, WI 54936
Product: Nutri-Pak® time-release fertilizer packets

Miracle-Gro
(800) 4-PRO-SOL
Product: Pro-Sol Plant Food
Catalogue: free

Schultz Company
14090 Riverport Drive
St. Louis, MO 63043
(314) 298-3045
(800) 325-3045
Product: Schultz-Instant fertilizers

Wilt-Pruf® Products, Inc.
Box 469
Essex, CT 06426
Product: Wilt-Pruf® antitranspirants

# Soil-Testing Laboratories

*Inexpensive home soil-testing kits are easily
available at any garden center, but they usually
test only for the pH of your soil. While knowing
the acidity or alkalinity of your soil is an important first step, more extensive testing is needed to
get detailed information about nutrient levels and
recommendations for soil amendments. Your local
USDA extension agent (see chapter 9) can provide some additional testing, usually for a nominal
fee. For thorough testing and recommendations,
try one of the professional soil-testing laboratories
listed below.*

A & L Analytical Laboratories, Inc.
411 North Third Street
Memphis, TN 38105
(901) 527-2780

A & L Eastern Agricultural
Laboratories, Inc.
7621 Whitepine Road
Richmond, VA 23237
(804) 743-9401

Biosystem Consultants
Box 43
Lorane, OR 97451

Cook's Consulting
RD 2, Box 13
Lowville, NY 13367
(315) 376-3002

Harmony Farm Supply
Box 460
3244 Highway 116 North
Graton, CA 95472
(707) 823-9125

Integrated Fertility Management
333 Ohme Gardens Road
Wenatchee, WA 98801
(509) 662-3179
(800) 332-3179

LaRamie Soils Service
Box 255
Laramie, WY 82070
(307) 742-4185

Ohio Earth Food, Inc.
5488 Swamp Street, NE
Hartville, OH 44632
(216) 877-9356

Peaceful Valley Farm Supply
Box 2209
Grass Valley, CA 95945
(916) 272-4769

Timberleaf
5569 State Street
Albany, OH 45710
(614) 698-3861

Wallace Laboratories
365 Coral Circle
El Segundo, CA 90245
(310) 615-0116

# Pest and Weed Control

DAMAGING INSECTS, *hungry deer, and weeds are all constant headaches for gardeners. Environmentally aware gardeners prefer to deal with these and other pests through nonchemical means. Many harmful insects, for example, can be controlled by introducing their natural insect predators to your garden. The retailers and manufacturers listed below sell beneficial insects, landscape fabrics, and other supplies for controlling garden pests. For the sake of completeness, the manufacturers of some popular herbicides and insecticides are listed as well. Although there are some rare instances when use of these products may be justified, their drawbacks almost always far outweigh their advantages. Responsible home gardeners should consider carefully before applying chemical herbicides and pesticides.*

## Beneficial Insects

### Publications

The Bio-Integral Resource Center
Box 7414
Berkeley, CA 94707
(415) 524-2567
Products: IPM publications
and newsletters
Catalogue: free

### Sources

A Natural Way to Grow
39 East Main Street
Sykesville, PA 15865
(800) 685-4769
Catalogue: free

Arbico, Inc.
Box 4247
Tucson, AZ 85712

(602) 825-9785
(800) 827-2847
Catalogue: free

Bob Bauer
311 Ford Road
Howell, NJ 07731
Product: praying mantis egg clusters
Catalogue: free

The Beneficial Insect Company
244 Forrest Street
Fort Mill, SC 29715
(803) 547-2301
Catalogue: free

Beneficial Resources, Inc.
Box 34
Turbotville, PA 17772
(717) 649-6289
Catalogue: free

Better Yield Insects
RR 3, Site 4, Box 48
Belle River, Ontario N5P 3R5
(519) 727-6108
Catalogue: $1.00

BioLogic
Box 177
Springtown Road
Willow Hill, PA 17271
(717) 349-2789
Product: nematodes
Catalogue: long SASE

Biological Control of Weeds
1418 Maple Drive
Bozeman, MT 59715
(406) 586-5111
Catalogue: free

Biosys
1057 East Meadow Circle
Palo Alto, CA 94303
(800) 821-8448
Product: nematodes
Catalogue: free

Bozeman Bio-Tech, Inc.
Box 3146
Bozeman, MT 59772
(800) 289-6656
Catalogue: free

The Bug Store
4472 Shaw Boulevard
St. Louis, MO 63110
(314) 773-7374
Catalogue: free

Charley's Greenhouse Supply
1569 Memorial Highway
Mount Vernon, WA 98273
(800) 322-4707
Catalogue: free

Cyline Biotic
Box 48
Goodyears Bar, CA 95944
(916) 289-3122
Product: ladybugs
Catalogue: free

Dirt Cheap Organics
5645 Paradise Drive
Corte Madera, CA 94925
(415) 924-0369
Catalogue: free

Foothill Agricultural Research, Inc.
510½ West Chase Drive
Corona, CA 91720
(714) 371-0120
Catalogue: free

GB Systems, Inc.
Box 19497
Boulder, CO 80308
(303) 863-1700
Catalogue: free

Gardener's Supply Co.
128 Intervale Road
Burlington, VT 05401
(800) 873-1700
Catalogue: free

Garden-Ville of Austin
8648 Old Bee Cave Road
Austin, TX 78735
(512) 288-6115
(800) 320-0724
Catalogue: free

Gardens Alive!
5100 Schenley Place
Lawrenceburg, IN 47025
(812) 537-8650
Catalogue: free

Great Lakes IPM
10220 Church Road NE

Vestaburg, MI 48891
(517) 268-5693
Catalogue: free

The Green Spot
93 Priest Road
Barrington, NH 03825
(603) 942-8925
Catalogue: $2.00

Harmony Farm Supply
Box 460
3244 Highway 116 North
Graton, CA 95444
(707) 823-9125
Catalogue: $2.00

Hydro-Gardens, Inc.
Box 25845
Colorado Springs, CO 80936
(800) 634-6362
Catalogue: free

Integrated Fertility Management
333 Ohme Gardens Road
Wenatchee, WA 98801
(509) 662-3179
(800) 332-3179
Catalogue: free

IPM Laboratories, Inc.
Box 300, Locke, NY 13092
(315) 497-2063
Catalogue: free

Johnny's Selected Seeds
Foss Hill Road
Albion, ME 04910
(207) 437-9294
Catalogue: free

Kunafin Trichogramma
Route 1, Box 39
Quemado, TX 78877
(800) 832-1113
Catalogue: free

The Lady Bug Company
8706 Oro-Quincy Highway
Berry Creek, CA 95916
(916) 589-5227
Catalogue: free

Land Steward
434 Lower Road
Souderton, PA 18964
Catalogue: free

M & R Durango
Box 886
Bayfield, CO 81122
(303) 259-3521
Catalogue: free

Natural Insect Control
RR 2
Stevensville, Ontario L0S 1S0
(905) 382-2904
Catalogue: $1.00

Nature's Alternative Insectary, Ltd.
Box 19, Dawson
Nanoose Bay, British Coumbia V0R 2R0
(604) 468-7912
Catalogue: free

Nature's Control
Box 35
Medford, OR 97501
(503) 899-8318
Catalogue: free

The Necessary Trading Company
1 Natures Way
New Castle, VA 24127
(703) 864-5103
Catalogue: free

Ohio Earth Food, Inc.
5488 Swamp Street NE
Hartville, OH 44632
(216) 877-9356
Catalogue: free

Organic Control, Inc.
Box 781147
Los Angeles, CA 90016
(213) 937-7444
Catalogue: free

Peaceful Valley Farm Supply
Box 2209
Grass Valley, CA 95945
(916) 272-4769
Catalogue: free

Pest Management Supply
311 River Drive
Hadley, MA 01035
(800) 272-7672
Catalogue: free

Richters
357 Highway 47
Goodwood, Ontario L0C 1A0
(416) 640-6677
Catalogue: $2.00

Rincon-Vitova Insectaries, Inc.
Box 95
Oak View, CA 93022
(800) 248-2847
Catalogue: free

Territorial Seed Company
Box 157
Cottage Grove, OR 97424
(503) 942-9547
Catalogue: free

Unique Insect Control
5504 Sperry Drive
Citrus Heights, CA 95621
(916) 961-7945
Catalogue: free

Worm's Way, Inc.
3151 South Highway 446
Bloomington, IN 47401
(812) 331-0300

(800) 274-9676
Catalogue: free

## Insect Control

*Many of the beneficial insect companies listed above also sell pheromone traps for insect control. The companies listed below sell additional insect control products.*

Bargyla Rateaver
9049 Covina Street
San Diego, CA 92126
(619) 566-8994
Product: organic pesticides
Catalogue: long SASE

Bonide Products, Inc.
2 Wurz Avenue
Yorkville, NY 13495
(315) 736-8233
Product: organic pesticides
Catalogue: $2.00

Dow Elanco
9002 Purdue Road
Indianapolis, IN 46268
(317) 875-8618
Product: Dursban insecticides
Catalogue: free

Enviro-Chem, Inc.
Box 1298
Walla Walla, WA 99362
(800) 247-9011
Product: Slug-Fest slug and snail control
Catalogue: free

Fairfax Biological Laboratory, Inc.
Box 300
Clinton Corners, NY 12514
(914) 266-3705
Product: organic pest control for
Japanese beetles
Catalogue: free

Garlic Research Labs
3550 Wilshire Boulevard
Los Angeles, CA 90010
(800) 424-7990
Product: garlic liquid insect repellents
Catalogue: free

Great Lakes IPM
10220 Church Road NE
Vestaburg, MI 48891
(517) 268-5911
Products: insect traps and pheromones
Catalogue: free

Naturally Scientific
726 Holcomb Bridge Road
Norcross, GA 30071
(800) 248-9970
Products: slug and snail baits
Catalogue: free

Phero Tech, Inc.
7572 Progress Way
Delta, British Columbia V4G 1E9
Products: insect traps and pheromones
Catalogue: free

Slugbuster™
827 Albemarle Avenue
Cuyahoga Falls, OH 44221
(216) 923-0631
Products: slug and snail killers
Catalogue: free

Sterling International, Inc.
Box 220
Liberty Lake, WA 99019
(800) 666-6766
Products: Rescue! insect control products
Catalogue: free

# Bird Control

Bird-X
(800) 662-5021

Product: bird repellents
Catalogue: free

InterNet, Inc.
2730 Nevada Avenue North
Minneapolis, MN 55427
(800) 328-8456
Product: bird netting
Catalogue: free

Reed-Joseph International
Box 894
Greenville, MS 38702
(800) 647-5554
Product: bird frightening balloons
Catalogue: free

Rice Lake Products
100 27th Street NE
Minot, ND 58701
(800) 998-7450
Product: scare owls
Catalogue: free

The Tanglefoot Company
314 Straight Avenue SW
Grand Rapids, MI 49504
(616) 459-4139
Products: crawling insect and
animal protectants
Catalogue: free

# Deer Control

Benner's Gardens
6974 Upper York Road
New Hope, PA 18938
(800) 753-4660
Product: mesh barriers
Catalogue: free

Bobbex, Inc.
52 Hattertown Road
Newtown, CT 06470
(203) 426-9696

Product: foliar repellent sprays
Catalogue: free

Burlington Scientific Corporation
222 Sherwood Avenue
Farmingdale, NY 11735
(516) 694-9000
Product: Ro-Pel animal repellents
Catalogue: free

Bye Deer
Stoll Road Associates
Box 1223
Woodstock, NY 12498
Product: deer repellents
Catalogue: free

Deer-B-Gone
Leticia Duenas
Box 4195
Santa Rosa, CA 95402
(707) 829-5872
Product: deer repellent containers
Catalogue: free

Deerbusters
(800) 248-DEER
Product: deer repellents
Catalogue: free

Deer No No
Box 112
West Cornwall, CT 06796
(800) 484-7107
Product: deer repellents
Catalogue: free

IntAgra, Inc.
8500 Pillsbury Avenue South
Minneapolis, MN 55420
(612) 881-5535
(800) 468-2472
Product: Deer-Away™ deer repellents
Catalogue: free

Tenax Corporation
8291 Patuxent Range Road
Jessup, MD 20794
(301) 725-5910
(800) 356-8495
Product: Tenax® deer fencing
Catalogue: free

Uniroyal Chemical Company, Inc.
Benson Road
Middlebury, CT 06749
(203) 573-2000
Product: Hinder® deer and rabbit
repellents
Catalogue: free

Varmint Guard
Box 8317
Portland, ME 04104
Product: deer repellents
Catalogue: free

## Fungus Control

Source Technology Biologicals, Inc.
(800) 356-8733
Products: Phyton® 27 bactericides
and fungicides
Catalogue: free

## Weed Control

AgrEvo Environmental Health
95 Chestnut Ridge Road
Montvale, NJ 07645
(800) 843-1702
Product: Finale™ and InterCept H&G™
weed killers
Catalogue: free

Agri-Tex, Inc.
Box 1106
Danbury, CT 06813
(800) 243-0989

Product: MagicMat™ landscape fabrics
Catalogue: free

American Agrifabrics, Inc.
1122D Cambridge Square
Alpharetta, GA 30201
(404) 664-7820
Product: landscape fabrics
Catalogue: free

DeWitt®
Route 3, Box 31
Sikeston, MO 63801
(800) 888-9669
Product: landscape fabrics
Catalogue: free

Dow Elanco
9002 Purdue Road
Indianapolis, IN 46268
(317) 875-8618
Product: Team and Gallery herbicides
Catalogue: free

Easy Gardener, Inc.
Box 21025
Waco, TX 76702
(817) 753-5353
(800) 327-9462
Product: landscape fabrics
Catalogue: free

Greenview®
1600 East Cumberland
Lebanon, PA 17042
(800) 233-0626
Product: Preen® weed preventers
Catalogue: free

Landmaster Products, Inc.
2395 West 4th Avenue
Denver, CO 80222
(303) 571-4636
Product: landscape fabrics
Catalogue: free

Monsanto Company
(800) 225-2883
Product: Roundup® weed killers
Catalogue: free

Reemay, Inc.
Box 511
Old Hickory, TN 37138
(800) 321-6271
Product: Typar landscape fabrics
Catalogue: free

Warp Brothers
4647 West Augusta Boulevard
Chicago, IL 60651
(312) 261-5200
(800) 621-3345
Product: No-Hoe landscape fabrics
Catalogue: free

# Garden Furnishings

GARDEN FURNISHINGS *are every bit as important to an enjoyable garden as the plants. An artfully placed garden bench or other ornament can add just the right touch; arbors and trellises can add height and interest. The retailers and manufacturers listed below sell garden furnishings and ornaments of all sorts, including benches, trellises, arbors, gazebos, lights, fencing, and plant markers.*

## Garden Furnishings Emporiums

Alsto's Handy Helpers
Box 1267
Galesburg, IL 61401
(309) 343-6181
(800) 447-0048
Catalogue: free

A Proper Garden
225 South Water Street
Wilmington, NC 28401
(800) 626-7177
Catalogue: $1.00

The Decorated Garden
5850 Bowcroft Street
Los Angeles, CA 90016
(310) 815-1077
Catalogue: free

The English Garden Emporium
Box 222
Manchester, VT 05254
(800) 347-8130
Catalogue: free

The Garden Concepts Collection
Box 241233
Memphis, TN 38124
(901) 756-1649
Catalogue: $5.00

Gardeners Eden
Box 7037
San Francisco, CA 94120
(800) 822-9600
Catalogue: free

The Garden Pantry
Box 1145
Folsom, CA 95673
(800) 916-3332
Catalogue: free

David Kay Garden & Gift Catalog
1 Jenni Lane
Peoria, IL 61614
(800) 535-9917
Catalogue: free

Kinsman Company
River Road
Point Pleasant, PA 18950

(800) 733-5613
Catalogue: free

Kenneth Lynch & Sons, Inc.
Box 488, Wilton, CT 06897
(203) 762-8363
Catalogue: $10.00

The Plow & Hearth
Box 830
Orange, VA 22960
(800) 627-1712
Catalogue: free

Elizabeth Schumacher's Garden Accents
4 Union Hill Road
West Conshohocken, PA 19428
(610) 825-5525
(800) 296-5525
Catalogue: $3.00

Smith & Hawken
25 Corte Madera
Mill Valley, CA 94941
(415) 383-2000
Catalogue: free

Winterthur Museum & Gardens
100 Enterprise Place
Dover, DE 19901
(800) 767-0500
Catalogue: free

# Gazebos and Other Garden Structures

Bow Bends™
Box 900
Bolton, MA 01740
(508) 779-2271
Products: gazebos and follies
Catalogue: $3.00

Dalton Pavilions, Inc.
20 Commerce Drive
Telford, PA 18969

(215) 721-1492
Product: red cedar garden pavilions
Catalogue: free

Garden Structures
5603 Friendly Avenue, Suite 102
Greensboro, NC 27410
Product: garden shed plans
Catalogue: free

Heritage Garden Houses
311 Seymour Avenue
Lansing, MI 48933
(517) 372-3385
Products: gazebos and other
garden structures
Catalogue: $3.00

Ivywood Gazebos
Box 9
Fairview Village, PA 19403
(215) 584-0206
Product: gazebos
Catalogue: $3.00

Oregon Timberframe
1389 Highway 99 North
Eugene, OR 97402
(503) 688-4940
Products: gazebos and other
garden structures
Catalogue: free

Vintage Wood Works
Box R
Quinlan, TX 78624
(903) 356-2158
Product: Victorian gazebos
Catalogue: $2.00

Vixen Hill Manufacturing Company
Main Street
Elverson, PA 19520
(800) 423-2766
Product: gazebos
Catalogue: $4.00

# Arbors, Arches, and Trellises

Anderson Design
Box 4057
Bellingham, WA 98227
(800) 947-7697
Products: red cedar arbors and trellises
Catalogue: $2.00

Architectural Brick Paving, Ltd.
1187 Wilmette Avenue
Wilmette, IL 60091
(708) 256-8432
Product: copper trellises
Catalogue: free

Bow Bends™
Box 900
Bolton, MA 01740
(508) 779-2271
Product: arbors
Catalogue: $3.00

Cross Industries, Inc.
3174 Marjan Drive
Atlanta, GA 30340
(770) 451-4531
(800) 521-9878
Product: vinyl arbors
Catalogue: free

Dr. TLC Greenthumb
1935 Yosemite Street
Denver, CO 80220
(303) 756-5286
Product: topiary frames
Catalogue: $1.00

Dulik Manufacturing
23 McKinley Street
Uniontown, PA 15401
Product: Waterboy trellises
Catalogue: free

Cliff Finch's Zoo
Box 54

Friant, CA 93626
(209) 822-2315
Product: topiary frames
Catalogue: SASE

French Wyres
Box 131655
Tyler, TX 75713
(903) 597-8322
Products: trellises and topiary frames
Catalogue: $3.00

Garden Architecture
719 South 17th Street
Philadelphia, PA 19146
(215) 545-5442
Product: tuteur trellises
Catalogue: free

The Garden Architecture Group
631 North 3rd Street
Philadelphia, PA 19123
(215) 627-5552
Product: cedar trellises
Catalogue: $3.00

Garden Trellises
Box 105
LaFayette, NY 13084
(315) 489-9003
Product: galvanized-steel trellises
Catalogue: free

Island Arbors
732 Sunrise Highway
West Babylon, NY 11704
(516) 669-3886
Product: red cedar arbors
Catalogue: free

M. R. Labbe, Company
Box 467
Biddeford, ME 04005
(207) 282-3420
Product: red cedar arbor kits
Catalogue: free

Moonstruck Designs
Box 177
Uniontown, OH 44685
(216) 699-7419
Product: latticed trellises
Catalogue: free

Nebraska Plastics, Inc.
Box 45
Cozad, NE 69130
(800) 445-2887
Products: Country Manor PVC arbors
and trellises
Catalogue: free

New England Garden Ornaments
38 East Brookfield Road
North Brookfield, MA 01535
(508) 867-4474
Product: Agriframes garden structures
Catalogue: free

Poly Concepts, Inc.
9176 Red Branch Road
Columbia, MD 21045
(800) 474-POLY
Product: PVC trellises
Catalogue: free

Rivertown Products
Box 5174
St. Joseph, MO 64505
(816) 232-8822
Product: handcrafted arbors
Catalogue: $1.00

Taylor Ridge Farm
Box 222
Saluda, NC 28773
(704) 749-4756
Products: steel and copper trellises
Catalogue: $3.00

Topiaries Unlimited
RD 2, Box 40C
Pownal, VT 05261

(802) 823-5536
Product: topiary frames
Catalogue: long SASE

Topiary, Inc.
41 Bering Street
Tampa, FL 33606
Product: topiary frames
Catalogue: long SASE

Valcovic Cornell Design
Box 380
Beverly, MA 01915
Product: sculptured trellises
Catalogue: $1.00

Westcoast Topiary
Box 20422, Portland, OR 97220
(503) 257-8340
Product: topiary frames
Catalogue: $1.00

# Landscape Lights

Copper Craft Lighting, Inc.
5100-1B Clayton Road, Suite 291
Concord, CA 94521
(510) 672-4337
Products: copper and bronze landscape
lights
Catalogue: free

Doner Design, Inc.
2175 Beaver Valley Pike
New Providence, PA 17560
(717) 786-8891
Product: copper landscape lights
Catalogue: free

Escort Lighting
201 Sweitzer Road
Sinking Spring, PA 19608
Fax: (610) 670-5170
Product: copper garden lights
Catalogue: free

Genie House
Box 2478
Vincentown, NJ 08088
(609) 859-0600
(800) 634-3643
Product: reproduction garden lights
Catalogue: $3.00

Great American Salvage Company
34 Cooper Square
New York, NY 10003
(212) 505-0070
Product: reproduction lighting
Catalogue: free

Hanover Lanterns
470 High Street
Hanover, PA 17331
(717) 632-6464
Product: Terralight® lighting fixtures
Catalogue: free

Heritage Lanterns
70A Main Street
Yarmouth, ME 04096
(207) 846-3911
(800) 544-6070
Product: garden lights
Catalogue: $3.00

Idaho Wood
Box 488
Sandpoint, ID 83864
(208) 263-9521
(800) 635-1100
Product: wooden garden lights
Catalogue: free

Landscape Resources
(800) 934-1448
Products: landscape lighting fixtures
and parts
Catalogue: free

Liteform Designs
Box 3316

Portland, OR 97208
(503) 257-8464
(800) 458-2505
Product: landscape lighting fixtures
Catalogue: free

Popovitch Associates, Inc.
346 Ashland Avenue
Pittsburgh, PA 15228
(412) 344-6097
Product: ornamental garden lighting
Catalogue: $2.00

Stonelight Corporation
2701 Gulf Shore Boulevard North
Naples, FL 33940
(813) 263-2208
Product: Vermont granite
lighting fixtures
Catalogue: free

## Benches and Other Garden Furniture

Acorn Services Corporation
Box 2854, Brewster, MA 02631
(508) 240-0072
(800) 472-4957
Product: redwood garden furniture
Catalogue: free

Adirondack Designs
350 Cypress Street
Fort Bragg, CA 95437
(707) 964-4940
(800) 222-0343
Product: redwood garden furniture
Catalogue: free

Alpine Millworks Company
1231 West Lehigh Place
Englewood, CO 80110
(303) 761-6334
Products: teak and mahogany garden
furniture
Catalogue: free

Ballard Designs
1670 DeFoor Avenue NW
Atlanta, GA 30318
(404) 351-5099
Products: metal and glass furniture
Catalogue: free

Barlow Tyrie, Inc.
1263 Glen Avenue
Moorestown, NJ 08067
(609) 273-1631
Product: English teak furniture
Catalogue: free

The BenchSmith
Box 86
Warrington, PA 18976
(800) 48-CEDAR
Products: cedar benches; planters
Catalogue: free

Celestial Creations
1427 Centre Circle
Downers Grove, IL 60515
(708) 629-9999
Product: cast-aluminum angel benches
Catalogue: free

The Chair That Fits
2628 Ridgewood Avenue
Charleston, SC 29414
(803) 766-6758
Product: wooden outdoor chairs
Catalogue: free

Charleston Battery Bench, Inc.
191 King Street
Charleston, SC 29401
(803) 722-3842
Product: cast-iron benches
Catalogue: free

Country Casual
17317 Germantown Road
Germantown, MD 20874
(301) 540-0040

Product: teak garden furniture
Catalogue: free

Country Wood™
Box 314
Sugar Loaf, NY 10981
Products: Adirondack rockers and chairs
Catalogue: free

Florentine Craftsmen, Inc.
46-24 28th Street
Long Island City, NY 11101
(718) 937-7632
Product: metal garden furniture
Catalogue: $5.00

The Garden Concepts Collection
Box 241233
Memphis, TN 38124
(901) 756-1649
Product: wooden garden furniture
Catalogue: $5,00

Kelly Grayson Woodcarving & Design
5111 Todd Road
Sebastopol, CA 95472
(707) 829-7764
Product: redwood garden furniture
Catalogue: $1.00

Green Enterprises
43 South Rogers Street
Hamilton, VA 22068
(703) 338-3606
Product: Victorian oak garden furniture
Catalogue: free

Hemlock Shop
RD 1, Box 273
Olyphant, PA 18447
(717) 586-8809
Product: Adirondack chairs
Catalogue: free

Heritage Garden Furniture
1209 East Island Highway

Parksville, British Columbia V9P 1R5
(604) 248-9598
Product: cedar garden furniture kits
Catalogue: free

Homeward
1007 Wisconsin Avenue
Washington, DC 20007
(800) 616-3667
Product: wooden garden benches
Catalogue: free

Kelly Pacific, Inc.
10260 SW Nimbus Avenue
Portland, OR 97223
(800) 999-3845
Product: wooden garden furniture
Catalogue: free

Kingsley-Bate
5587B Guinea Road
Fairfax, VA 22032
(703) 978-7222
Product: teak garden furniture
Catalogue: free

McKinnon and Harris, Inc.
Box 4885
Richmond, VA 23220
(804) 358-2385
Product: metal garden furniture
Catalogue: $4.00

Park Place
2251 Wisconsin Avenue NW
Washington, DC 20007
(202) 342-6294
Product: bentwood garden furniture
Catalogue: free

Reed Brothers
Turner Station
Sebastopol, CA 95472
(707) 795-6261
Product: redwood garden furniture
Catalogue: free

Richardson Allen Furniture
Box 701
Cape Porpoise, ME 04014
(207) 967-8482
Product: wooden garden furniture
Catalogue: free

Seth Rolland
HCR 74, Box 22203
El Prado, NM 87529
(800) 858-9053
Product: redwood garden furniture
Catalogue: free

Sloan Designs
Route 1, Box 183A
Linden, VA 22642
(703) 636-1626
Products: wooden benches;
Adirondack chairs
Catalogue: free

Southerlands
10 Biltmore Avenue
Asheville, NC 28801
(704) 252-0478
(800) 968-5596
Product: garden furniture
Catalogue: free

The Thaxted Cottage Gardener
121 Driscoll Way
Gaithersburg, MD 20878
(301) 330-6211
Product: historic English benches
Catalogue: $2.00

Tidewater Workshop
Oceanville, NJ 08231
(800) 666-TIDE
Product: cedar Classic English
Garden Bench[TM]
Catalogue: free

Vermont Outdoor Furniture
Box 375

East Barre, VT 05649
(800) 588-8834
Product: white cedar garden furniture
Catalogue: free

The Virginia Bench Company
Keswick, VA 22947
(804) 295-7299
Product: pine folding garden bench
Catalogue: free

Wetherend Estate Furniture
Box 648
Rockland, ME 04841
(207) 596-6483
Product: wooden garden furniture
Catalogue: free

Wikco Industries, Inc.
4931 North 57th Street
Lincoln, NE 68507
(402) 464-2070
(800) 872-8864
Product: wrought-iron garden benches
Catalogue: free

Willsboro Wood Products
Box 509
Keesville, NY 12944
(518) 834-5200
(800) 342-3373
Product: cedar Adirondack
garden furniture
Catalogue: free

Windsor Designs
37 Great Valley Parkway
Malvern, PA 19355
(215) 640-5896
(800) 722-5434
Products: wooden and cast-aluminum
garden furniture
Catalogue: free

Wood Classics, Inc.
Osprey Lane
Gardiner, NY 12525
(914) 255-5599
Product: wooden garden furniture
Catalogue: free

Woodbrook Furniture
Manufacturing Company
Box 175
Trussville, AL 35173
(800) 828-3607
Product: cypress garden furniture
Catalogue: free

## Garden Ornaments

Adams & Adkins, Inc.
104 South Early Street
Alexandria, VA 22304
(703) 823-3404
(800) 928-3588
Product: Water Flute? fountain-pond
Catalogue: free

American Weather Enterprises
Box 1383
Media, PA 19063
(215) 565-1232
Products: weather instruments; sundials
Catalogue: free

The Artisans Group
1039 Main Street
Dublin, NH 03444
(603) 563-8782
(800) 528-2035
Product: handcrafted garden ornaments
Catalogue: $1.00

Asian Artifacts
Box 2494
Oceanside, CA 92051
(619) 723-3039
Product: Japanese garden ornaments
Catalogue: $2.00

Baker's Lawn Ornaments
RD 5, Box 265
Somerset, PA 15501
(814) 445-7028
Product: gazing globes
Catalogue: free

Bridgeworks
306 East Lockwood Street
Covington, LA 70433
(504) 893-7933
Product: bridges
Catalogue: free

Carruth Studio, Inc.
1178 Farnsworth Road
Waterville, OH 43566
(800) 225-1178
Product: cast-limestone garden art
Catalogue: free

Claycraft
807 Avenue of the Americas
New York, NY 10001
(212) 242-2903
Product: fiberglass planters
Catalogue: $2.00

Robert Compton, Ltd.
RD 3, Box 3600
Bristol, VT 05443
(802) 453-3778
Product: fountains
Catalogue: $2.00

Design Toscano, Inc.
17 East Campbell Street
Arlington Heights, IL 60005
(800) 525-0733

Product: historical reproduction
outdoor sculptures
Catalogue: $4.00

Elizabeth Street
210 Elizabeth Street
New York, NY 10012
(212) 941-4800
Products: garden ornaments; fountains
Catalogue: free

Florentine Craftsmen, Inc.
46-24 28th Street
Long Island City, NY 11101
(718) 937-7632
Products: ornaments; statuary; fountains
Catalogue: $5.00

French Wyres
Box 131655
Tyler, TX 75713
(903) 597-8322
Product: planters
Catalogue: $3.00

Granite Impressions
342 Carmen Road
Talent, OR 97540
(503) 535-6190
Product: Japanese garden ornaments
Catalogue: $1.00

Haddonstone (USA), Ltd.
201 Heller Place
Interstate Business Park
Bellmawr, NJ 08031
(609) 931-7011
Product: ornamental cast stonework
Catalogue: $10.00

Hollowbrook Pottery and Tile
26 Anton Place
Lake Peekskill, NY 10537
Product: stoneware planters
Catalogue: free

The Joiner's Workshop
2006 43rd Avenue
San Francisco, CA 94116
(415) 681-7271
Product: planters
Catalogue: free

Made in the Shade Umbrellas
810 West 6th Street, Suite 2
Chico, CA 95928
(916) 342-3025
Product: garden umbrellas
Catalogue: free

D. F. Mangum Company
5311 Acoma SE
Albuquerque, NM 87108
(800) 859-6399
Product: garden bridge kits
Catalogue: free

MDT-Muller Design, Inc.
971 Dogwood Trail
Tyrone, GA 30290
(404) 631-9074
Product: garden umbrellas
Catalogue: $2.00

Mister Boardwalk
Box 789
Point Pleasant, NJ 08742
(908) 341-4800
Product: wooden walkways
Catalogue: free

Mitchells & Son
13558 Sunrise Drive NE
Bainbridge Island, WA 98110
(206) 842-9827
Product: cedar planters
Catalogue: free

New England Garden Ornaments
38 East Brookfield Road
North Brookfield, MA 01535
(508) 867-4474

Products: ornaments; statuary; fountains
Catalogue: free

P & R International, Inc.
Box 939
Norwalk, CT 06852
(203) 846-2989
Products: ornaments; planters; fountains
Catalogue: $3.00

Pennoyer Castings Company
Box 597
Locust Valley, NY 11560
(516) 676-1920
Product: classic garden ornaments
Catalogue: free

Pompeian Studios
90 Rockridge Road
Bronxville, NY 10708
(914) 337-5595
(800) 457-5595
Products: stone and wrought-iron
garden ornaments
Catalogue: $10.00

Redwood Arts
Box 419
Airway Heights, WA 99001
(509) 244-9669
Product: redwood planters
Catalogue: free

Salt Creek Traders
Route 1, Box 189W
Effingham, IL 62401
(800) 360-1512
Product: sundials
Catalogue: free

Seibert & Rice
Box 365
Short Hills, NJ 07078
(201) 467-8266
Product: terra-cotta planters
Catalogue: free

Spademan Pottery
218 Chestnut Street
Cambridge, MA 02139
(617) 354-1704
Product: terra-cotta planters
Catalogue: free

Stone Forest
Box 2840
Santa Fe, NM 87504
(505) 986-8883
Product: granite garden ornaments
Catalogue: $3.00

Stoneworks Gallery
Box 35
Tuxedo, NY 10987
(800) STONE-08
Product: Riverstones™
Catalogue: free

Sun Garden Specialties
Box 52382
Tulsa, OK 74152
Product: Japanese garden ornaments
Catalogue: free

Utopian Designs
Box 1434
Eugene, OR 97440
(503) 683-5530
Product: gazing globes
Catalogue: free

Wind & Weather
Box 2320
Mendocino, CA 95460
(800) 922-9463
Products: weather instruments; sundials;
gazing globes
Catalogue: free

Wood Classics, Inc.
Osprey Lane
Gardiner, NY 12525
(914) 255-5599

Product: market umbrellas
Catalogue: free

Wood Garden
11 Fitzrandolph Street
Green Brook, NJ 08812
(201) 968-4325
Product: wooden planters
Catalogue: free

Wundrella, Inc.
8239 SW 64th Street
Miami, FL 33143
(305) 598-8202
Product: market umbrellas
Catalogue: free

# Fencing

Architectural Iron Company
Route 6 West, Box 126
Milford, PA 18337
(717) 296-7722
Product: wrought-iron fences
Catalogue: free

Bamboo & Rattan Works
470 Oberlin Avenue South
Lakewood, NJ 08701
(908) 370-0220
(800) 4-BAMBOO
Products: bamboo and reed fencing
Catalogue: free

Bamboo Fencer
31 Germania Street
Jamaica Plain, MA 02130
(617) 524-6137
(800) 775-8641
Product: bamboo fencing
Catalogue: $3.00

Bufftech
2525 Walden Avenue
Buffalo, NY 14225

(800) 333-0569
Product: polyvinyl fencing
Catalogue: free

Country Estate Fence
Nebraska Plastics, Inc.
Box 45
Cozad, NE 69130
(800) 445-2887
Product: polyvinyl fencing
Catalogue: free

Invisible Fence Company
355 Phoenixville Pike
Malvern, PA 19355
(800) 538-DOGS
Product: pet containment fencing
Catalogue: free

Jerith Manufacturing Company
3939 G Street
Philadelphia, PA 19124
Product: aluminum fencing
Catalogue: free

Materials Unlimited
2 West Michigan Avenue
Ypsilanti, MI 48197
(313) 483-6980
IProduct: wrought-iron fencing
Catalogue: free

Moultrie Manufacturing Company
Drawer 1179, Moultrie, GA 31768
(912) 985-1312
(800) 841-8674
Product: metal fencing
Catalogue: free

Stewart Iron Works Company
20 West 18th Street
Covington, KY 41012
(606) 431-1985
Products: Victorian and Edwardian
fences and gates
Catalogue: free

Walpole Woodworkers
767 East Street
Walpole, MA 02081
(508) 668-2800
(800) 343-6948
Product: cedar fencing
Catalogue: free

## Garden Gates

Fine Architectural Metalsmiths
Box 30, Chester, NY 10918
(914) 651-7550
Product: wrought-iron gates
Catalogue: $3.50

The Timeless Garden
Box 500998
Atlanta, GA 31150
(404) 518-9127
Product: historic garden gate replicas
Catalogue: free

## Edging

Proline Edging
13505 Barry Street
Holland, MI 49424
(800) 356-9660
Product: aluminum edging
Catalogue: free

The Victoriana Collection
(905) 627-4035
Product: terra-cotta edging
Catalogue: free

Warp Brothers
4647 West Augusta Boulevard
Chicago, IL 60651
(312) 261-5200
(800) 621-3345
Product: Easy Edge landscape borders
Catalogue: free

# Plant Markers

AAA Quality Engravers
5754 Oxford Place
New Orleans, LA 70131
(504) 391-2225
Products: engraved markers
Catalogue: free

Amaranth Stoneware
Box 243
Sydenham, Ontario K0H 2T0
(800) 465-5444
Products: stoneware and terra-cotta
garden signs
Catalogue: free

Art Line, Inc.
600 North Kibourn
Chicago, IL 60624
(312) 722-8100
Catalogue: free

Beason Engraving
731 Springhill Avenue
Spartanburg, SC 29303
(803) 583-8913
Product: custom engraved markers
Catalogue: free

Berkshire Brass
162 Chipman Road
Chester, MA 01011
(413) 623-5649
Product: brass markers
Catalogue: free

Blackburn Manufacturing Company
Box 86
Neligh, NE 68756
(402) 887-4161
Catalogue: free

Brass Butterfly, Inc.
58 Garin Mill Park
Poultney, VT 05764

(802) 287-9818
Product: brass markers
Catalogue: free

Eon Industries
Box 11
Liberty Center, OH 43532
(419) 533-4961
Product: metal markers
Catalogue: free

Evergreen Garden Plant Labels
Box 922
Cloverdale, CA 95425
Product: galvanized-steel markers
Catalogue: one stamp

Forget-Me-Not Marker Company
1917 Kenneth Street
Urbana, IL 61801
Product: metal markers
Catalogue: long SASE

Garden Expressions
Box 1358
Loveland, CO 80539
(303) 663-7989
Catalogue: $1.00

Garden Fonts
RFD 1, Box 54
Barnstead, NH 03218
Product: custom printed peel-and-stick
labels
Catalogue: free

Garden Graphics
17 Woodfield Road
Pomona, NY 10970
(914) 354-3981
Product: custom engraved markers
Catalogue: free

Harlane Company, Inc.
266 Orangeburgh Road
Old Tappan, NJ 07675

Product: plastic markers
Catalogue: free

Mark Kit Company
Box 1667
San Pedro, CA 90733
Catalogue: free

MIS-Q
1865 Laraway Lake Drive SE
Grand Rapids, MI 49546
Product: custom engraved terra-cotta
markers
Catalogue: SASE

Permanent Metal Labels
Box 93
Paw Paw, MI 49070
Product: metal markers
Catalogue: SASE

S & D Enterprises
1280 Quince Drive
Junction City, OR 97448
(503) 998-2060
Product: anodized aluminum markers
Catalogue: long SASE

Spring Valley Roses
7637 330th Street
Spring Valley, WI 54767
Product: rose plaques
Catalogue: $1.00

TK Company
Box 610
Walker, MN 56484
(218) 547-1530
Product: custom markers
Catalogue: free

F. R. Unruh
37 Oaknoll Road
Wilmington, DE 19808
(302) 994-2328
Product: metal markers
Catalogue: SASE

Versamax Company
Box 918
East Troy, WI 53120
(800) 642-4408
Product: large plastic markers
Catalogue: free

Wingfoot Studios
Box 951
Langley, WA 98260
(360) 321-3974
Product: porcelain herb tags; custom tags
Catalogue: SASE

The Wood Rapture
6369 SW 10th Street
Topeka, KS 66615
Catalogue: free

# Organizations for Gardeners

GARDENERS ARE a well-organized group, both by geography and by interest. General gardening organizations that promote the hobby overall are active at the national, state, and provincial levels, while gardening clubs and societies exist in almost every state and municipality. In the interest category, many national organizations—such as the American Orchid Society—have local chapters that sponsor get-togethers and flower shows. Native plant societies are active in many states and provinces.

The listings below start with national gardening organizations and go on to state and provincial organizations. They are followed by listings of specialty gardening organizations and native plants groups, organized first nationally, then by state or province. A listing of professional organizations ends this section.

Most organizations put out some sort of publication for their members—the subscription price is part of your annual dues. Publications can range from sophisticated magazines with paid advertising to simple newsletters produced at the local copy shop. In any case, these publications generally provide a lot of information and give schedules of upcoming events.

An enjoyable and interesting feature of some plant societies is the chance to participate in round-robins. A round-robin is basically a sort of circulating bulletin board that travels around a small group of gardeners (usually no more than ten) with common interests—orchid fanciers with an interest in cattleyas, for example. One member agrees to be the volunteer director. The director writes a letter about cattleyas, perhaps describing something interesting about them or asking a cultivation question. The letter is then mailed to the next person on the list, who reads it and writes his or her own letter, perhaps answering the question. The two letters are mailed on to the next person on the list, who repeats the process. The entire packet of letters eventually arrives back at the director, who removes the original letter, writes a new one, and starts the process all over again.

At the state and local level, many plant societies are run on a shoestring by volunteers. Membership dues are usually nominal. The headquarters of the organization is often the home of whoever is president or membership chair that year, so the contact addresses change rapidly. Your inquiry will almost certainly be forwarded to the proper person, but it may take a little time—be patient. Be considerate as well. Don't call very early in the morning or late at night, bear time zone differences in mind, and send a stamped, self-addressed envelope when you write for information.

# National Organizations

American Community Gardening
Association
325 Walnut Street
Philadelphia, PA 19106
(215) 625-8280
Dues: $25.00
Publication: *Journal of Community Gardening*
(quarterly)

American Horticultural Society
7931 East Boulevard Drive
Alexandria, VA 22308
(703) 768-5700
(800) 777-7931
Dues: $35.00
Publication: *American Horticulturist*
(monthly magazine)

The Garden Club of America
598 Madison Avenue
New York, NY 10022
(212) 753-8287
Publications: GCA *Bulletin* (biannual);
GCA Newsletter (bimonthly)

Garden Clubs Canada
6 Compton Place
London, Ontario N6C 4G4
(519) 681-7089
Publication: *Garden Clubs Canada Newsletter*
(three times annually)

Indoor Gardening Society
of America, Inc.
1082 Hillstone Road
Cleveland Heights, OH 44121
(800) 892-7594
Dues: $22.00
Publication: *House Plant Magazine*
(bimonthly)

Men's Garden Club of America, Inc.
5560 Merle Hay Road
Johnston, IA 50131

(515) 278-0295
Publication: *The Gardener* (bimonthly)

National Arbor Day Foundation
100 Arbor Avenue
Nebraska City, NE 68410
(402) 474-5655
Dues: $15.00
Publication: *Arbor Day* (bimonthly)

National Council for
State Garden Clubs, Inc.
4401 Magnolia Avenue
St. Louis, MO 63110
(314) 776-7574
Publication: *The National Gardener*
(bimonthly)

National Gardening Association
1800 Flynn Avenue
Burlington, VT 05401
(802) 863-1308
(800) LETSGRO
Dues: $18.00
Publication: *National Gardening*
(bimonthly magazine)

National Junior Horticultural Association
401 North 4th Street
Durant, OK 74701
(405) 924-0771
Publication: *Going & Growing*
(three times annually)

National Xeriscape Council
Box 163172
Austin, TX 78716
(512) 392-6225
Publication: *Xeriscape News* (bimonthly)

The Royal Horticultural Society
Membership Secretary
80 Vincent Square
London SW1P 2PE
England
(071) 834-4333

Publication: *The Garden*
(monthly magazine)

Women's National Farm and Garden
Association, Inc.
2402 Clearview Drive
Glenshaw, PA 15116
(412) 486-7964

# State and Provincial Organizations

## Alabama

Garden Club of Alabama
c/o Mrs. Gene Castleberry
124 Highland Place
Sheffield, AL 35660

South Alabama Botanical and
Horticultural Society
c/o John Bowen
Box 8382
Mobile, AL 36608

## Alaska

Alaska Federation of Garden Clubs
c/o Mrs. Albert Silk
2801 Bennett Drive
Anchorage, AK 99517

Alaska Horticultural Association
Box 1909
Palmer, AK 99645

## Arizona

Arizona Federation of Garden Clubs
c/o Mrs. Harry Wagner
508 Highland Drive
Prescott, AZ 86303

## Arkansas

Arkansas State Horticultural Society
University of Arkansas
Plant Science Building, Room 306
Fayetteville, AR 72701
(501) 575-2603

## California

California Garden Clubs, Inc.
c/o Mrs. Allan Nielsen
7540 Granite Avenue
Orangeville, CA 95662

The California Horticultural Society
California Academy of Sciences
Elsie Mueller, Secretary
1847 34th Avenue
San Francisco, CA 94122
(415) 566-5222
Dues: $35.00
Publication: *Pacific Horticulture* (quarterly)

Southern California Horticultural Society
c/o Joan DeFato
Box 41080
Los Angeles, CA 90041
(818) 567-1496
Dues: $20.00
Publications: *Pacific Horticulture* (quarterly);
monthly bulletin

Western Horticultural Society
Treasurer
Box 60507
Palo Alto, CA 94306
(415) 941-1332
Dues: $25.00
Publications: *Pacific Horticulture* (quarterly);
newsletter (ten times annually)

## Colorado

Colorado Federation of Garden Clubs, Inc.
c/o Mrs. Dode Mehrer

Box 186
Idaho Springs, CO 80452

## Connecticut

Connecticut Horticultural Society
150 Main Street
Wethersfield, CT 06109
(203) 529-8713
Publication: *CHS Newsletter* (ten times
annually)

Federated Garden Clubs of Connecticut
c/o Lee Bauerfield
Box 672
Wallingford, CT 06492

## Delaware

Delaware Federation of
Garden Clubs, Inc.
c/o Mrs. Robert Weeks
2306 Jamaica Drive
Wilmington, DE 19810

## Florida

Florida Federation of Garden Clubs
c/o Mrs. Kenton Haymans
Box 1604
Winter Park, FL 32790
(407) 647-7016

## Georgia

Garden Club of Georgia, Inc.
c/o Mrs. E. Carl White
7 Woodland Drive
Cartersville, GA 30120

## Hawaii

Hawaii Federation of Garden Clubs, Inc.
c/o Mrs. John Johnson
Box 25401
Honolulu, HI 96825

## Idaho

Idaho State Federation of
Garden Clubs, Inc.
c/o F. Ruth Thacker
1218 North 25th Street
Boise, ID 83702

## Illinois

Garden Clubs of Illinois, Inc.
c/o Mrs. William Laycock
23W163 Blackberry Lane
Glen Ellyn, IL 60137

## Indiana

Garden Club of Indiana
c/o Barbara Yoder
Route 1, Box 34
Geneva, IN 46740
(219) 334-5453

## Iowa

Federated Garden Clubs of Iowa
c/o Mrs. G. B. Cox
Windsong
Route 4, Box 223
Marshalltown, IA 50158

Iowa State Horticultural Society
Wallace State Office Building
Des Moines, IA 50319
(515) 281-5402
Publication: *Horticulturist* (quarterly)

## Kansas

Kansas Associated Garden Clubs
c/o Mrs. Vernon Carlsen
811 Sunset Drive
Lawrence, KS 66044

## Kentucky

Garden Club of Kentucky
c/o Mrs. Charles Huddleston
Box 1653
Middleboro, KY 40965

## Louisiana

Federated Council of New Orleans
Garden Clubs, Inc.
c/o Mrs. Donald Miester
787 Jewell Street
New Orleans, LA 70124
(540) 282-5077

Louisiana Garden Club Federation
c/o Mrs. E. Massa
139 Citrus Road
River Ridge, LA 70123

New Orleans Garden Society
3914 Prytania Street
New Orleans, LA 70115

## Maine

Garden Club Federation of Maine, Inc.
c/o Mrs. Steen Meryweather
Box 56
Salisbury Cove, ME 04672

Maine Federated Garden Club
c/o Mrs. Phillip Burril
RFD 1, Box 1040
Corinna, ME 04928
(207) 278-5994

## Maryland

Federated Garden Clubs
of Maryland, Inc.
c/o Mrs. Hal Tray
128 Round Bay Road
Severna Park, MD 21146

Horticultural Society of Maryland
1563 Sherwood Avenue
Baltimore, MD 21239
(301) 352-7863

## Massachusetts

Garden Club Federation of
Massachusetts, Inc.
c/o Mrs. George Dennett
547 Central Avenue
Needham, MA 01294

Massachusetts Horticultural Association
300 Massachusetts Avenue
Boston, MA 02115
(617) 536-9280
Dues: $45.00
Publication: *Horticulture*
(monthly magazine)

Worcester County Horticultural Society
Tower Hill Botanic Garden
11 French Drive
Boylston, MA 01505
(508) 869-6111
Dues: $25.00
Publication: *Grow With Us* (bimonthly)

## Michigan

Federated Garden Club of Michigan
c/o Mrs. Peter Butus
1509 Orchard Lane
Niles, MI 49120
(616) 683-3030

Garden Club of Michigan
c/o Mrs. Douglas Roby
7113 Greer Road
Howell, MI 48843
(517) 546-2649

Michigan Botanical Club
Dorothy Sibley
7951 Walnut Avenue

Newaygo, MI 49337
(616) 652-2036
Dues: $17.00
Publication: *The Michigan Botanist*
(quarterly)

## Minnesota

Federated Garden Clubs of Minnesota
c/o Mrs. Herbert Larson
1295 Dodd Road West
St. Paul, MN 55118

Minnesota State Horticultural Society
1755 Prior Avenue North
Falcon Heights, MN 55113
(612) 645-7066
Dues: $25.00
Publication: *Minnesota Horticulturalist*
(nine times annually)

## Mississippi

Garden Clubs of Mississippi
c/o Mrs. H. T. Miller
Box 265
Drew, MS 38737

## Missouri

Federated Garden Clubs of Missouri, Inc.
c/o Mrs. J. Herman Belz
10 Chipper Road
St. Louis, MO 63131

Garden Club of St. Louis
c/o Peggy Jones
33 Granada Way
St. Louis, MO 63124
(314) 997-5185

## Montana

Montana Federation of Garden Clubs
c/o Mrs. Anthony Hanic
Box 356, Ashland, MT 59003

## Nebraska

Federated Garden Clubs of Nebraska
c/o Mrs. Robert Keating
Route 1, Box 70
Palisade, NE 69040

Omaha Council of Garden Clubs
4014 South 14th Street
Omaha, NE 68107

## Nevada

Nevada Garden Clubs, Inc.
c/o Mrs. Charles Gorley
Box 27624
Las Vegas, NV 89126

## New Hampshire

New Hampshire Federation
of Garden Clubs
c/o Mrs. William Murdock
Box 10
Windham, NH 03087

## New Jersey

Garden Club of New Jersey
c/o Mrs. Carmine Grossi
Box 622
West Milford, NJ 07480

New Jersey State Horticultural Society
Box 116
Clayton, NJ 08312
(609) 863-0110

## New Mexico

New Mexico Garden Clubs, Inc.
c/o Mrs. Donald Wood
7000 Seminole Road NE
Albuquerque, NM 87110

## New York

Federated Garden Clubs of New York
State, Inc.
5432 Collett Road
Shortsville, NY 14548
(716) 289-3539
(518) 869-6311

Horticultural Society of New York
128 West 58th Street
New York, NY 10019
(212) 757-0915
Dues: $35.00
Publication: *HSNY Newsletter* (quarterly)

Long Island Horticultural Society
c/o David Carrody
9 Anita Avenue
Syosset, NY 11791
(516) 921-4661
Publication: monthly newsletter

## North Carolina

Garden Club of North Carolina, Inc.
c/o Mrs. E. L. Swaim
848 Shoreline Road
Winston-Salem, NC 27106

## North Dakota

North Dakota Federation of Garden
Clubs
c/o Lois Forrest
RR 3
Jamestown, ND 58401

North Dakota State Horticultural Society
Box 5658
North Dakota State University
Fargo, ND 58105
(701) 237-8161
Publication: *North Dakota Horticulture*
(monthly)

## Ohio

Garden Club of Ohio, Inc.
c/o Mrs. Donald De Cessna
883 Bexley Drive
Perrysburg, OH 43551

Ohio Association of Garden Clubs
c/o Jan Harman
402 Craggy Creek Drive
Chippewa Lake, OH 44215
(216) 769-2210

Ohio Horticulture Council
c/o David Kelly
4680 Indianola Avenue
Columbus, OH 43314
(614) 261-6834

Ohio Junior Horticulture Association
Dennis Waldman, Executive Officer
5759 Sandalwood NE
North Canton, OH 44721
(216) 492-3252

## Oklahoma

Oklahoma Garden Clubs, Inc.
c/o Mrs. W. A. Williams
115 West 1st
Atoka, OK 74525

Oklahoma Horticulture Society
OSU Technical Branch
900 North Portland
Oklahoma City, OK 73107
(405) 945-3358
Publication: Horizons (quarterly)

## Oregon

Oregon State Federation of Garden
Clubs, Inc.
c/o Mrs. Sam Roller
820 NW Elizabeth Drive
Corvallis, OR 97330

## Pennsylvania

Garden Club Federation of Pennsylvania
c/o Mrs. Henry Hermani
445 North Front Street
Milton, PA 17847

Horticultural Society of Western
Pennsylvania
Box 5126
Pittsburgh, PA 15206
(412) 392-8540

The Pennsylvania Horticultural Society
325 Walnut Street
Philadelphia, PA 19106
(215) 625-8250
Dues: $40.00
Publications: Green Scene (bimonthly
journal); PHS News (monthly newsletter)

## Rhode Island

Rhode Island Federation of Garden Clubs
c/o Mrs. G. Dickson Kenney
130 Waterway
Saunderstown, RI 02874

## South Carolina

Garden Club of South Carolina
c/o Mrs. John F. C. Hunter
912 Santee Drive
Florence, SC 29501

## South Dakota

South Dakota Federation of Garden Clubs
c/o Catherine Hladky
Box 540
Yankton, SD 57078

## Tennessee

Tennessee Federation of Garden Clubs
c/o Mrs. D. V. Pennington

958 Brownlee Road
Memphis, TN 38116

## Texas

Rio Grande Valley Horticultural Society
Box 107
Weslaco, TX 78596
(512) 968-5000

Texas Garden Clubs, Inc.
c/o Mrs. Ben P. Denman
7173 Kendallwood
Dallas, TX 75240

Texas State Horticultural Society
4348 Carter Creek Parkway
Bryan, TX 77802
(409) 846-1752
Publication: The Texas Horticulturist
(monthly)

## Utah

Utah Associated Garden Clubs, Inc.
c/o Mrs. Arlan Headman
4060 South 1500 East
Salt Lake City, UT 84124

Utah Horticulture Association
Chad Rowley, President
Box 567
Santaquin, UT 48655
(801) 754-5601

## Vermont

Federated Garden Clubs of Vermont
c/o Mrs. Howard A. Allen
Overlake #15
545 South Prospect Street
Burlington, VT 05401

## Virginia

Virginia Federation of Garden Clubs, Inc.
c/o Mrs. Dewitt B. Casler
205 Culpepper Road
Richmond, VA 23229

Virginia Horticulture Council, Inc.
383 Coal Hollow Road
Christiansburg, VA 24073
(703) 382-0904

## Washington

Northwest Horticultural Society
c/o Yoosun Park
Isaacson Hall, University of Washington
Seattle, WA 98195
(206) 527-1794
Dues: $35.00
Publication: *Pacific Horticulture*

Washington State Federation
of Garden Clubs, Inc.
c/o Mrs. Ralph Swenson
2314 108th Street SE
Bellevue, WA 98004

## West Virginia

West Virginia Garden Club, Inc.
c/o Mrs. Robert L. Swoope
1978 Smith Road
Charleston, WV 25314

## Wisconsin

Milwaukee Horticultural Soceity
c/o Boerner Gardens
5879 South 92nd Street
Hales Corners, WI 53130

Wisconsin Garden Club Federation, Inc.
c/o Mrs. Walter Seeliger
75 East Water Street
Markesan, WI 53946

## Wyoming

Wyoming Federation
of Garden Clubs, Inc.
c/o Mrs. Harry Pelliccione
Box 1208
Pinedale, WY 82941

# CANADA

## Alberta

Alberta Horticultural Association
Box 223
Lacombe, Alberta T0C 1S0
(403) 782-3053

Calgary Horticultural Society
2405 9th Avenue SE
Calgary, Alberta T2G 4T4
(403) 262-5609
Dues: Canada $20.00
Publication: *CHS Newsletter*
(eight times annually)

Edmonton Horticultural Society
Arlene Smith, Director
11707 150th Avenue
Edmonton, Alberta T5X 1C1
(403) 456-7986

Lethbridge and District
Horticultural Society
D. L. Weightman, Secretary
74 Eagle Road North
Lethbridge, Alberta T1H 4S5

St. Albert and District Garden Club
25 Lombard Crescent
St. Albert, Alberta T8N 3N1

Western Canadian Society
for Horticulture
University of Alberta
Devonian Botanic Garden

Edmonton, Alberta T6G 2E1
(403) 987-3054
Publication: *WCSH Grapevine* (quarterly)

## British Columbia

Garden Club of Vancouver
3185 West 45th Avenue
Vancouver, British Columbia V6N 3L9

Victoria Horticultural Society
Box 5081, Station B
Victoria, British Columbia V8R 6N3

## New Brunswick

Fredericton Garden Club
107 Summer Street
Fredericton, New Brunswick E3A 1X7

## Newfoundland

Newfoundland Horticultural Society
Box 10099
St. John's, Newfoundland A1A 4L5
(709) 712-4604
Publication: *Down to Earth*
(eleven times annually)

## Nova Scotia

Nova Scotia Association of Garden Clubs
Box 550
Truro, Nova Scotia B2N 5E3

## Ontario

Garden Club of Ancaster
50 Academy Street
Ancaster, Ontario L9G 2Y1

Garden Club of Burlington
c/o Mrs. R. D. Shots
RR 3
Campbelville, Ontario L0P L8O

Garden Club of Hamilton
2070 Watson Drive
Burlington, Ontario L7R 3X4

Garden Club of Kitchener-Waterloo
284 Shakespeare Drive
Waterloo, Ontario N2L 2T6

Garden Club of London
34 Bromleigh Avenue
London, Ontario N6G 1T9

Garden Club of Ontario
c/o Mrs. W. J. E. Spence
228 Dunvegan Road
Toronto, Ontario M5P 2P2

Garden Club of Toronto
777 Lawrence Avenue East
Don Mills, Ontario M3C 1P2

Garden Research Exchange
536 MacDonnell Street
Kingston, Ontario K7K 4W7
(613) 542-6547

Men's Garden Club
173 Joycey Boulevard
Toronto, Ontario M5M 2V3

Ontario Horticultural Association
c/o Bonnie Warner
RR 3
Englehart, Ontario P0J 1H0
(705) 544-2474

Woodstock Horticultural Society
c/o Mary Yeoman
RR 2
Burgessville, Ontario N0J 1C0

## Quebec

Diggers and Weeders Garden Club
20 Thornhill Avenue
Westmount, Quebec K3Y 2E2

Garden Club of Montreal
66 St. Sulpice Road
Montreal, Quebec M3Y 2B7

La Société d'Animation du Jardin
et de l'Institut Botaniques
Botanical Garden
4101 East Sherbrooke Avenue
Montreal, Quebec H1X 2B2
(514) 872-1493

*Saskatchewan*

Evergreen Garden Club
13 Kootenay Drive
Saskatoon, Saskatchewan S7K 1T2

Prairie Flower Club
Box 35
White City, Saskatchewan S9G 5B0

Prairie Garden Guild
Monty Zary, Treasurer
Box 211
Saskatoon, Saskatchewan S7K 3K4

Saskatoon Horticultural Society
Box 161
Saskatoon, Saskatchewan S7K 3K4

# Plant Species Organizations
*See also chapter 1,* **Plant Sources,** *and*
*chapter 2,* **Specialty Gardening**

African Violet Society of America, Inc.
2375 North Street
Beaumont, TX 77702
(409) 839-4725
(800) 770-AVSA
Dues: $18.00
Publication: *African Violet* (bimonthly
magazine)

African Violet Society of Canada
c/o Bonnie Scanlan

1573 Arbourdale Avenue
Victoria, British Columbia V8N 5J1
(604) 477-7561
Dues: Canada $12.00; US $14.00
Publication: *Chatter* (quarterly)

Alpine Garden Society
The Secretary
AGS Centre
Avon Bank, Pershore
Worcestershire WR10 3JP
England
(0386) 55-4790
Dues: £18.00
Publications: quarterly bulletin;
newsletter

American Bamboo Society
666 Wagnon Road
Sepastopol, CA 95472
(518) 765-3507
Dues: $20.00
Publications: *ABS Newsletter* (bimonthly);
*Journal of the ABS* (irregular)

American Begonia Society
c/o John Ingles Jr.
157 Monument Road
Rio Bell, CA 95562
(707) 764-5407
Dues: $21.00
Publication: *The Begonian*
(bimonthly magazine)

American Calochortus Society
c/o H. P. McDonald
Box 1128
Berkeley, CA 94701
Dues: $4.00
Publication: *Mariposa* (quarterly)

American Camellia Society
Massee Lane Gardens
1 Massee Lane
Fort Valley, GA 31030
(912) 967-2358

Dues: $20.00
Publication: *The Camellia Journal*
 (quarterly)

American Conifer Society
827 Brooks Street
Ann Arbor, MI 48103
(313) 665-1871
Dues: $25.00
Publication: quarterly bulletin

American Daffodil Society, Inc.
c/o Mary Lou Gripshover
1686 Grey Fox Trails
Milford, OH 45150
(513) 248-9137
Dues: $20.00
Publication: *Daffodil Journal* (quarterly)

American Dahlia Society
Terry Shaffer, Membership Chair
422 Sunset Boulevard
Toledo, OH 43612
(419) 478-4159
Dues: $20.00
Publication: *Bulletin* (quarterly)

The American Dianthus Society
c/o Rand B. Lee
Box 22232
Santa Fe, NM 87502
(505) 438-7038
Dues: $15.00
Publication: *The Gilliflower Times*
(quarterly newsletter)

American Fern Society
c/o Richard Hauke
456 McGill Place
Atlanta, GA 30312
(404) 525-3147
Dues: $15.00
Publications: *American Fern Journal*
(quarterly); *Fiddlehead Forum*
(bimonthly newsletter)

American Fuchsia Society
County Fair Building
9th Avenue and Lincoln Way
San Francisco, CA 94122
(707) 643-0449
Dues: $15.00
Publication: *American Fuchsia Society*
Bulletin (bimonthly)

American Ginger Society
Box 100
Archer, FL 32618
(904) 495-9168
Publication: *Zingiber* (irregular)

American Gloxinia and Gesneriad
Society, Inc.
New York Horticultural Society
128 West 58th Street
New York, NY 10019
(212) 757-0915
Dues: $20.00
Publication: *The Gloxinian*
(bimonthly journal)

American Hemerocallis
(Daylilies) Society
c/o Elly Launius, Executive Secretary
1454 Rebel Drive
Jackson, MS 39211
(601) 366-4362
Dues: $18.00
Publication: *The Daylily Journal* (quarterly)

American Hepatica Association
c/o Paul Held
195 North Avenue
Westport, CT 06880
Dues: $20.00
Publication: newsletter

American Hibiscus Society
Jeri Grantham, Executive Secretary
Box 321540
Cocoa Beach, FL 32932
(407) 783-2576

Dues: $17.50
Publication: The Seed Pod (quarterly)

American Hosta Society
c/o Robyn Duback
7802 NE 63rd Street
Vancouver, WA 98662
Dues: $19.00
Publication: *Hosta Journal* (semiannual)

American Iris Society
Marilyn Harlow, Membership Secretary
Box 8455
San Jose, CA 95155
(408) 971-0444
Dues: $12.50
Publication: *Bulletin of the AIS* (quarterly)

American Ivy Society
Daphne Pfaff, Membership Chair
696 16th Avenue South
Naples, FL 33940
(813) 261-0388
Dues: $15.00
Publications: *The Ivy Journal* (annual);
*Between the Vines* (semiannual newsletter)

American Orchid Society
6000 South Olive Avenue
West Palm Beach, FL 33405
(407) 585-8666
Dues: $30.00
Publication: *Orchids* (monthly journal)

American Penstemon Society
Ann W. Bartlett, Membership Secretary
1569 South Holland Court
Lakewood, CO 80232
(303) 986-8096
Dues: $10.00
Publication: *APS Bulletin* (semiannual)

American Peony Society
c/o Greta Kessenich
250 Interlachen Road
Hopkins, MN 55343

(612) 938-4706
Dues: $10.00
Publication: *Bulletin* (quarterly)

American Primrose, Primula,
and Auricula Society
c/o Addaline Robinson
9705 SE Spring Crest Drive
Portland, OR 97225
Dues: $15.00
Publication: *Primroses* (quarterly)

American Rhododendron Society
Barbara R. Hall, Executive Director
Box 1380
Gloucester, VA 23061
(804) 693-4433
Dues: $25.00
Publication: *Journal of the ARS* (quarterly)

American Rose Society
Box 30,000
Shreveport, LA 71130
(318) 938-5402
Dues: $32.00
Publication: *The American Rose Magazine*
(eleven times annually); special interest
quarterlies

Azalea Society of America, Inc.
Membership Chair
Box 34536
West Bethesda, MD 20827
(301) 585-5269
Dues: $20.00
Publication: *The Azalean* (quarterly)

British Cactus and Succulent Society
Mr. P. A. Lewis, FBCSS
Firgrove, 1 Springwoods, Courtmoor
Fleet, Hants. GU13 9SU
England
Dues: £13.00
Publications: *British Cactus and Succulent
Journal* (quarterly); Bradleya (annual)

The British Clematis Society
Mrs. B. Risdon, Membership Secretary
The Tropical Bird Gardens, Rode
Bath, Somerset BA3 6QW
England
(0373) 83-0326
Dues: £12.00
Publication: *The Clematis Journal* (annual)

British and European Geranium Society
Leyland Cox
Norwood Chine, 26 Crabtree Lane
Sheffield, Yorkshire S5 7AY
England
(0742) 426-2000
Dues: $15.00
Publication: *The Geranium Gazette* (three
times annually);*The Geranium Yearbook*

British Fuchsia Society
Membership Secretary
20 Brodawel, Llannon
Llanelli, Dyfed SA14 6BJ
Wales
Dues: £5.00
Publication: *Bulletin* (semiannual)

British Iris Society
Mrs. E. M. Wise
197 The Parkway, Iver Heath
Iver, Bucks. SL0 0RQ
England
Publication: *The Iris Year Book*

British Pelargonium and Geranium
Society
c/o Carol Helyar
134 Montrose Avenue
Welling, Kent DA16 2QY
England
(081) 856-6137
Dues: £12.00
Publications: *Pelargonium News*
(three times annually);*Yearbook*

Bromeliad Society, Inc.
2488 East 49th Street
Tulsa, OK 74105
Dues: $20.00
Publication: *BSI Journal* (bimonthly)

Cactus and Succulent Society of America
c/o Dr. Seymour Linden
1535 Reeves Street
Los Angeles, CA 90035
(310) 556-1923
Dues: $30.00
Publication: *Cactus & Succulent Journal*
(bimonthly)

Canadian Begonia Society
70 Enfield Avenue
Toronto, Ontario M8W 1T9
Dues: Canada $20.00

Canadian Chrysanthemum
and Dahlia Society
c/o Karen Ojaste
17 Granard Boulevard
Scarborough, Ontario M1M 2E2
(416) 269-6960
Dues: Canada $10.00

Canadian Gladiolus Society
c/o W. L. Turbuck
3073 Grant Road
Regina, Saskatchewan S4S 5G9
Dues: Canada $10.00
Publication: *Canadian Gladiolus Annual*

Canadian Iris Society
c/o Verna Laurin
199 Florence Avenue
Willowdale, Ontario M2N 1G5
(415) 225-1088
Dues: Canada $5.00
Publication: *CIS Newsletter* (quarterly)

Canadian Orchid Congress
c/o Peter Root
Box 241

Goodwood, Ontario L0C 1A0
(416) 640-5643
Publication: *Canadian Orchid Journal*
(annual)

Canadian Pelargonium
and Geranium Society
Kathleen Gammer, Membership
Secretary
101-2008 Fullerton Avenue
North Vancouver, British Columbia
V7P 3G7
(604) 926-2190
Dues: Canada $10.00
Publication: *Storksbill* (quarterly)

Canadian Peony Society
1246 Donlea Crescent
Oakville, Ontario L6J 1V7
(416) 845-5380

Canadian Prairie Lily Society
M. E. Driver, Secretary
22 Red River Road
Saskatoon, Saskatchewan S7K 1G3
(306) 242-5329
Dues: Canada $5.00
Publication: *Newsletter* (quarterly)

Canadian Rose Society
Anne Graber, Secretary
10 Fairfax Crescent
Scarborough, Ontario M1L 1Z8
(416) 757-8809
Dues: Canada $18.00
Publications: *The Rosarian* (three times
annually); *Canadian Rose Annual*

The Cryptanthus Society
2355 Rusk
Beaumont, TX 77702
(409) 835-0644
Dues: $15.00
Publications: *The Cryptanthus Journal*
(quarterly); *Yearbook*

The Cycad Society
c/o David Mayo
1161 Phyllis Court
Mountain View, CA 94040
(415) 964-7898
Dues: $15.00
Publication: *The Cycad Newsletter*
(three times annually)

Cyclamen Society
Dr. D. V. Bent
Little Pilgrims, 2 Pilgrims Way East
Otford, Sevenoaks, Kent TN14 5QN
England
(0959) 52-2322
Dues: £7.00
Publication: *Cyclamen* (semiannual)

Cymbidium Society of America
533 South Woodland
Orange, CA 92669
(714) 532-4719
Dues: $25.00
Publication: *The Orchid Advocate*
 (bimonthly magazine)

The Daffodil Society (UK)
c/o Don Barnes
32 Montgomery Avenue
Sheffield S7 1NZ
England
Dues: £15.00

The Delphinium Society
Mrs. Shirley E. Bassett
"Takakkaw," Ice House Wood
Oxted, Surrey RH8 9DW
England
Dues: £10.00
Publication: *Delphinium Year Book*

Epiphyllum Society of America
Betty Berg, Membership Secretary
Box 1395
Monrovia, CA 91017
(818) 447-9688

Dues: $10.00
Publication: *The Bulletin* (bimonthly)

Gardenia Society of America
c/o Lyman Duncan
Box 879
Atwater, CA 95301
(209) 358-2231
Dues: $5.00
Publication: *Gardenia News*
 (3 times annually)

The Geraniaceae Group
c/o Penny Clifton
9 Waingate Bridge Cottages
Haverigg, Cumbria LA18 4NF
England
Dues: $16.00
Publication: *The Geraniaceae Group News*
(quarterly)

Gesneriad Society International
Richard Dunn
11510 124th Terrace North
Largo, FL 34648
(813) 585-4247
Dues: $16.50
Publication: *Gesneriad Journal* (bimonthly)

Hardy Fern Foundation
Box 166
Medina, WA 98039
(206) 747-2998
Dues: $20.00
Publication: quarterly newsletter

The Heather Society
c/o Mrs. A. Small
Denbeigh, All Saints Road,
Creeting St. Mary
Ipswich, Suffolk 1P6 8PJ
England
(0449) 71-1220
Dues: £6.00
Publications: *Bulletin* (three times
annually); yearbook

Heliconia Society International
Flamingo Gardens
3750 Flamingo Road
Fort Lauderdale, FL 33330
(305) 473-2955
Dues: $35.00
Publication: HSI Bulletin (quarterly)

Herb Research Foundation
1007 Pearl Street, Suite 200
Boulder, CO 80301
(303) 449-2265
Dues: $35.00
Publication: HerbalGram (quarterly)

Herb Society of America, Inc.
9019 Kirtland Chardon Road
Mentor, OH 44060
(216) 256-0514
Dues: $35.00
Publications: *HSA News* (quarterly);
*The Herbalist* (annual)

Heritage Rose Group
Miriam Wilkins
925 Galvin Drive
El Cerrito, CA 94530
(510) 526-6960
Dues: $5.00
Publication: *Heritage Rose Letter* (quarterly)

Holly Society of America, Inc.
c/o Linda Parsons
11318 West Murdock
Wichita, KS 67212
(301) 825-8133
Dues: $15.00
Publication: *Holly Society Journal*
(quarterly)

The Hoya Society International
Box 1043
Porterdale, GA 30270
Dues: $20.00
Publication: *The Hoyan* (quarterly)

International Aroid Society
Box 43-1853
Miami, FL 33143
(305) 271-3767
Dues: $18.00
Publications: *IAS Newsletter* (bimonthly);
*Aroideana* (annual)

International Bulb Society
Box 4928
Culver City, CA 90230
Dues $30.00
Publication: *Herbertia* (annual journal)

International Camellia Society
c/o Thomas H. Perkins III
Box 750
Brookhaven, MS 39601
(601) 833-7351
Dues: $13.00
Publication: *International Camellia Journal*
(annual)

International Carnivorous Plant Society
Fullerton Arboretum
California State University
Fullerton, CA 92634
(714) 773-2766
Dues: $15.00
Publication: *Carnivorous Plant Newsletter*
(quarterly)

International Geranium Society
Membership Secretary
Box 92734
Pasadena, CA 91109
(818) 908-8867
Dues: $12.50
Publication: *Geraniums Around the World*
(quarterly journal)

International Lilac Society
The Holden Arboretum
9500 Sperry Road
Mentor, OH 44060
(216) 946-4400

Dues: $15.00
Publication: *Lilac Journal* (quarterly)

International Oleander Society
Elizabeth Head, Corresponding
Secretary
Box 3431
Galveston, TX 77552
(409) 762-9334
Dues: $10.00
Publication: *Nerium News* (quarterly)

International Ornamental Crabapple
Society
c/o Thomas L. Green
Department of Agriculture
Western Illinois University
Macomb, IL 61455
Dues: $15.00
Publication: *Malus* (semiannual)

The International Palm Society
Box 1897
Lawrence, KS 66044
(913) 843-1235
Dues: $25.00
Publication: *Principes* (quarterly)

International Tropical Fern Society
8720 SW 34th Street
Miami, FL 33165
(305) 221-0502

International Violet Association
c/o Elaine Kudela
8604 Main Road
Berlin Heights, OH 44814
(419) 588-2616
Dues: $15.00
Publication: *Sweet Times* (quarterly)

International Water Lily Society
c/o Dr. Edward Schneider
Santa Barbara Botanic Gardens
Santa Barbara, CA 93105
(805) 682-4726

Dues: $18.00
Publication: *Water Garden Journal*
(quarterly)

Los Angeles International Fern Society
Box 90943
Pasadena, CA 91109
Dues: $20.00
Publication: *LAIFS Journal*
(bimonthly)

Marigold Society of America, Inc.
c/o Jeannette Lowe
Box 5112
New Britain, PA 18901
(215) 348-5273
Dues: $12.00
Publication: *Amerigold Newsletter* (quarterly)

National Auricula and Primula Society
Mr. D. G. Hadfield
146 Queens Road, Cheadle Hulme
Cheadle, Cheshire SK8 5HY
England
Publication: yearbook

National Chrysanthemum Society (UK)
H. B. Locke
2 Lucas House, Craven Road
Rugby, Warwickshire CV21 3HY
England
(0788) 56-9039
Dues: $15.00
Publications: fall and spring bulletins;
yearbook

National Chrysanthemum Society, Inc.
(US)
Galen L. Goss
10107 Homar Pond Drive
Fairfax Station, VA 22039
(703) 978-7981
Dues: $12.50
Publication: *The Chrysanthemum*
(quarterly)

National Fuchsia Society
c/o Agnes Rietkerk
11507 East 187th Street
Artesia, CA 90701
(213) 865-1806
Dues: $15.00
Publication: *Fuchsia Fan* (bimonthly)

North American Gladiolus Council
c/o William Strawser
701 South Hendricks Avenue
Marion, IN 46953
(317) 664-3857
Dues: $10.00
Publication: *Bulletin* (quarterly)

North American Heather Society
c/o Pauline Croxton
3641 Indian Creek Road
Placerville, CA 95667
Dues: $10.00
Publication: *Heather News* (quarterly)

North American Lily Society, Inc.
Dr. Robert Gilman, Executive Secretary
Box 272
Owatonna, MN 55060
(507) 451-2170
Dues: $12.50
Publications: *Lily Yearbook*;
quarterly bulletin

Passiflora Society International
c/o Anna Zinno
Butterfly World
3900 West Sample Road
Coconut Creek, FL 33073
(305) 977-4434
Dues: $15.00
Publication: quarterly newsletter

Peperomia and Exotic Plant Society
c/o Anita Baudean
100 Neil Avenue
New Orleans, LA 70131
(504) 394-4146

Dues: $7.50
Publication: *The Gazette*
(three times annually)

The Plumeria Society of America, Inc.
Box 22791
Houston, TX 77227
Dues: $15.00
Publication: *Plumeria Potpourri* (quarterly
newsletter)

Rare Conifer Foundation
Box 100
Potter Valley, CA 95469
Dues: $25.00
Publications: newsletter, yearbook

Rhododendron Society of Canada
c/o R. S. Dickhout
5200 Timothy Crescent
Niagara Falls, Ontario L2E 5G3
(416) 357-5981
Note: See American Rhododendron
Society

Rhododendron Species Foundation
Box 3798
Federal Way, WA 98063
(206) 838-4646
Dues: $30.00
Publication: *RSF Newsletter* (quarterly)

Rose Hybridizers Association
c/o Larry D. Peterson
3245 Wheaton Road
Horseheads, NY 14845
(607) 562-8592
Dues: $7.00
Publication: quarterly newsletter

The Royal National Rose Society
The Secretary
Chiswell Green
St. Albans, Herts. AL2 3NR
England
(0727) 50-461

Dues: £13.50
Publication: *The Rose* (quarterly journal)

Royal Saintpaulia Club
c/o Ms. A. Moffett
Box 198
Sussex, New Brunswick E0E 1P0

Saintpaulia and Houseplant Society
The Secretary
33 Church Road, Newbury Park
Ilford, Essex 1G2 7ET
England
(081) 590-3710
Dues: £5.00
Publication: quarterly bulletin

Saintpaulia International
1650 Cherry Hill Road South
State College, PA 16803
(814) 237-7410
Publication: *Saintpaulia International News*
(bimonthly)

Saxifrage Society
Adrian Young, Secretary
31 Eddington Road
London SW16 5BS
England
Dues: £10.00

The Sedum Society
c/o Micki Crozier
10502 North 135th Street West
Sedgwick, KS 67135
(316) 796-0496
Dues: $17.50
Publication: quarterly newsletter

Sempervivum Fanciers Association
37 Ox Bow Lane
Randolph, MA 02368
(617) 963-6737
Dues:
Publication: *SFA Newsletter* (quarterly)

The Sempervivum Society
The Secretary
11 Wingle Tye Road
Burgess Hill, West Sussex RH15 9HR
England
(0444) 23-6848
Dues: £2.50
Publication: *Newsletter*
(three times annually)

Solanaceae Enthusiasts
3370 Princeton Court
Santa Clara, CA 95051
(408) 241-9440
Publication: *Solanaceae Enthusiasts*
(quarterly)

Woody Plant Society
c/o Betty Ann Mech
1315 66th Avenue NE
Minneapolis, MN 55432
(612) 574-1197
Dues: $15.00
Publication: *Bulletin* (biannual)

World Federation of Rose Societies
c/o Jill Bennell
46 Alexandra Road
St. Albans, Herts. AL1 3AZ
England
(0727) 833-648
Dues: £25.00
Publication: *World Rose News* (semiannual)

# Specialty Garden Organizations

Alpine Garden Club of British Columbia
Main Post Office Box 5161
Vancouver, British Columbia V6B 4B2
Publication: *Alpine Garden Club Bulletin*
(five times annually)

American Rock Garden Society
Secretary
Box 67

Millwood, NY 10546
(914) 762-2948
Dues: $25.00
Publication: *Rock Garden Quarterly*

Aquatic Gardeners Association
c/o Dorothy Reimer, Membership
83 Cathcart Street
London, Ontario N6C 3L9
Dues: $15.00
Publication: *The Aquatic Gardener*
(bimonthly journal)

Bonsai Clubs International
c/o Virginia Ellermann
2636 West Mission Road
Tallahassee, FL 32304
(904) 575-1442
Dues: $25.00
Publication: *Bonsai* (bimonthly magazine)

Cottage Garden Society
c/o Mrs. C. Tordorff
5 Nixon Close, Thornhill
Dewsbury, West Yorkshire. WF12 0JA
England
(0924) 46-8469
Dues: $20.00
Publication: *CGS Newsletter* (quarterly)

Desert Plant Society of Vancouver
Box 145-790
6200 McKay Avenue
Barnaby, British Columbia V5H 4MY
(604) 525-5315
Dues: Canada $15.00

Hardy Plant Society (UK)
Little Orchard, Great Comberton
Pershore WR10 3DP
England
(0386) 71-0317
Dues: £8.50
Publications: *The Hardy Plant*
(semiannual);
*Newsletter* (three times annually)

Hardy Plant Society (US)
c/o Betty Mackey
440 Louella Avenue
Wayne, PA 19087
Dues: $12.00
Publication: *The Newsletter* (quarterly)

Hobby Greenhouse Association
18517 Kingshill Road
Germantown, MD 20874
(410) 275-0377
Dues: $12.00
Publications: *Hobby Greenhouse* (quarterly);
*HGA News* (quarterly)

Hydroponic Society of America
2819 Crow Canyon Road, Suite 218
San Ramon, CA 94583
(510) 743-9605
Dues: $30.00
Publication: *Soilless Grower* (bimonthly)

Indoor Gardening Society of America
Sharon Zentz, Membership Secretary
944 South Munro Road
Tallmadge, OH 44278
(216) 733-8414
Dues: $20.00

International Society of Greenhouse
Gardeners
Box 7567
Olympia, WA 98507
Publication: newsletter

Northern Horticultural Society
Harlow Carr Gardens, Crag Lane
Harrogate, North Yorkshire HG3 1QB
England
(0423) 56-5418
Dues: £19.00
Publication: *Northern Gardener* (quarterly)

Pioneer Plant Society
c/o Ms. P. A. Puryear
708 Holland Street

Navasota, TX 77868
(409) 825-3220
Dues: $7.00
Publication: *PPS Newsletter* (quarterly)

Scottish Rock Garden Club
c/o Mrs. J. Thomlinson
1 Hillcrest Road
Bearsden, Glasgow G61 2EB
Scotland
Dues: $28.00
Publication: *The Rock Garden* (semiannual
journal)

The Terrarium Association
c/o Robert C. Baur
Box 276
Newfane, VT 05345
(802) 365-4721

# Native Plant Societies and Botanical Clubs

*National and Regional Organizations*

American Association of Field Botanists
Box 23542
Chattanooga, TN 37422

American Floral Meadow Society
c/o John M. Krouse
University of Maryland
Cherry Hill Turf Research Facility
3120 Gracefield Road
Silver Spring, MD 20904
(301) 572-7247
Dues: $35.00
Publication: quarterly newsletter

American Wildflower Society
c/o John Rough, Treasurer
11 Johnson Avenue
Chicopee, MA 02138

Center for Plant Conservation
The Missouri Botanical Garden

4344 Shaw Boulevard
St. Louis, MO 63166
(314) 577-5100

Eastern Native Plant Alliance
Box 6101
McLean, VA 22106

National Wildflower Research Center
4801 La Crosse Avenue
Austin, TX 78739
(512) 292-4100
Dues: $25.00
Publication: bimonthly newsletter;
semiannual journal

New England Wild Flower Society, Inc.
Garden in the Woods
180 Hemenway Road
Framingham, MA 01701
(508) 877-7630
Dues: $35.00
Publication: newsletter
(three times annually)

Operation Wildflower
National Council of State Garden Clubs
9516 Glenbrook Drive
Charlotte, NC 28175

Southern Appalachian Botanical Club
c/o Charles N. Horn, Secretary/Treasurer
Biology Department
Newberry College
2100 College Street
Newberry, SC 29108

## Alabama

Alabama Wildflower Society
c/o Dottie Elam, Treasurer
240 Ivy Lane
Auburn, AL 36830

## Alaska

Alaska Native Plant Society
Box 141613
Anchorage, AK 99514

## Arizona

Arizona Native Plant Society
Box 41206, Sun Station
Tucson, AZ 85717

## Arkansas

Arkansas Native Plant Society
Route 2, Box 256BB
Mena, AR 71953
(501) 394-4666

## California

California Native Grass Association
Box 566
Dixon, CA 95620
(916) 678-6282
Dues: $35.00
Publication: *Grasslands* (quarterly)

California Native Plant Society
1722 J Street, Suite 17
Sacramento, CA 95814
(916) 447-2677
Dues: $25.00
Publications: *Fremontia*
(quarterly magazine); *Bulletin* (newsletter)

Regional Parks Botanic Garden
Tilden Regional Park
Berkeley, CA 94708
(510) 841-8732
Publication: *The Four Seasons* (quarterly)

Southern California Botanists
c/o Alan Romspert
Department of Biology
Fullerton State University

Fullerton, CA 92634
(714) 449-7034
Dues: $8.00
Publication: *Crossosoma* (semiannual)

## Colorado

Colorado Native Plant Society
Box 200
Fort Collins, CO 80522
Dues: $12.00
Publication: *Aquilegia*
(four to six times annually)

## Connecticut

Connecticut Botanical Society
c/o Margaret Taylor, Secretary
10 Hillside Circle
Storrs, CT 06268

## District of Columbia

Botanical Society of Washington
Department of Botany, NHB 166
Smithsonian Institution
Washington, DC 20560

## Florida

Florida Native Plant Society
Box 680008
Orlando, FL 32868
(407) 299-1472
Dues: $20.00
Publication: *The Palmetto* (quarterly)

## Georgia

Georgia Botanical Society
c/o Ted Reissing, President
5102 Hidden Branches Drive
Atlanta, GA 30338

## Hawaii

Hawaii Botanical Society
Botany Department
University of Hawaii
3190 Maille Way
Honolulu, HI 96822

Hawaii Plant Conservation Center
National Tropical Botanical Garden
Box 340, Lawai
Kauai, HI 96765
(808) 332-7324

## Idaho

Idaho Native Plant Society
Box 9451
Boise, ID 83707
Dues: $8.00
Publications: *Sage Notes* (bimonthly);
*Sage Briefs* (bimonthly)

## Illinois

Illinois Native Plant Society
Forest Glen Preserve
20301 East 900 North Road
Westville, IL 61883

## Indiana

Indiana Native Plant and
Wildflower Society
c/o Caroline Harstad
5952 Lieber Road
Indianapolis, IN 46208

## Kansas

Kansas Wildflower Society
c/o R. L. McGregor Herbarium
University of Kansas
2045 Constant Avenue
Lawrence, KS 66047

## Kentucky

Kentucky Native Plant Society
c/o Dr. Douglas N. Reynolds
Department of Natural Sciences
East Kentucky University
Richmond, KY 40475

## Louisiana

Louisiana Native Plant Society
c/o Ella Price
Box 393
Blanchard, LA 71009
Dues: $10.00
Publication: *LNPS Newsletter* (quarterly)

Louisiana Project Wildflower
Lafayette Natural History Museum
637 Girard Park Drive
Lafayette, LA 70503

## Maine

Josselyn Botanical Society
c/o Marilyn Dwelley, Treasurer
Box 41
China, ME 04926

## Maryland

Maryland Native Plant Society
Box 4877
Silver Spring, MD 20914

## Massachusetts

New England Botanical Club
22 Divinity Avenue
Cambridge, MA 02138

## Michigan

Michigan Botanical Club
c/o Dr. Peter Kaufman
Biology Department

University of Michigan
Ann Arbor, MI 48109

Wildflower Association of Michigan
Box 80527
6011 West St. Joseph, Suite 403
Lansing, MI 48908

## Minnesota

Friends of the Eloise Butler Wildflower
Garden
Box 11592
Minneapolis, MN 55412

Minnesota Native Plant Society
220 BioScience Center
University of Minnesota
1445 Gortner Avenue
St. Paul, MN 55108

## Mississippi

Mississippi Native Plant Society
c/o Victor Rudis
Box 2151
Starkville, MS 38759
(601) 324-0430
Dues: $7.50
Publication: quarterly newsletter

## Missouri

Missouri Native Plant Society
Box 20073
St. Louis, MO 63144
(314) 577-9522
Dues: $9.00
Publications: *Petal Pusher*
(bimonthly newsletter);
*Missouriensis* (semiannual journal)

## Montana

Montana Native Plant Society
Box 8783, Missoula, MT 59807

## Nevada

The Mohave Native Plant Society
8180 Placid Street
Las Vegas, NV 89123

Northern Nevada Native Plant Society
c/o Loring Williams
Box 8965
Reno, NV 89507
(702) 358-7759
Dues: $10.00
Publication: newsletter (nine times
annually)

## New Jersey

Native Plant Society of New Jersey
Box 231
Cook College
New Brunswick, NJ 08903

## New Mexico

Native Plant Society of New Mexico
443 Live Oak Loop NE
Albuquerque, NM 87122
(505) 356-3942
Dues: $10.00
Publication: bimonthly newsletter

## New York

Amherst Museum Wildflower Society
3755 Tonawanda Creek Road
East Amherst, NY 14501

Long Island Botanical Society
45 Sandy Hill Road
Oyster Bay, NY 11771

New York Flora Association
New York State Museum
3132 CEC
Albany, NY 12230

Niagara Frontier Botanical Society
Buffalo Museum of Science
1020 Humboldt Parkway
Buffalo, NY 14211

Syracuse Botanical Club
c/o Janet Holmes
101 Ambergate Road
DeWitt, NY 13214

Torrey Botanical Club
c/o Margaret Basile, Treasurer
Department of Biological Science
Herbert H. Lehman College
Bronx, NY 10468

## North Carolina

North Carolina Wild Flower
Preservation Society
UNC Botanical Garden
Chapel Hill, NC 27517
(919) 962-0522
Dues: $15.00
Publication: semiannual newsletter

Western Carolina Botanical Club
c/o Dick Smith
6 Tenequa Drive
Connestee Falls
Brevard, NC 28712

University Botanical Gardens at Asheville
151 W. T. Weaver Boulevard
Asheville, NC 28804

## Ohio

Native Plant Society of Northeastern
Ohio
2651 Kerwick Road
University Heights, OH 44118

Ohio Native Plant Society
c/o A. K. Malmquist
6 Louise Drive

Chagrin Falls, OH 44022
(216) 338-6622
Publication: *Trillium* (bimonthly)

## Oklahoma

Oklahoma Native Plant Society
Tulsa Garden Center
2435 South Peoria
Tulsa, OK 74114

## Oregon

Native Plant Society of Oregon
c/o Jan Dobak, Membership Chair
2584 NW Savier Street
Portland, OR 97210
(503) 248-9242
Dues: $12.00
Publications: *Kalmiopsis* (annual);
*Bulletin* (monthly)

## Pennsylvania

Botanical Society of Western
Pennsylvania
c/o Robert F. Bahl, Secretary
401 Clearview Avenue
Pittsburgh, PA 15205

Delaware Valley Fern and
Wildflower Society
c/o Dana Cartwright
263 Hillcrest Road
Wayne, PA 19087

Muhlenberg Botanical Society
North Museum
Franklin and Marshall College
Box 3003
Lancaster, PA 17604

Pennsylvania Native Plant Society
1806 Commonwealth Building
316 4th Avenue
Pittsburgh, PA 15222

Philadelphia Botanical Club
Academy of Science
19th and Parkway
Philadelphia, PA 19103

## Rhode Island

Rhode Island Wild Plant Society
12 Sanderson Road
Smithfield, RI 01917

## South Dakota

Great Plains Botanical Society
Box 461
Hot Springs, SD 57747

## Tennessee

Tennessee Native Plant Society
Department of Botany
University of Tennessee
Knoxville, TN 37996
(615) 691-0077
Dues: $15.00
Publication: bimonthly newsletter

The Wildflower Society
c/o Goldsmith Civic Garden Center
750 Cherry Road
Memphis, TN 38119

## Texas

El Paso Native Plant Society
7760 Maya Avenue
El Paso, TX 79912

Native Plant Society of Texas
c/o Dana Tucker
Box 891
Georgetown, TX 78627
(512) 863-7794
Dues: $20.00
Publication: *Texas Native Plant Society News*
(bimonthly)

Native Prairies Association of Texas
301 Nature Center Drive
Austin, TX 78746
(512) 327-8181
Dues: $15.00
Publication: quarterly journal

## Utah

Utah Native Plant Society
c/o Pam Poulson
Box 520041
Salt Lake City, UT 84152
Dues: $10.00
Publication: *Sego Lily* (bimonthly)

## Vermont

Vermont Botanical and Bird Clubs
c/o Deborah Benjamin, Secretary
Box 327
Warren Road
Eden, VT 05652

## Virginia

Virginia Native Plant Society
c/o Nicky Staunton
Box 844
Annandale, VA 22003
Dues: $15.00
Publication: *Bulletin* (quarterly)

## Washington

Washington Native Plant Society
c/o Shirly Post
Box 576
Woodinville, WA 98072
(206) 485-2193
Dues: $12.00
Publication: *Douglasia* (quarterly)

## West Virginia

West Virginia Native Plant Society
Corresponding Secretary
Box 2755
Elkins, WV 26241
Dues: $8.00
Publication: *Native Notes*

## Wisconsin

Botanical Club of Wisconsin
Wisconsin Academy of Arts,
Sciences, and Letters
1922 University Avenue
Madison, WI 53705

Wild Ones Natural Landscapers, Ltd.
c/o Judy Crane
Box 23576
Milwaukee, WI 53223
(414) 251-2185
Dues: $15.00
Publication: bimonthly newsletter

## Wyoming

Wyoming Native Plant Society
3165 University Station
Laramie, WY 82071
Publication: newsletter

## Canada

The Canadian Wildflower Society
John Craw, Business Secretary
Unit 12A, Box 228
4981 Highway 7 East
Markham, Ontario L3R 1N1
(416) 294-9075
Dues: $30.00
Publication: *Wildflower* (quarterly)

Newfoundland Chapter
Canadian Wildflower Society
c/o Sue Meades

633 Pouch Cove Highway
Flatrock, Newfoundland A1K 1C8

Nova Scotia Wild Flora Society
Nova Scotia Museum
1747 Summer Street
Halifax, Nova Scotia B3H 3A6
Dues: Canada $12.00
Publication: *NSWFS Newsletter*

Wellington/Waterloo Chapter
Canadian Wildflower Society
c/o Allan Anderson
Botany Department
University of Guelph
Guelph, Ontario N1G 2W1

## Professional Organizations

American Association of
Nurserymen/Garden Centers of America
1250 I Street, Suite 500
Washington, DC 20005
(202) 789-2900

American Seed Trade Association
1030 15th Street NW, Suite 964
Washington, DC 20005
(202) 223-4080

American Society of Consulting Arborists
5130 West 101st Circle
Westminster, CO 80030
(303) 466-2722

American Society for Horticultural
Science
113 South West Street, Suite 400
Alexandria, VA 22314
(703) 836-4606

American Society of
Landscape Architects
4401 Connecticut Avenue NW
Washington, DC 20008
(202) 686-2752

Canadian Horticultural Council
1101 Prince of Wales Drive, Suite 310
Ottawa, Ontario K2C 3W7
(613) 226-4187

Canadian Nursery Trades Association
1293 Matheson Boulevard
Mississauga, Ontario L4W 1R1
(416) 629-1367

Garden Writers Association of America
c/o J. C. McGowan
10210 Leatherleaf Court
Manassas, VA 22111
(703) 257-1032

Mailorder Association of Nurseries, Inc.
8683 Doves Fly Way
Laurel, MD 20723
(301) 490-9143

National Garden Bureau/All-America
Selections
1311 Butterfield Road, Suite 310
Downers Grove, IL 60515
(708) 963-0770

Perennial Plant Association
3383 Schirtzinger Road
Hilliard, OH 43026
(614) 771-8431

Professional Plant Growers Association
Box 27517
Lansing, MI 48909
(800) 647-7742

# Government Sources for Gardeners

THE UNITED STATES Department of Agriculture provides a number of valuable services to gardeners, at little or no cost, through the Cooperative Extension Service. Extension Service offices are located in over three thousand counties in all fifty states. For obvious reasons of space, only the horticulture specialists at state headquarters offices are listed here. Check the government blue pages of your local phone book or call the USDA Information Office (see below) for your local county extension office. For a list of on-line USDA information servers, see chapter 11.

Extension Service agents provide information and advice on all aspects of gardening. Through them, you can arrange for soil and water testing, have your garden pests identified, receive pamphlets and other publications, get cultivation advice, attend classes, organize a 4-H club, and participate in many other activities and services. The Cooperative Extension Service also sponsors the Master Gardener program (see below) and operates the National Agricultural Library (see chapter 10).

## United States Department of Agriculture

Infomation Office
United States Department of Agriculture
Washington, DC 20250
(202) 447-8005

For information regarding permits to import plants from abroad, and regarding plant inspection stations, contact:

United States Department of Agriculture
Animal and Plant Health Inspection
Service
Permit Unit
Federal Building
Hyattsville, MD 20782

## USDA Cooperative Extension Service

### Alabama

Dr. Ronald Shumack
Extension Horticulture Department
Auburn University
Auburn, AL 36849
(205) 826-4985

### Alaska

Wayne G. Vandre
Extension Horticulturist
2221 East Northern Lights Boulevard
University of Alaska
Anchorage, AK 99508
(907) 279-6576

## Arizona

Dr. Michael Kilby
Extension Horticulturist
University of Arizona
Tucson, AZ 85721
(602) 621-1400

## Arkansas

Kenneth R. Scott
Extension Horticulturist
Box 391
Little Rock, AR 72203
(501) 376-6301

Dr. Gerald Klingaman
Extension Horticulturist
316 Plant Science Building
University of Arkansas
Fayetteville, AR 72701
(501) 575-2603

## California

William B. Davis
Extension Environmental Horticulturist
University of California
Davis, CA 95616
(916) 752-0412

Dr. Tokuji Furuta
Extension Environmental Horticulturist
4114 Batchelor Hall
University of California
Riverside, CA 92521
(714) 787-3318

## Colorado

Dr. Kenneth W. Knutson
Extension Associated Professor
Department of Horticulture
University of Colorado
Fort Collins, CO 80523
(303) 491-7068

## Connecticut

Edmond L. Marotte
Consumer Horticulturist
Department of Plant Science
University of Connecticut
Storrs, CT 06268
(203) 486-3435

## Delaware

Susan Barton
Extension Horticulturist
Townsend Hall
University of Delaware
Newark, DE 19711
(302) 451-2532

## District of Columbia

Pamela Marshall
Extension Horticulturist
1351 Nicholson Street NW
Washington, DC 20011
(202) 282-7410

## Florida

Dr. Robert J. Black
Extension Urban Horticulture Specialist
Ornamental Horticulture Department
University of Florida
Gainesville, FL 32611
(904) 392-1835

## Georgia

Dr. A. Jefferson Lewis
Extension Horticulturist
University of Georgia
Athens, GA 30602
(404) 542-2340

## Hawaii

Dr. Harry Bittenbender
Extension Horticulturist
University of Hawaii
Honolulu, HI 96822
(808) 948-6043

## Idaho

Larry O'Keeffe
Department of Plant, Soil and
Entomological Sciences
University of Idaho
Moscow, ID 83843
(208) 885-6277

## Illinois

James Schmidt
Extension Specialist
104 Ornamental Horticulture Building
University of Illinois
Urbana, IL 61801
(217) 333-2125

## Indiana

B. R. Lerner
Extension Horticulturist
Department of Horticulture
Purdue University
West Lafayette, IN 47907
(317) 494-1311

## Iowa

Dr. Michael L. Agnew
Extension Horticulturist
Department of Horticulture
Iowa State University
Ames, IA 50011
(515) 294-0027

## Kansas

Dr. Frank Morrison
Extension Program Leader
Water Hall 227
Kansas State University
Manhattan, KS 66506
(913) 532-6173

## Kentucky

Dr. John Strang
Extension Horticulturist
Agriculture Science Center North
University of Kentucky
Lexington, KY 40546
(606) 257-5685

## Louisiana

Dr. Thomas Pope
Horticulture Specialist
J. C. Miller Horticulture Building
Louisiana State University
Baton Rouge, LA 70803
(504) 388-2222

## Maine

Dr. Lois Berg Stack
Ornamental Horticulture Specialist
University of Maine
Orono, ME 04469
(207) 581-2949

## Maryland

Dr. Francis Gouin
Department of Horticulture
University of Maryland
College Park, MD 20742
(301) 454-3143

## Massachusetts

Kathleen Carool
Extension Specialist, Horticulture
French Hall
University of Massachusetts
Amherst, MA 01003
(413) 545-0895

## Michigan

Dr. Jerome Hull Jr.
Department of Horticulture
Michigan State University
East Lansing, MI 48824
(517) 355-5194

## Minnesota

Deborah L. Brown
Extension Horticulturist
1970 Folwell Avenue
University of Minnesota
St. Paul, MN 55108
(612) 624-7419

## Mississippi

Dr. Richard Mullenax
Extension Horticulturist
Department of Horticulture
Box 5446
Mississippi Valley State College, MS
39762

## Missouri

Dr. Gary C. Long
Extension Ornamental Plant Specialist
University of Missouri
Columbia, MO 65211
(314) 882-9625

## Montana

Dr. James W. Bauder
Extension Specialist
Plant and Soil Science Department
Montana State University
Bozeman, MT 59717
(406) 994-4605

## Nebraska

Dr. Donald Steinegger
Extension Horticulturist
377 Plant Science Building
University of Nebraska
Lincoln, NE 68503
(402) 472-2550

## Nevada

William J. Carlos
Extension Horticulturist
1001 East 9th Street
Reno, NV 89520
(702) 328-2650

## New Hampshire

Dr. Charles Williams
Extension Ornamentals Specialist
Plant Science Department
University of New Hampshire
Durham, NH 03824
(603) 862-3207

## New Jersey

Lawrence D. Little Jr.
Extension Horticulturist
Blake Hall
Rutgers—The State University
New Brunswick, NJ 08903
(201) 932-9559

## New Mexico

George Dickerson
Extension Horticulturist
9301 Indian School Road
New Mexico State University
Albuquerque, NM 87112
(505) 292-0097

## New York

Robert Kozlowski
Senior Extension Associate
Homes and Grounds
17 Plant Science Building
Cornell University
Ithaca, NY 14853
(607) 255-1791

## North Carolina

Dr. Joseph Love
Extension Horticulturist
Department of Horticultural Science
North Carolina State University
Raleigh, NC 27695
(919) 737-3322

## North Dakota

Dr. Ronald Smith
Extension Horticulturist
North Dakota State University
Fargo, ND 58105
(701) 237-8161

## Ohio

Barbara J. Williams
Extension Horticulturist
2001 Fyffe Court
Ohio State University
Columbus, OH 43210
(614) 292-3852

## Oklahoma

Paul J. Mitchell
Extension Horticulturist
Oklahoma State University
Stillwater, OK 74078
(405) 624-6593

## Oregon

Dr. James L. Green
Extension Ornamentals Specialist
Department of Horticulture
Oregon State University
Corvallis, OR 97331
(503) 754-3464

## Pennsylvania

Dr. J. Robert Nuss
Extension Horticulturist
Department of Horticulture
Pennsylvania State College
102 Tyson Building
University Park, PA 16802
(814) 863-2196

## Rhode Island

Kathy Mallon
Extension Specialist
Department of Plant Science
University of Rhode Island
Kingston, RI 02881
(401) 792-5999

## South Carolina

Dr. Alta Kingman
Extension Horticulturist
173 Plant and Agriculture Science
Building
Clemson University
Clemson, SC 29634
(803) 656-4962

## South Dakota

Dean M. Martin
Extension Horticulturist
South Dakota State University
Brookings, SD 57007
(605) 688-5136

## Tennessee

Dr. Elmer Ashburn
Department of Plant and Soil Science
Box 1071
University of Tennessee
Knoxville, TN 37901
(615) 974-7208

## Texas

Dr. William Welch
Extension Horticulturist
225 Horticulture Building
Texas A & M University
College Station, TX 77843
(409) 845-7341

## Utah

Dr. Gerald Olson
UMC 4900
Utah State University
Logan, UT 84322
(801) 750-2194

## Vermont

Dr. Leonard Perry
Extension Horticulturist
Hills Building
University of Vermont
Burlington, VT 05405
(802) 656-2630

## Virginia

Dr. Paul Smeal
Extension Horticulturist
Virginia Polytechnical Institute
Blacksburg, VA 24061
(703) 961-5609

## Washington

Dr. Robert Thornton
Extension Horticulturist
Washington State University
Pullman, WA 99164
(509) 335-2811

## West Virginia

Dr. Richard Zimmerman
Extension Horticulturist
2088 Agricultural Sciences Building
West Virginia University
Morgantown, WV 26506
(304) 293-4801

## Wisconsin

Dr. R. C. Newman
Extension Horticulturist
University of Wisconsin
Madison, WI 53706
(608) 262-1624

## Wyoming

Dr. James Cook
Extension Horticulturist
University of Wyoming
Laramie, WY 82071
(307) 766-2243

# Master Gardener Program

*The Master Gardener program has been sponsored by the USDA Extension Service since 1972. This valuable program provides free or inexpensive horticultural training to volunteers, who then repay the training costs—through volunteer service in their communities—by participating in local beautification efforts, answering plant information hotlines, or working with local gardening groups, for example. The training programs vary considerably, especially in length and focus, from state to state. For more information about participating in the program, contact the Master Gardener Coordinator at your state extension office (see above) or:*

Master Gardeners International
Corporation (MaGIC)
Membership Services
2904 Cameron Mills Road
Alexandria, VA 22302
(703) 920-6677
Dues: $10.00
Publication: MaGIC Lantern (quarterly)

# Canada

For information about government programs regarding horticulture, contact:

Agriculture Canada
Communications Branch
Ottawa, Ontario K1A 0C7
(613) 995-5222

# The Well-Read Gardener

$\mathbf{A}$S A GROUP, gardeners are big readers. They read lots of plant catalogues, of course, but they also read pretty much anything else they can find about gardens, gardening, and other gardeners. This section lists commercial magazines and newsletters about general, regional, and specialty gardening. (See chapter 8 for the interesting publications put out by gardening organizations.) Also listed here are dealers in new and old gardening books, book clubs, and libraries with significant horticultural collections.

## Magazines and Newsletters

If you're looking for articles about a particular aspect of gardening, these two indexes (often carried by large public libraries and specialized horticultural libraries—see below) may help you find what you need:

*Gardener's Index*
CompuDex Press
Box 27041
Kansas City, MO 64110
Frequency: annual
Subscription: $18.00

*Garden Literature*
Garden Literature Press
398 Columbus Avenue, Suite 181
Boston, MA 02116
Frequency: quarterly
Subscription: $50.00

### General Gardening

*Allen Lacy's Homeground*
Allen Lacy

Box 271
Linwood, NJ 08221
Frequency: quarterly newsletter
Subscription: $38.00

*The Avant Gardener*
Horticultural Data Processors
Box 489
New York, NY 10028
Frequency: monthly newsletter
Subscription: $18.00

*Baer's Garden Newsletter*
John Baer's Sons
Box 328
Lancaster, PA 17608
Frequency: quarterly
Subscription: $5.00

*Backyard Gardener Idea Letter*
James J. Martin
Box 605
Winfield, IL 60190

*Beautiful Gardens*
CMK Publishing

350 Brannan Street
San Francisco, CA 94107
(800) 677-6411
Frequency: bimonthly
Subscription: $17.00

*Canadian Gardening*
Camar Publications, Ltd.
130 Spy Court
Markham, Ontario L3R 5H6
Frequency: bimonthly
Subscription: Canada $23.00

*Country Home Country Gardens*
Meredith Corporation
Box 55154
Boulder, CO 80322
(800) 677-0484
Frequency: quarterly
Subscription: $15.00

*Country Journal*
Box 8200
Harrisburg, PA 17105
(717) 657-9555
(800) 435-9610
Frequency: bimonthly
Subscription: $20.00

*Country Living*
Hearst Corporation
Box 10557
Des Moines, IA 50340
(800) 777-0102
Frequency: monthly
Subscription: $28.00

*Country Living Gardener*
Hearst Corporation
Box 10557
Des Moines, IA 50340
(800) 777-0102
Frequency: quarterly
Subscription: $10.00

*Fine Gardening*
The Taunton Press
Box 5506
Newtown, CT 06470
(203) 426-8171
Frequency: bimonthly
Subscription: $28.00

*Flower & Garden*
KC Publishing
700 West 47th Street, Suite 310
Kansas City, MO 64112
(816) 531-5730
Frequency: bimonthly
Subscription: $15.00

*Garden Clippin's*
Gene E. Bush
323 Woodside Drive
Depauw, IN 47115
(812) 633-4858
Frequency: monthly
Subscription: $15.00

*Garden Design*
Evergreen Publishing Company
Box 55458
Boulder, CO 80322
(800) 234-5118
Frequency: bimonthly
Subscription: $28.00

*Garden Gate*
Woodsmith Corporation
2200 Grand Avenue
Des Moines, IA 50312
(800) 341-4769
Frequency: bimonthly
Subscription: $20.00

*Gardens and Nature*
Box 394
Sound Beach, NY 11789
Frequency: bimonthly
Subscription: $12.00

*Gardens Illustrated*
John Brown Publishing, Ltd.
Frome, Somerset 8A11 1YA
England
US phone: (516) 627-3836
Frequency: bimonthly
Subscription: $50.00

*Green Prints: The Weeder's Digest*
Pat Stone
Box 1355
Fairview, NC 28730
(800) 569-0602
Frequency: quarterly
Subscription: $14.00

*Grow America*
Ames Lawn and Garden Tools
Box 1485
Mansfield, OH 44901
Frequency: bimonthly
Subscription: free

*Harrowsmith Country Life*
Camden House Publishing
Ferry Road
Charlotte, VT 05445
Frequency: bimonthly
Subscription: $18.00

*Home Garden*
Meredith Corporation
1716 Locust Street
Des Moines, IA 50309
(800) 413-9748
Frequency: bimonthly
Subscription: $20.00

*Horticulture: The Magazine of American Gardening*
Horticulture, Inc.
Box 53879
Boulder, CO 80321
(617) 742-5600
Frequency: ten times annually
Subscription: $26.00

*Hortideas*
Greg and Pat Williams
460 Black Lick Road
Gravel Switch, KY 40328
Frequency: monthly
Subscription: $15.00

*Hortus*
David Wheeler
The Neuadd
Rhayader, Powys LD6 5HH
Wales
Frequency: quarterly
Subscription: £35.00

*HousePlant Magazine*
HousePlant, Inc.
Route 1, Box 271–2
Elkins, WV 26241
Frequency: bimonthly
Subscription: $20.00

*Indoor & Patio Gardening*
Box 1182
Fort Washington, PA 19034
Frequency: bimonthly
Subscription: $17.85

*National Gardening*
National Gardening Association
180 Flynn Avenue
Burlington, VT 05401
(802) 863-1308
(800) 727-9097
Frequency: bimonthly
Subscription: $18.00

*On the Garden Line*®
The YardenCare Company
Box 6047
Wixom, MI 48393
(800) 336-5885
Frequency: eight times annually
Subscription: $28.00

*Organic Flower Gardening*
Rodale Press, Inc.
33 East Minor Street
Emmaus, PA 18098
(800) 666-2206
Frequency: semiannual
Subscription: $2.95/issue; newsstand sales
only

*Organic Gardening*
Rodale Press, Inc.
33 East Minor Street
Emmaus, PA 18098
(800) 666-2206
Frequency: nine times annually
Subscription: $25.00

*Plant & Garden*
Gardenvale Publishing Company, Ltd.
1 Pacifique
Ste. Anne de Bellevue, Quebec H9X 1C5
(514) 457-2744
Frequency: quarterly
Subscription: $17.00

*Plants & Gardens*
Brooklyn Botanic Garden
1000 Washington Avenue
Brooklyn, NY 11225
Frequency: quarterly
Subscription: $25.00

*The Plantsman*
Maxwell Publishing
80 Vincent Square
London SW1P 2PE
England
Frequency: quarterly
Subscription: £19.50

*Weekend Gardening*
Harris Publications, Inc.
1115 Broadway
New York, NY 10010
Frequency: monthly
Subscription: $20.00

# Regional Gardening Periodicals

*John E. Bryan Gardening Newsletter*
John E. Bryan, Inc.
300 Valley Street, Suite 206
Sausalito, CA 94965
Region: northern California
Frequency: monthly
Subscription: $30.00

*California Garden*
San Diego Floral Association
Casa del Prado
Balboa Park
San Diego, CA 92101
Region: California
Frequency: bimonthly
Subscription: $7.00

*Carolina Gardener*
Carolina Gardener, Inc.
Box 4504
Greensboro, NC 27404
(800) 245-0142
Region: North and South Carolina
Frequency: bimonthly
Subscription: $15.00

*The Four Seasons*
Regional Parks Botanic Garden
Tilden Regional Park
Berkeley, CA 94708
(510) 841-8732
Region: California-native plants
Frequency: quarterly
Subscription: $12.00

*The Gardener's Gazette*
Michael Henry
Box 786
Georgetown, CT 06829
Region: New England
Frequency: ten times annually
Subscription: $15.00

*Gardening Newsletter by Bob Flagg*
Morningside Associates
5002 Morningside
Houston, TX 77005
Region: Sun Belt and Gulf Coast
Frequency: monthly
Subscription: $16.00

*Gardens West*
Dorothy Horton
Box 2690
Vancouver, British Columbia V6B 3W8
Region: western Canada
Frequency: nine times annually
Subscription: Canada $20.00

*Growing Native*
Growing Native Research Institute
Box 489
Berkeley, CA 94701
Region: western US
Frequency: bimonthly
Subscription: $30.00

*The Island Grower*
Greenheart Publications
RR 4
Sooke, British Columbia V0S 1N0
Region: Pacific Northwest
Frequency: ten times annually
Subscription: Canada $19.00

*Minnesota Horticulturist: The Magazine of
Northern Gardening*
Minnesota State Horticultural Society
1970 Folwell Avenue
St. Paul, MN 55108
(800) 676-6747
Frequency: nine times annually
Subscription: $25.00

*Native Notes*
Joseph L. Collins
Route 2, Box 550
Heiskell, TN 37754
Region: eastern US

Frequency: quarterly
Subscription: $17.00

*New England Farm Bulletin and Garden Gazette*
Jacob's Meadow, Inc.
Box 67
Taunton, MA 02780
Region: New England
Frequency: twenty-four times annually
Subscription: $17.00

*Pacific Horticulture*
Pacific Horticulture Foundation
Circulation Department
Box 485
Berkeley, CA 94701
(510) 849-1627
Region: California/Pacific Northwest
Frequency: quarterly
Subscription: $15.00

*Rocky Mountain Gardener*
Box 1230
Gunnison, CO 81230
Region: Rocky Mountain states
Frequency: quarterly
Subscription: $12.00

*The Southern California Gardener*
610 20th Street
Santa Monica, CA 90402
Region: southern California
Frequency: bimonthly
Subscription: $20.00

*Southern Living*
Box 830219
Birmingham, AL 35283
Region: Southeast and Texas
Frequency: monthly
Subscription: $25.00

*Neil Sperry's Gardens*
Gardens South
Box 864
McKinney, TX 75070

Region: Texas and Gulf Coast
Frequency: ten times annually
Subscription: $21.50

*Sundew Garden Reports*
Tom Carey
Box 214
Oviedo, FL 32765
Region: Florida and Southeast
Frequency: bimonthly
Subscription: $15.00

*Sunset Magazine*
Sunset Publishing Company
80 Willow Road
Menlo Park, CA 94025
(800) 777-0117
Region: western US
Frequency: monthly
Subscription: $21.00

*Texas Gardener*
Chris S. Corby
Box 9005
Waco, TX 76714
Region: Texas
Frequency: bimonthly
Subscription: $15.00

*The Weedpatch Gazette*
229 Gage Road
Riverside, IL 60546
Region: Chicago area
Frequency: quarterly
Subscription: $18.00

## Specialty Gardening Periodicals

*The American Cottage Gardener*
131 East Michigan Street
Marquette, MI 49855
Frequency: quarterly
Subscription: $35.00

*Birds & Blooms*
5400 South 60th Street
Greendale, WI 53129
(414) 423-0100
Frequency: bimonthly
Subscription: $17.00

*Garden Railways*
Sidestreet Bannerworks
Box 61461
Denver, CO 80206
Frequency: bimonthly
Subscription: $21.00

*Hardy Enough: Experimental Gardeners Journal*
351 Pleasant Street
Northampton, MA 01060
Frequency: bimonthly
Subscription: $27.00

*HerbalGram*
American Botanical Council
Box 201660
Austin, TX 78720
(512) 331-8868
Frequency: quarterly
Subscription: $25.00

*The Herb Companion*
Interweave Press, Inc.
201 East 4th Street
Loveland, CO 80537
(970) 669-7672
(800) 645-3675
Frequency: bimonthly
Subscription: $24.00

*The Herb Quarterly*
Long Mountain Press, Inc.
Box 689
San Anselmo, CA 94960
Frequency: quarterly
Subscription: $24.00

# Gardening Book Dealers

*Most large bookstores carry a good selection of recent horticulture titles, but not many carry specialized titles, serious reference works, or books that are more than a few years old. Fortunately, a number of specialized book dealers are available to help you find both new and old titles. Most issue catalogues on a more or less regular basis. Most dealers in used and rare titles will search for out-of-print books for you for a modest fee or even for free.*

ABT Books
6673 Chadbourne Drive
North Olmsted, OH 44070
Specialties: used and out-of-print

Acres U.S.A. Book Sales
Box 9547
Kansas City, MO 64133
Specialties: general organic gardening

agAccess
Box 2008
603 4th Street
Davis, CA 95616
(916) 756-7177
Specialties: agriculture and horticulture

Agave Books
Box 2539
Providence, RI
(401) 831-3833
Specialties: used, rare, and out-of-print

The American Botanist
Box 532
1103 West Truitt
Chillicothe, IL 61523
(309) 274-5254
Specialties: used, rare, and out-of-print

Anchor & Dolphin Books
Box 823
30 Franklin Street

Newport, RI 02840
(401) 846-6890
Specialties: used, rare, and out-of-print garden history

Andover Books & Prints
68 Park Street
Andover, MA 01810
(508) 475-1645
Specialties: used, rare, and out-of-print herbs

Carol Barnett Books
3562 NE Liberty Street
Portland, OR 97211
(503) 282-7036
Specialties: used, rare, and out-of-print

J. F. Beattie Book Company
105 North Wayne Avenue
Wayne, PA 19087
(215) 687-3347
Specialties: used, rare, and out-of-print

Bell's Book Store
536 Emerson Street
Palo Alto, CA 94301
(415) 323-7822
Specialties: new, used, rare, and out-of-print

B. L. Bibby Books
1225 Sardine Creek Road
Gold Hill, OR 97525
(503) 855-1621
Specialties: used, rare, and out-of-print

Robin Bledsoe, Bookseller
1640 Massachusetts Avenue
Cambridge, MA 02138
(617) 576-3634
Specialties: used, rare, and out-of-print

Book Arbor
Box 20885
Baltimore, MD 21215

(410) 367-0338
Specialties: used, rare, and out-of-print

Book Orchard
1379 Park Western Drive
San Pedro, CA 90732
(310) 548-4279
Specialties: western gardening

The Bookpress, Ltd.
Box KP
411 West Duke of Gloucester Street
Williamsburg, VA 23187
(804) 229-1260

The Book Tree
12 Pine Hill Road
Englishtown, NJ 07726
(908) 446-3853
Specialties: general gardening

The Botana Collection
Box 085756
Racine, WI 53408
(414) 633-2772
(800) 723-8502
Specialties: orchids

Warren F. Broderick Books
Box 124
Lansingburgh, NY 12182
(518) 235-4041
Specialties: used, rare, and out-of-print

Brooks Books
Box 21473
Concord, CA 94521
(510) 672-4566
Specialties: new, used, rare, and out-of-print

Builders Booksource
1817 4th Street
Berkeley, CA 94710
(800) 843-2028
Specialties: general gardening

A. C. Burke & Company
2554 Lincoln Boulevard, Suite 1058
Marina Del Ray, CA 90291
(310) 574-2770
Specialties: general gardening

Calendula Horticultural Books
Box 930
Picton, Ontario K0K 2T0
(613) 476-3521
Specialties: used, rare, and out-of-print

Capability's Books
2379 Highway 48
Deer Park, WI 54007
(800) 247-8154
Specialties: general gardening

Cape Cod Book Center
Box 1380
Mashpee, MA 02649
Specialties: general gardening

The Captain's Bookshelf, Inc.
Box 2258
Asheville, NC 28802
(704) 253-6631
Specialties: used, rare, and out-of-print

Cascadia Company
375 Candalaria Boulevard South
Salem, OR 97302
(503) 364-5127
Specialties: general gardening

Chimney Sweep Books
419 Cedar Street
Santa Cruz, CA 95060
Specialties: general gardening

Copper Fox Farm Books
Box 763
Millbrook, NY 12545
Specialties: general gardening

Cover to Cover
5499 Belfast Road
Batavia, OH 45103
Specialties: general gardening

Discount Garden Books
Box 8354
Portland, OR 97207
(800) 327-1828
Specialties: general gardening

Exeter Rare Books
200 High Street
Exeter, NH 03833
(603) 772-0618
Specialties: used, rare, and out-of-print

Barbara Farnsworth, Bookseller
Box 9
West Cornwall, CT 06796
(203) 672-6571
Specialties: used, rare, and out-of-print

Flora & Fauna Books
121 1st Avenue South
Seattle, WA 98104
(206) 623-4727
Specialties: new, used, rare, and out-of-print

Footnote
179 Washington Park
Brooklyn, NY 11205
Specialties: new and used general gardening

Fortner Books
155 Winslow Way
Bainbridge Island, WA 98110
Specialties: general gardening

Gardeners Bookshelf
Box 16416
Hooksett, NH 03106
Specialties: general gardening

The Gardener's Bookshop
Route 9
Rhinebeck, NY 10572
(914) 876-3786
Specialties: new and used general gardening

Garden Works
31 Old Winter Street
Lincoln, MA 01773
Specialties: used, rare, and out-of-print

V. L. T. Gardner Botanical Books
625 East Victoria Street
Santa Barbara, CA 93103
(805) 966-0256
Specialties: used, rare, and out-of-print

Greenfield Herb Garden
Box 9
Shipshewana, IN 46565
(219) 768-7110
Specialties: herbs

Hannon House
5310 Mountain Road
Cheyenne, WY 82009
Specialties: general gardening

Hortulus
139 Marlborough Place
Toronto, Ontario M5R 3J5
(416) 920-5057
Specialties: used, rare, and out-of-print

Hurley Books
RR 1, Box 160
Westmoreland, NH 03467
(603) 399-4342
Specialties: used, rare, and out-of-print

Ian Jackson
Box 9075
Berkeley, CA 94709
(415) 548-1431
Specialties: used, rare, and out-of-print

John Johnson, Natural History Books
RD 1, Box 513
North Bennington, VT 05257
(802) 442-6738
Specialties: used, rare, and out-of-print
botany

Myron Kimnach
5508 North Astell Avenue
Azusa, CA 91702
(818) 334-7349
Specialties: cacti and succulents

J. Kramer
Box 243, Whitehall, PA 18052
Specialties: used, rare, and out-of-print

Landscape Architecture Bookstore
4401 Connecticut Avenue NW
Washington, DC 20008
(800) 787-2665
Specialties: gardening and landscape
architecture

Landscape Books
Box 483
Exeter, NH 03833
(603) 964-9333
Specialties: landscape architecture,
garden history

Laurelbrook Book Services
5468 Dundas Street West
Toronto, Ontario M9B 6E3
Specialties: general gardening

Diane Lewis Associates
4747 Hollywood Boulevard
Hollywood, FL 33021
Specialties: general gardening

Limberlost Roses
7304 Forbes Avenue
Van Nuys, CA 91406
(818) 901-7798
Specialties: roses

Linden House
148 Sylvan Avenue
Scarborough, Ontario M1M 1K4
(416) 261-0732
Specialties: general gardening

Timothy Mawson Books
New Preston, CT 06777
(203) 868-0732
Specialties: used, rare, and out-of-print

McQuerry Orchid Books
5700 West Salerno Road
Jacksonville, FL 32244
(904) 387-5044
Specialties: new, used, rare, and out-of-
print books about orchids

Nelson Books
RR 2, Box 212
Newport, NH 03773
Specialties: new and used general
gardening

New Moon Gardening Books
Box 1027
Corvallis, OR 97339
(503) 757-0027
Specialties: hydroponics and high-tech
gardening

Mary Odette Books
3831 North Cherry Creek Place
Tucson, AZ 85749
(520) 749-2285
Specialties: cacti and succulents

Pomona Book Exchange
Box 111
Rockton, Ontario L0R 1X0
(519) 621-8897
Specialties: new, used, rare, and out-of-
print

Larry W. Price Books
353 NW Maywood Drive
Portland, OR 97210
(503) 221-1410
Specialties: used, rare, and out-of-print

Quest Rare Books
774 Santa Ynez
Stanford, CA 94305
(415) 324-3119
Specialties: used, rare, and out-of-print

Rainbow Gardens Bookshop
1444 East Taylor Street
Vista, CA 92084
(619) 758-4290
Specialties: cacti and succulents

Savoy Books
Box 271
Lanesboro, MA 01237
(413) 499-9968
Specialties: used, rare, and out-of-print

Robert Shuhi Books
Box 268
Morris, CT 06763
(203) 567-5231
Specialties: used, rare, and out-of-print

Edward F. Smiley Bookseller
43 Liberty Hill Road
Bedford, NH 03110
(603) 472-5800
Specialties: used, rare, and out-of-print

Spectrum
Box 891617
Oklahoma City, OK 73189
Specialties: bonsai

Sperling Books
160 East 38th Street
New York, NY 10016
Specialties: African violets

Storey's Books for Country Living
Schoolhouse Road
Pownal, VT 05261
(800) 441-5700

Stroud Booksellers
Star Route Box 94
Williamsburg, WV 24991
(304) 645-7169
Specialties: used, rare, and out-of-print

Stubbs Books and Prints
835 Madison Avenue
New York, NY 10021
(212) 772-3120
Specialties: used, rare, and out-of-print

Raymond M. Sutton Jr.
Box 330
430 Main Street
Williamsburg, KY 40769
(606) 549-3464
Specialties: new, used, rare, and out-of-print

Tiny Trees Book, Sales
Box 5834
Hauppauge, NY 11788
Specialties: bonsai

Tools and Books, Ltd.
16 High Street
Westerly, RI 02891
Specialties: general gardening

Gary Wayner Bookseller
Route 3, Box 18
Fort Payne, AL 35967
(205) 845-7828
Specialties: used, rare, and out-of-print

Wilkerson Books
31 Old Winter Street
Lincoln, MA 01773
(617) 259-1110

Elizabeth Woodburn
Box 398
Booknoll Farm
Hopewell, NJ 08525
(609) 466-0522
Specialties: new, used, rare, and out-of-print

Wood Violet Books
3814 Sunhill Drive
Madison, WI 53704
(608) 837-7207
Specialties: new, used, rare, and out-of-print

Gary W. Woolson Bookseller
RR 1, Box 1576
Hampden, ME 04444
(207) 234-4931
Specialties: used, rare, and out-of-print

## Gardening Book Clubs

Country Homes & Gardens Book Club
Box 11436
1716 Locust Street
Des Moines, IA 50336

The Garden Book Club
3000 Cendel Drive
Delran, NJ 08370
(609) 786-1000

Organic Gardening Book Club
Box 4515
Des Moines, IA 50336

## Libraries with Significant Horticultural Collections

*With over two million books and more than 27,000 periodical titles, the National Agricultural Library is the largest horticultural library in the country. It's open to the public for reference only; many titles are available through interlibrary loan.*

National Agricultural Library
United States Department of Agriculture
10301 Baltimore Boulevard
Beltsville, MD 20705
(301) 504-5204

*A number of horticultural libraries at botanical gardens, universities, museums, and organizations are open to the public for research. Indeed, free access to the library is often one of the privileges of membership in a botanical garden. These libraries are an excellent way to look at back issues of horticultural journals, hard-to-find or rare volumes, and big, expensive scholarly reference books. Contact the library well in advance to check on the hours and to arrange permission to visit. As a rule, permission to use the collection is granted if you have an area of serious research, but there may be a small fee and some restrictions. If you can't get to a distant library, speak to your local librarian about interlibrary loan programs.*

## Alabama

Horace Hammond Memorial Library
Birmingham Botanical Gardens
2612 Lane Park Road
Birmingham, AL 35223
(205) 879-1227
Note: interlibrary loans

## Arizona

Boyce Thompson Southwestern
Arboretum
37615 US Highway 60
Superior, AZ 85273
(602) 689-2723

Desert Botanical Garden
Richter Memorial Library
1201 North Galvin Parkway
Phoenix, AZ 85008
(602) 941-1225

## California

Fullerton Arboretum
California State University
1900 Associated Road
Fullerton, CA 92631
(714) 773-3579

Los Angeles Arboretum
Plant Sciences Library
301 North Baldwin Avenue
Arcadia, CA 91007
(818) 821-3213
Note: interlibrary loans

Rancho Santa Ana Botanic Garden
1500 North College Avenue
Claremont, CA 91711
(909) 625-8767

San Diego Floral Association
Library and Information Center
Casa del Prado, Balboa Park
San Diego, CA 92101
(619) 232-5762

Santa Barbara Botanic Garden
1212 Mission Canyon Road
Santa Barbara, CA 93105
(805) 682-4726

Strybing Arboretum and Botanical Gardens
Helen Crocker Russell Library of
Horticulture
9th Avenue and Lincoln Way
San Francisco, CA 94122
(415) 661-1514

## Colorado

Denver Botanic Gardens
Helen Fowler Library
1005 York Street
Denver, CO 80206
(303) 370-8014
Note: interlibrary loans

## Connecticut

Bartlett Arboretum
George E. Bye Library
University of Connecticut
151 Brookdale Road
Stamford, CT 06903
(203) 322-6971
Note: interlibrary loans

Connecticut Horticultural Society
150 Main Street
Wethersfield, CT 06109
(203) 529-8713

Nurserymen's Gardens
Connecticut Agricultural Experiment
Station
Box 1106
123 Huntington
New Haven, CT 06504
(203) 789-7272

## Delaware

Delaware Center for Horticulture
1810 North DuPont Street
Wilmington, DE 19806
(302) 658-1913

## District of Columbia

Dumbarton Oaks Garden
1703 32nd Street NW
Washington, DC 20007
(202) 342-3280

Smithsonian Institution
Botany Library
10th and Constitution
Washington, DC 20560
(202) 357-2715

Smithsonian Institution
Horticulture Branch Library
Arts & Industries Building, Room 2282

Washington, DC 20560
(202) 357-1544
Note: interlibrary loans

United States National Arboretum
USDA Agricultural Research Service
3501 New York Avenue NE
Washington, DC 20002
(202) 475-4815
Note: interlibrary loans

## Florida

Fairchild Tropical Garden
Montgomery Library
10901 Old Cutler Road
Miami, FL 33156
(305) 667-1651

Marie Selby Botanical Garden
811 South Palm Avenue
Sarasota, FL 34236
(941) 366-5730

## Georgia

Atlanta Botanical Garden
Sheffield Botanical Library
Piedmont Park
Atlanta, GA 30309
(404) 876-5859

Cherokee Garden Club
Atlanta Historical Society
3101 Andrews Drive NW
Atlanta, GA 30305
(404) 814-4040

Fernbank Science Center
156 Heaton Park Drive NE
Atlanta, GA 30307
(404) 378-4311

## Hawaii

Bernice Pauani Bishop Museum
1525 Bernice Street
Honolulu, HI 96817
(808) 848-4148
Note: interlibrary loans

Honolulu Botanic Gardens
Rock Library
50 North Vineyard Boulevard
Honolulu, HI 96817
(808) 533-3406

National Tropical Botanical Garden
Halima Road
Lawai, HI 96765
(808) 332-7324
Note: interlibrary loans

## Illinois

Chicago Botanic Garden Library
Lake–Cook Road
Glencoe, IL 60022
(708) 835-8200
Note: interlibrary loans

Field Museum of Natural History
Roosevelt Road and Lake Shore Drive
Chicago, IL 60605
(312) 922-9410
Note: interlibrary loans

Morton Arboretum
Sterling Morton Library
Route 53, Lisle, IL 60532
(708) 968-0074
Note: interlibrary loans

University of Illinois
Agricultural Library
1301 West Gregory Drive
Urbana, IL 61801
(217) 333-2416
Note: interlibrary loans

## Indiana

Indianapolis Museum of Art Horticultural
Society
Horticultural Science Library
1200 West 38th Street
Indianapolis, IN 46208
(317) 923-1331

## Iowa

Dubuque Arboretum and Botanical
Gardens
3125 West 32nd Street
Dubuque, IA 52001
(319) 556-2100

## Kansas

Botanica, The Wichita Gardens
Frank Good Library
701 North Amidon
Wichita, KS 67203
(316) 264-0448

## Maryland

Brookside Gardens
1500 Glenallan Avenue
Wheaton, MD 20902
(301) 949-8231

Cylburn Garden Center
Horticultural Library
4915 Greenspring Avenue
Baltimore, MD 21209
(410) 367-2217

## Massachusetts

Arnold Arboretum of Harvard University
125 Arborway
Jamaica Plain, MA 02130
(617) 524-1718

Berkshire Garden Center
Routes 102 and 183, Box 826
Stockbridge, MA 01262
(413) 298-3926

The Botany Libraries
Harvard University Herbaria Building
22 Divinity Avenue
Cambridge, MA 02138
(617) 495-2366
Note: interlibrary loans

Massachusetts Horticultural Library
300 Massachusetts Avenue
Boston, MA 02155
(617) 536-9280

New England Wild Flower Society, Inc.
Lawrence Newcomb Library
180 Hemenway Road
Framingham, MA 01701
(508) 877-7630

Worcester County Horticultural Society
Tower Hill Botanic Garden
11 French Hill Drive
Boylston, MA 01505
(508) 869-6111

## Michigan

Chippewa Nature Center
400 South Badour Road
Midland, MI 48640
(517) 631-0803

Detroit Garden Center
1460 East Jefferson Avenue
Detroit, MI 48207
(313) 259-6363

Detroit Public Library
5201 Woodward Avenue
Detroit, MI 48202
(313) 833-1400
Note: interlibrary loans

The Dow Gardens
1018 West Main Street
Midland, MI 48640
(517) 631-2677

Fernwood Garden and Nature Center
13988 Range Line Road
Niles, MI 49120
(616) 683-8653

Hidden Lake Gardens
Michigan State University
Tipton, MI 49287
(517) 431-2060

Matthaei Botanical Gardens
University of Michigan
1800 North Dixboro Road
Ann Arbor, MI 48105
(313) 763-7061

## Minnesota

Minnesota Landscape Arboretum
Andersen Horticultural Library
University of Minnesota
3675 Arboretum Drive
Box 39
Chanhassen, MN 55317
(612) 443-2460

Minnesota State Horticultural Society
1970 Folwell Avenue
St. Paul, MN 55108
(612) 624-7752

## Missouri

The Missouri Botanical Garden
4344 Shaw Boulevard
St. Louis, MO 63110
(314) 577-5155
Note: interlibrary loans

## New Jersey

Deep Cut Park Horticultural Center
Elvin McDonald Horticultural Library
352 Red Hill Road
Middletown, NJ 07748
(908) 671-6050

George Griswold Frelinghuysen
Arboretum
Elizabeth Donnell Kay Botanical Library
53 East Hanover Avenue
Morristown, NJ 07962
(201) 326-7600

## New York

Liberty Hyde Bailey Hortorium
462 Mann Library
Cornell University
Ithaca, NY 14853
(607) 255-2131

Brooklyn Botanic Garden
1000 Washington Avenue
Brooklyn, NY 11225
(718) 941-4044

Mary Flagler Cary Arboretum
Institute of Ecosystem Studies
Box AB
Millbrook, NY 12545
(914) 677-5343

Garden Center of Rochester
5 Castle Park
Rochester, NY 14620
(716) 473-5130

Garden Club of America Library
598 Madison Avenue
New York, NY 10022
(212) 753-8287

Horticultural Society of New York
128 West 58th Street

New York, NY 10019
(212) 757-0915
Note: interlibrary loans

New York Botanical Garden
200th Street and Kazimiroff Boulevard
Bronx, NY 10458
(718) 817-8604
Note: interlibrary loans

Planting Fields Arboretum Garden Library
Planting Fields Road
Oyster Bay, NY 11771
(516) 922-9024

## North Carolina

North Carolina Botanical Garden
Addie Williams Totten Library
University of North Carolina
Chapel Hill, NC 27599
(919) 962-0522

## Ohio

Civic Garden Center of Cincinnati
Hoffman Horticultural Library
2715 Reading Road
Cincinnati, OH 45206
(513) 221-0981

Cox Arboretum
6733 Springboro Pike
Dayton, OH 45449
(513) 434-9005

Dawes Arboretum
7770 Jacksontown Road SE
Newark, OH 43056
(614) 323-2355

Garden Center of Greater Cleveland
Eleanor Squire Library
11030 East Boulevard
Cleveland, OH 44106
(216) 721-1600

Gardenview Horticultural Park Library
16711 Pearl Road
Strongsville, OH 44136
(216) 238-6653

Holden Arboretum
Warren H. Corning Library
9500 Sperry Road
Mentor, OH 44060
(216) 256-1110

Kingwood Center Library
900 Park Avenue West
Mansfield, OH 44906
(419) 522-0211
Note: interlibrary loans

Lloyd Library
917 Plum Street
Cincinnati, OH 45202
(513) 721-3707

## Oklahoma

Tulsa Garden Center
2435 South Peoria Avenue
Tulsa, OK 74114
(918) 749-6401

## Oregon

Berry Botanic Garden
11505 SW Summerville Avenue
Portland, OR 97219
(503) 636-4112

## Pennsylvania

Academy of Natural Sciences of
Philadelphia
Stewart Memorial Library
1900 Benjamin Franklin Parkway
Philadelphia, PA 19103
(215) 299-1140
Note: interlibrary loans

Carnegie Museum of Natural History
4400 Forbes Avenue
Pittsburgh, PA 15213
(412) 622-3264
Note: interlibrary loans

Delaware Valley College
Joseph Krauskopf Memorial Library
Route 202
Doylestown, PA 18901
(215) 345-1500

Hunt Institute for Botanial
Documentation
Hunt Botanical Library
Carnegie Mellon University
Frew Street
Pittsburgh, PA 15213
(412) 268-2436
Note: interlibrary loans

Longwood Gardens
Route 1
Kennett Square, PA 19348
(215) 388-6745
Note: interlibrary loans

Pennsylvania Horticultural Society
325 Walnut Street
Philadelphia, PA 19106
(215) 625-8261
Note: interlibrary loans

Pittsburgh Civic Garden Center
1059 Shady Avenue
Pittsburgh, PA 15232
(412) 441-4442

University of Pennsylvania
Morris Arboretum Library
9414 Meadowbrook Avenue
Philadelphia, PA 19118
(215) 247-5777
Note: interlibrary loans

## Tennessee

Memphis Botanic Garden
Sybil G. Malloy Memorial Library
750 Cherry Road
Memphis, TN 38117
(901) 685-1566

Tennessee Botanical Gardens at
Cheekwood
Minnie Ritchey and Joel Owsley Cheek
Library
1200 Forrest Park Drive
Nashville, TN 37205
(615) 353-2148

## Texas

Fort Worth Botanical Garden
3220 Botanic Garden Boulevard
Fort Worth, TX 76107
(817) 870-7682

## Virginia

American Horticultural Society
Harold B. Tukey Memorial Library
7931 East Boulevard Drive
Alexandria, VA 22308
(703) 768-5700

Norfolk Botanical Gardens
Huette Horticultural Library
Azalea Garden Road
Norfolk, VA 23158
(804) 441-5380
Note: interlibrary loans

## Washington

University of Washington
Center for Urban Horticulture
Elisabeth C. Miller Library
Seattle, WA 98195
(206) 543-8616

Yakima Area Arboretum
Walker Horticultural Library
1207 Arboretum Drive
Yakima, WA 98901
(509) 248-7337

## West Virginia

Wheeling Civic Garden Center
Oglebay Park
Wheeling, WV 26003
(304) 242-0665

## Wisconsin

Boerner Botanical Gardens
Whitnall Park
5879 South 92nd Street
Hales Corners, WI 53130
(414) 425-1131

Olbrich Botanical Gardens
Schumacher Library
3330 Atwood Avenue
Madison, WI 53704
(608) 246-5805

# CANADA

## British Columbia

University of British Columbia
Botanical Garden Library
6804 SW Marine Drive
Vancouver, British Columbia V6T 1W5
(604) 822-3928

VanDusen Botanical Garden
5251 Oak Street
Vancouver, British Columbia V6M 4H1
(604) 266-7194

## Ontario

Canadian Agriculture Library
Agriculture Canada
Ottawa, Ontario K1A 0C5
(613) 995-7829
Note: interlibrary loans

Civic Garden Centre
777 Lawrence Avenue East
North York, Ontario M3C 1P2
(416) 397-1340
Note: interlibrary loans

Niagara Parks Commission
School of Horticulture Library
Niagara Parkway North
Niagara Falls, Ontario L2E 6T2
(416) 356-8554

Royal Botanical Gardens
680 Plains Road West
Hamilton, Ontario L8N 3H8
(416) 527-1158
Note: interlibrary loans

## Quebec

Montreal Botanical Garden
4101 Sherbrooke Road East
Montreal, Quebec H1X 2B2
(514) 872-1824
Note: interlibrary loans

# Computer Gardening

Gardening Software and on-line services for the home computer have opened up a new world for gardeners. Numerous plant databases and software packages for keeping garden records, designing your garden, and other applications are now available. Improvements to existing programs and new programs come along all the time.

The dynamic new world of on-line services provides some fascinating sources of free information for gardeners. The major on-line services such as Compuserve, Prodigy, and America Online offer gardening forum areas where gardeners—from all over the country and the world—can "meet" to discuss their favorite pastime and share information. Depending on which service you subscribe to, you can also access the texts of some gardening magazines and check garden reference works.

The Internet and the World Wide Web provide numerous sites from all over the world, both general and specific, for gardeners to visit. These sites often have links to other, related sites that can send you off on an interesting journey through cyberspace in search of information, fellow gardeners, and fun.

The listings below for on-line sites are as current as possible. Cyberspace changes fast, however. The sites listed may no longer be accessible by the time you read this, and there will doubtless be new sites that are not listed here.

## Software

### Software Emporiums

A. C. Burke & Company
2554 Lincoln Boulevard, Suite 1058
Marina Del Rey, CA 90291
(310) 574-2770
Products: software; CD-ROMs; videos; books
Catalogue: free

Cascadia Company
375 Candalaria Boulevard South
Salem, OR 97302
(503) 364-5127

Products: software; CD-ROMs; books
Catalogue: free

### Software

Abracadata
Box 2440
Eugene, OR 97402
(503) 342-3030
(800) 451-4871
Programs: Sprout!™ vegetable garden design program; Design Your Own Home landscaping program
System requirements: DOS 3.3+, Windows 3.1+, or Macintosh

Autodesk
18911 North Creek Parkway, Suite 105
Bothell, WA 98011
(206) 487-2233
(800) 228-3601
Program: Home Series Landscape
CAD program
System requirements: DOS 3.0+

Books That Work
2300 Geng Road
Palo Alto, Ca 94303
(800) 242-4546
CD-ROMs: 3D Landscape;
The Garden Encyclopedia
System requirements: IBM 386+,
Windows 3.1+, 4 MB RAM

Capstan Distributing Company
Box 245
Manchester, IA 52057
(319) 927-5948
Program: English Country Garden
design program
System requirements: IBM DOS 3.1+,
VGA, 640K RAM

Cornucopia Publishing
Box 307
West Boxford, MA 01885
Program: Garden Designer's Helper
design program

The Designing Gardener
Box 837
Harrison, NY 10528
(914) 698-7425
Program: Enter the Perennial database
System requirements: IBM DOS 3.1+

Double-Pawed Software
432 Bigelow Hollow
Eastford, CT 06242
Program: perpetual garden
calendar/journal
System requirements: IBM DOS 3.1+

Elemental Software
2218 North 1200 Street East
Logan, UT 84321
(801) 755-0701
Program: The Plant Doctor
plant disorder diagnosis program
System requirements: IBM 386+,
DOS 3.1+

FLOWERscape
(800) 258-2088 (Windows)
(800) 248-0800 (Macintosh)
Program: FLOWERscape design program
System requirements: IBM: Windows
3.0+, VGA, 4MB RAM; Mac: System
6.0.4+, 256 color driver, 1.5MB

Garden in Time
(800) 228-0705
Program: Garden in Time flower garden
design program
System requirements: IBM 386DX+,
Windows 3.1+, 4MB RAM,
VGA color monitor

Green Thumb Software, Inc.
75 Manhattan Drive
Boulder, CO 80303
(303) 499-1388
(800) 336-3127
Programs: LandDesigner® for Windows
(DOS available); LandDesigner
Multimedia CD-ROM; plant libraries
for LandDesigner
System requirements: IBM: 386SX+,
VGA, 4MB RAM; CD-ROM: IBM
386SX+, Windows 3.1+ VGA,
4MB RAM

J & L Bluebonnet Plantation
Box 559
Hempstead, TX 77445
(409) 826-8975
(800) 204-5614
Program: Gardner Pardner™
record-keeping program

System requirements: IBM 386+,
Windows 3.1+, 4MB RAM

Lifestyle Software Group
63 Orange Street
St. Augustine, FL 32084
(800) 289-1157
Program: Garden Companion CD
System requirements: Windows 3.1

Look Systems
105 Cascadilla Park Road
Ithaca, NY 14850
(607) 277-5665
(800) 698-LOOK
Program: Look Into The Garden
design program
System requirements: IBM 386+,
Windows 3.1+, 4MB RAM,
VGA color monitor

Mindsun
RD 2, Box 710
Andover, NJ 07821
(201) 398-8082
Program: Gardenviews 5.3 plant database
System requirements: IBM  EGA/VGA

MoonOwl Software, Inc.
Box 693
Chelsea, Quebec J0X 1N0
(800) 228-0705
Program: Garden in Time design program
System requirements: IBM 386DX+,
Windows 3.1+, 4MB RAM,
VGA color monitor

Paradise Information, Inc.
Box 1701
East Hampton, NY 11937
(516) 324-2334
(800) 544-2721
Program: CHIP2 computerized
horticultural information planner

Plant Care Information Systems, Inc.
500 SE 17th Street
Ft. Lauderdale, FL 33316
(954) 522-1334
(800) 498-8383
Program: Plant Care 2000 for house-
plants care

Saroh
Box 8375
Springfield, IL 62791
Program: plant care and propagation
database
System requirements: DOS 3.1+,
10MB hard disk storage

Shapeware Corporation
520 Pike Street, Suite 1800
Seattle, WA 98101
(206) 521-4500
Program: Visio Home 3.0
System requirements: Windows 3.1

Sierra Online
Box 3403
Salinas, CA 93912
(800) 757-7707
Program: LandDesigner 3D
System requirements: 486, Windows
5.0+, VGA, CD-ROM, at least 8 MB
RAM

Surgicad Corporation
115 Etna Road
Lebanon, NH 03766
(800) 522-6695
Program: InfoSavers' floral screen saver
System requirements: Windows 3.1+

Terrace Software
Box 271
Medford, MA 02155
(617) 396-0382
Programs: Mum's the Word (Mac) design
program; Florafile (IBM) plant database

## World Wide Web and Other On-Line Sources

### General World Wide Web and Internet Sites

*The sites listed below are general gardening areas that contain a lot of useful gardening information. Most offer book reviews, new product information, seasonal advice, areas for posting and answering queries, and the like. Some sites also offer unique information. For example, within the GardenNet site you can jump to useful state listings of public gardens and garden events. General gardening sites also include many hypertext links to other Web pages and Internet gardening sites. Some of these sites are sponsored by commercial entities, while others are put together by individuals or volunteers.*

Garden Gate
http://www.prairienet.org/ag/garden/
homepage.html

Garden Gate at SunSITE
http://sunsite.unc.edu/garden-gate/

Gardening (Leisure and Recreation)
http://www.einet.net/galaxy/Leisure-and-Recreation/Gardening.html

Gardening Launch Pad
http://www.tpoint.net/neighbor/

Gardening List WWW
http://www.cog.brown.edu/gardening/

GardenNet from Wayside Gardens
http://www.olympus.net/gardens/
welcome.html

The Garden Patch
http://mirror.wwa.com/mirror/garden/
patch/htm

The Garden Spider's Web
http://www.gardenweb.com/spdrsweb/

GardenWeb
http://www.gardenweb.com/

General Gardening Sites
http://www.btw.com/urls/garden/
general.htm

Links to Gardening-Related Home Pages
http://weber.u.washington.edu/~trav/
garden_links.html

Master Gardener files at Texas A&M
http://leviathan.tamu.edu:70/1s/mg

My Garden
http://www.hal-pc.org/~trobb/horticul.html

The Trellis: Garden Links on the Internet
http://wormsway.com/trellis.html

The Virtual Garden from Time-Life Inc.
http://www.timeinc.com/vg/

### Interesting Web Pages

*The sites listed below are Web pages oriented directly to specific interests, such as bonsai. Many of these pages are linked to the general areas listed above; many also contain links to other Web sites. Most of the sites listed below are run by volunteers or organizations. Some are commercial or sponsored areas that provide interesting information along with advertising. This list is by no means complete—new sites arise daily. For reasons of space, local and personal home pages have not been listed. However, there are separate listings below of sites for books and magazines, botanic gardens, flower photos, bulletin boards, mailing lists, newsgroups, and USDA Cooperative Extension Service information servers.*

## SPECIAL INTEREST WEB PAGES

American Bamboo Society Home Page
http://www.halcyon.com/plrabbit/
bamboo/abs.html

American Bonsai Society Home Page
http://www.paonline.com/abs

American Rose Society Home Page
http://www.ars.org

Bonsai Home Page
http://www.pass.wayne.edu/~dan/

Books That Work Complete Guide to
Garden Stuff
http://www.btw.com/garden.htm

Botany Department at the University of
Georgia
http://dogwood.botany.uga.edu/

The Carnivorous Plant Archive Page
http://randomaccess.unm.edu/www/cp/
cparchive.html

Carnivorous Plants Database
http://www.hpl.hp.com/bot/cp_home

City Farmer: Canada's Office of Urban
Agriculture
http://unixg.ubc.ca:880/cityfarm/
gardsites65.html

Cornell University Fruit and Vegetable
Information
gopher://gopher.cce.cornell.edu/11/cenet/
submenu/fruit-veg/

The Cyber-Plantsman
http://mirror.www.com/mirror/garden/
cyberplt.htm

Designing Gardens for Butterflies
http://www.gardenweb.com/bbg/
butterfl.html

Don't Panic Eat Organic
http://www/rain.org/~sals/my.html

Daylilies Growing along the Information
Highway
http://www.daylilies.com/daylilies

Earth Matters
http://192.216.191.71/ng/earth/earth.htm

Expo Garden Tours
http://www.olympus.net/gardens/
expotour.htm

Friends of the Daylilies
http://www.primenet.com/utilehr/daylily.
html

Garden Catalogs List
http://www.cog.brown.edu/gardening

Garden Earth
http://www.interworld.com.au/garden/

Gardening for Vegetarians
http://www.veg.org/veg/Orgs/VegSocUK/
Info/gardenin.html

Garden South Africa
http://www.pix.za/garden/

Gardens & Gardening
http://www.cfn.cs.dal.ca/Recreation/Gard
ening/G_G_Home.html

General Gardening Catalogs and
Supplies
http://www.btw.com/urls/garden/
vendors.htm

Herbs & Spices
http://www.teleport.com/~ronl/herbs/
herbs.html

Horticulture Solutions
http://www.ag.uiuc.edu/~robsond/
solutions/hort.html

International Camellia Society Home
Page
http://www.med_rzuni—sb.de/med_fak/
physiol2/camellia/home.htm

Irises
http://alepho.clarke.edu/~djoyce/Iris

Hortus—A Gardening Journal
http://www.kc3ltd.co.uk/business/hortus.
html

National Museum of Natural History,
Smithsonian Institution, Department of
Botany
http://nmnhwww.si.edu/departments/
botany.html

New York Botanical Garden Library catalogue on Telnet
librisc.nybg.org

Northern Gardening
http://www/geocities.com/BainForest/1329

The Orchid House
http://cougar.uwaterloo.co/orchids.html

OrchidWeb
http://www.pathfinder.com/vg/Gardens/
AOS

Ortho Online
http://www.ortho.com

Palm trees information
http://www.geopages.com/TheTropics/
1811/

Pinetree Garden Seeds
http://www.olympus.net/gardens/
pinetree.htm

PrairieNet
http://sunsite.unc.edu/gardengate/www.
hort.htm

Pukeiti Rhododendron Trust
http://pluto.taranaki.ac.nz/pukeiti/
welcome.html

The Rhododendron Page
http://haven.los.com/~mckenzie/rhodo05
.html

Rooftop Gardens
http://unixg.ubc.ca:880/cityfarm/rooftop5
9.html

The Rose Page
http://www.mc.edu/~nettles/rofaq/
rofaq-top.html

The Seven Wonders: The Hanging
Gardens of Babylon
http://ce.ecn.purdue/edu/~ashmawy/
7WW/gardens.html

The Succulent Plant Page
http://www.graylab.oc.uk/usr/hogkiss/
succule.htm

Sunshine Farm & Gardens
http://mirror.wwwa.com/mirror/busdir/
sunshine/sunshine.htm

Tele-Garden Robotic Gardening Project
http://www.usc.edu/dept/garden

Time-Life Complete Gardener Encyclopedia
http://www.timeinc.com/vg/TimeLife/CG/
vg-search.html

USDA Growing Zone Finder
http://www.timeinc.com/cgibin/
vgzonefinder

University of Connecticut
http://florawww.eeb.uconn.edu/
homepage.htm

University of Florida Herbarium
http://nabalu.flas.ufl.edu/flashome.html

The Weekend Gardener
http://www.chestnut-sw.com

## BOOKS AND GARDENING MAGAZINES ON LINE

*A number of Web sites offer book reviews; some also provide ordering information. The magazines listed here include both the on-line versions of print gardening magazines and some new "e-zines" available only on line.*

The American Cottage Gardener Home Page
http://www.olympus.net/gardens/acg.htm

The Cyber-Plantsman magazine on Garden Web
http://www.gardenweb.com/cyberplt/

The Garden Bookshelf of the Virtual Garden
http://www.timeinc.com/vg/
or
http://pathfinder.com/@@91Z2X2HbdAI
AQLRr/vg/Bookshelf/index.html

The Garden Gate: The Gardener's Reading Room
http://prairienet.org/ag/garden/
readroom.htm

The Gardening Bookshelf Page
http://www.atlgarden.com/books.html

Garden Literature Press
http://www.olympus.net/gardens/gardlit.
htm

GardenNet Book Reviews
http://www.olympus.net/gardens/review.
htm

GardenNet's *The Ardent Gardener* magazine
http://www.olympus.net/gardens/gmg.htm

GardenNet's *The Ardent Gardener Over The Fence* e-zine
http://www.olympus.net/gardens/otf.htm

The Gourmet Gardener—Books
http://metroux.tetrobbs.com/tgg/books.htm

*Homeground* Newsletter on the Virtual Garden
http://pathfinder.com/@@95CA29Flc
QIAQG9s/vg/Magazine-
Rack/Homeground

*Hortus—A Gardening Journal*
http://www.ke3ltd.co.uk/business/hortus.
html

*Southern Garden Gate* for Florida Gardeners
http://www.gate.net/good-green-fun/
ggp_1.htm

*Southern Living* magazine on the Virtual Garden
http://pathfinder.com/@@1UflcBFEdAIA
QHdv/vg/Magazine-Rack/SoLiving

*Sunset* magazine on the Virtual Garden
http://pathfinder.com/@@@soLSIFbdwIA
QNZu/vg/Magazine-Rack/Sunset

## BOTANIC GARDENS ON LINE

American Association of Botanical Gardens and Arboreta (AABGA)
http://192.104.39.4/AABGA/aabga1.html

Australian National Botanic Gardens
http://155.187.10.12:80/anbg.html

Brooklyn Botanic Garden
http://mirror.wwa.com/mirror/orgs/bbg/
bbg.htm

Devonian Botanic Garden
http://gause.biology/ualberta.ca/
devonian.hp/dbg.html

Directory of Australian Botanic Gardens
and Arboreta
http://osprey.erin.gov.au/chabg/bg-dir/
bg-dir.html

Georgeson Botanical Garden
http://www.lter.alaska.edu/html/gbg.html

Hello Riviera #2: The Hambury Botanic
Gardens
http://www.doit.it/News/HelloRiviera/
Giugno/hambury.uk.html

Missouri Botanic Garden
http://straylight.tamu.edu/MoBot/
welcome.html

Claude Monet's Garden at Giverny
http://www.monash.edu.au/visarts/diva/
monet.html

New York Botanical Garden
http://www.pathfinder.com/vg/Gardens/
NYBG/index.html

Park and Tilford Gardens, North Vancouver
http://www.fleethouse.com/fhcanada/
ptg_home.htm

Royal Botanic Gardens, Kew
http://www.rbgkew.org.uk/

University of Delaware Botanic Gardens
gopher://bluehen.ags.udel.edu:71/hh/.
botanic_garden/botanicg.html

## GARDENING PHOTOS ON LINE

The Armchair Gardener
http://www.mailer.fsu.edu/~dansley

Australian flora and fauna
http://rs306.ccs.bbk.ac.uk/flora/
welcome.html

Botany Image Archive
http://muse.bio.cornell.edu/images/

Daylilies Online (experimental project)
http://www.assumption.edu/HTML/
daylilies/about.html

DIVA (Digital Images for the Visual Arts)
gardens and landscape design
http://www.monash.edu.au/diva/gardens.
htm

Electronic Orchid Greenhouse
http://yakko.cs.wmich.edu/~charles/
orchids/greenhouse.html

Flowers pictures archive
http://sunsite.sut.ac.jp/multimed/pics/
flowers/

Hungarian flora and fauna
http://www.unigiessen.de/~gdg3/mud/
firstl.html

Madagascar flora and fauna
http://lalo.inria.fr/~andry/Mada.html

The Rose Gallery
http://www.halcyon.com/cirsium/
rosegal/welcom.htm

WWW Server of the University of Costa
Rica
http://www.ucr.ac.cr/

## Bulletin Boards, Mailing Lists, Discussion Lists, and Newsgroups

Alpines and rock gardening (ALPINE-L)
LISTSERV@hearn.nic.surfnet.nl

Aroids (AROID-L)
LISTPROC@MOBOT.ORG

Gesneriad bulletin board
listproc@lists.Colorado.edu
Greenhouses (HGA-L)
LISTSERV@ULKYVM.LOUISVILLE.EDU

Herbs
LISTSERV@vm.ege.edu.tr
LISTSERV@trearn.bitnet

Home Composting discussion list
(COMPOST)
LISTPROC@listproc.wsu.edu

Home gardening e-mail list
LISTSERV@UKCC.UKY.EDU

Residential gardening (RES-GARD)
LISTSERV@TAMVM1.TAMU.EDU

Gardening newsgroups via Usenet
rec.gardens
red.gardens.orchids
rec.gardens.roses

## USDA COOPERATIVE EXTENSION SERVICE INFORMATION SERVERS

*This listing is adapted from USDA listings. The detailed list is available from the USDA at:*
http://eos.esusda.gov/partners/ceslocs.htm.

USDA Extension Service
gopher://esusda.gov/1/

Alabama Extension System
http://www.acenet.auburn.edu

Arizona Agriculture and Resource
Economics Extension
http://ag.arizona.edu/AREC/exthome.html

Colorado State Cooperative Extension
On Line
http://www.colostate.educ/Depts/CoopExt/

Delaware College of Agricultural
Sciences (AGINFO)
http://bluehen.ags.undel.edu

Florida Institute of Food and Agricultural
Sciences (IFAS)
http://bnv.ifas.ufl.edu

Illinois Cooperative Extension Service
http://www.ag.uiuc.edu

Indiana—Purdue University Cooperative
Extension
gopher://hermes.ecn.purdue.edu

Iowa State University Cooperative
Extension
http://www.exnex.iastate.edu/

Kansas State University, Extension
Systems and Agricultural Research
Programs (ESARP)
http://www.oznet.ksu.edu/

Kentucky—University of Kentucky
College of Agriculture
http://www.uky.edu/CampusGuide/uk.html

Michigan State University
http://lep.cl.msu.edu/msueimp/

Minnesota National Extension
gopher://tinman.mes.umn.edu

Mississippi—University Extension,
Mississippi State University
http://www.ces.msstate.edu/

Missouri—University Extension, Missouri
http://etcs.ext.missouri.edu:70/

Nebraska Institute of Agriculture and
Natural Resources (IANR)
http://unlvm.unl.edu

New Jersey—Rutgers Cooperative
Extension
http://aesop.rutgers.edu/~huntzinger/rce.
htm
New York—Cornell University
Cooperative Extension Service
http://empire.cse.cornell.edu/

North Carolina Cooperative Extension
Service
http://www.ces.ncsu.edu

North Dakota State University Extension
Service
gopher://ndsuext.nodak.edu

Oregon Extension Service Information
System
http://gopher://gopher.oes.orst.edu

Pennsylvania—PENPages
gopher://penpages.psu.edu

Texas A&M University (DOS)
http://leviathan.tamu.edu

Utah State University Extension
http://ext.us.edu:80/

Virginia Cooperative Extension (VCE)
gopher://gopher.ext.vt.edu

Washington State University College of
Agriculture and Home Economics
gopher://cru1.cahe.wsu.edu

Wisconsin—University of Wisconsin
Extension
gopher://wisdom.uwex.edu:70/1

# Botanical Gardens and Arboretums

THE LISTING BELOW *is a somewhat arbitrary compilation of large or notable botanical, estate, and display gardens. For reasons of space, only arboretums with extensive or very unusual display gardens have been included. (Information about All-America Rose Selections display gardens is in chapter 2.) If you're planning a visit to any botanical garden, be sure to call ahead. Hours and admission fees (if any) vary seasonally, as do peak displays.*

*For an extensive and detailed listing of many North American gardens open to the public, see the two invaluable volumes by Everitt L. Miller and Jay S. Cohen: The American Garden Guidebook (NY: M. Evans, 1987) and The American Garden Guidebook West (NY: M. Evans, 1989).*

## Botanical Gardens and Arboretums by State and Province

### Alabama

Bellingrath Gardens and Home
12401 Bellingrath Gardens Road
Theodore, AL 36582
(205) 973-2217
Notable plantings: azaleas; camellias; chrysanthemums; roses; tulips

Birmingham Botanical Gardens
2612 Lane Park Road
Birmingham, AL 35223
(205) 879-1227
Notable plantings: roses; lilies

### Arizona

The Arizona–Sonora Desert Musuem
2021 North Kinney Road
Tucson, AZ 85743
(520) 883-2702
Notable plantings: plants of the Sonoran Desert

The Boyce Thompson Southwestern Arboretum
Box AB
Superior, AZ 85273
(602) 689-2811
Notable plantings: plants of the Sonoran Desert

The Desert Botanical Garden
1201 North Galvin Parkway
Phoenix, AZ 85008
(602) 941-1225
Notable plantings: plants
of the Sonoran Desert

## Arkansas

Arkansas State Capitol Rose Garden
Information Services Division
State Capitol
Little Rock, AR 72201
(501) 371-5164
Notable plantings: All-American Rose
Selections garden; over 1,200 rosebushes

## California

All-America Gladiolus Selections
11734 Road 33$^{1}/_{2}$
Madera, CA 93638
(209) 645-5329
Notable plantings: gladioli

Balboa Park
Laurel Street and 6th Avenue
San Diego, CA 92101
(619) 236-5984
Notable plantings: Casa del Rey Moro
garden; Alcazar garden

Berkeley Rose Garden
Euclid Avenue and Bayview Place
Berkeley, CA 94720
(415) 644-6530
Notable plantings: 4,000 rosebushes

Descanso Gardens
1418 Descanso Drive
La Cañada Flintridge, CA 91011
(818) 952-4400
Notable plantings: camellias; roses

Exposition Park Rose Garden
701 State Drive

Los Angeles, CA 90012
(213) 748-4772
Notable plantings: over 12,000
rosebushes

Filoli
Cañada Road
Woodside, CA 94062
(415) 364-2880
Notable plantings: rhododendrons;
roses; spring bulbs

Golden Gate Park. See Strybing
Arboretum

Hearst San Simeon State Historical
Monument
Micheltorena and Santa Barbara Streets
San Simeon, CA 93452
(619) 452-1950
Notable plantings: formal gardens

The Huntington Botanical Gardens
1151 Oxford Road
San Marino, CA 91108
(818) 405-2100
Notable plantings: fifteen
specialty gardens

Los Angeles State and County Arboretum
301 North Baldwin Avenue
Arcadia, CA 91007
(818) 446-8251
Notable plantings: begonias; tropical
plants; Australian plants; water garden

Mildred E. Mathias Botanical Garden
University of California at Los Angeles
405 Hilgard Avenue
Los Angeles, CA 90024
(213) 835-3620
Notable plantings: desert plants

Hortense Miller Garden
3035 Bert Drive
Laguna Beach, CA 92651

(714) 497-7692
Notable plantings: over 1,200
subtropical and native species

Moorten Botanic Garden
1702 South Palm Canyon Drive
Palm Springs, CA 92264
(619) 327-6555
Notable plantings: desert plants

Morcom Amphitheater of Roses
1520 Lakeside Drive
Oakland, CA 94612
(415) 273-3090
Notable plantings: over 8,000 rosebushes

Pageant of Roses Garden
3900 South Workman Mill Road
Whittier, CA 90608
(213) 699-0921
Notable plantings: over 7,000 rosebushes

Theodore Payne Foundation
10459 Tuxford Street
Sun Valley, CA 91352
(818) 768-1802
Notable plantings: wildflowers

Quail Botanical Gardens
230 Quail Gardens Drive
Encinitas, CA 92024
(619) 436-3036
Notable plantings: bamboos;
cycads; palms

Rancho Santa Ana Botanic Garden
1500 North College Avenue
Claremont, CA 91711
(909) 625-8767
Notable plantings: California-native
plants

San Diego Zoo
Box 551
Balboa Park
San Diego, CA 92112

(619) 231-1515
Notable plantings: over 6,500 exotic
species

Santa Barbara Botanic Garden
1212 Mission Canyon Road
Santa Barbara, CA 93105
(805) 682-4726
Notable plantings: California-native
plants

South Coast Botanical Garden
26300 Crenshaw Boulevard
Palos Verdes Peninsula, CA 90274
(310) 544-6815
Notable plantings: over 2,000 species

Strybing Arboretum and Botanical
Gardens
Golden Gate Park
9th Avenue and Lincoln Way
San Francisco, CA 94122
(415) 661-1316
Notable plantings: geographic collections
from Australia, New Zealand, Chile, and
Cape Province

University of California at Berkeley
Botanical Garden
200 Centennial Drive
Berkeley, CA 94720
(510) 642-3343
Notable plantings: California-native
plants

University of California at Irvine
Arboretum
Irvine, CA 92717
(714) 856-5833
Notable plantings: flowering bulbs

## Colorado

Denver Botanic Gardens
1005 York Street
Denver, CO 80206

(303) 331-4000
Notable plantings: alpine and
rock garden plants

## Connecticut

Audubon Fairchild Garden of the
National Audubon Society
613 Riversville Road
Greenwich, CT 06831
(203) 869-5272
Notable plantings: wildflowers;
medicinal plants

Bartlett Arboretum
University of Connecticut
151 Brookdale Road
Stamford, CT 06903
(203) 322-6971
Notable plantings: dwarf conifers;
flowering shrubs; ericaceous plants

Connecticut College Arboretum
5625 Connecticut College
New London, CT 06320
(203) 447-7700
Notable plantings: northeastern-
native plants

Elizabeth Park
25 Stonington Street
Hartford, CT 06106
(203) 722-6541
Notable plantings: over 15,000 rosebushes

## Delaware

Nemours Mansion and Gardens
1600 Rockland Road
Wilmington, DE 19803
(302) 651-6905
Notable plantings: formal gardens

Winterthur Museum and Gardens
Winterthur, DE 19735
(302) 888-4600

(800) 448-3883
Notable plantings: azaleas; daffodils;
rhododendrons; tulips

## District of Columbia

Dumbarton Oaks Gardens
1703 32nd Street NW
Washington, DC 20007
(202) 342-3200
Notable plantings: Italian gardens

Kenilworth Aquatic Gardens
National Park Service
Anacostia Avenue and Douglass Street
NE
Washington, DC 20019
(202) 426-6905
Notable plantings: aquatic gardens

United States Botanic Garden
245 1st Street SW
Washington, DC 20024
(202) 225-8333
Notable plantings: begonias; orchids;
annuals

United States National Arboretum
3501 New York Avenue NE
Washington, DC 20002
(202) 475-4815
Notable plantings: herbs; Japanese garden; bonsai; azaleas; rhododendrons

## Florida

Fairchild Tropical Garden
10901 Old Cutler Road
Miami, FL 33156
(305) 667-1651
Notable plantings: tropical plants;
bromeliads; ferns; orchids; palms

Flamingo Gardens
3750 Flamingo Road
Fort Lauderdale, FL 33330

(305) 473-2955
Notable plantings: Heliconia species

Florida Cypress Gardens
State Route 540
Cypress Gardens, FL 33880
(813) 324-2111
Notable plantings: over 8,000 plant
species

H. P. Leu Botanical Gardens
1730 North Forest Avenue
Orlando, FL 32803
(407) 849-2620
Notable plantings: camellias

Orchid Jungle
26715 SW 157th Avenue
Homestead, FL 33030
(305) 247-4824
Notable plantings: orchids

Marie Selby Botanical Garden
811 South Palm Avenue
Sarasota, FL 34236
(941) 366-5731
Notable plantings: tropical plants;
epiphytes

Sunken Gardens
1825 4th Street North
St. Petersburg, FL 33704
(813) 896-3186
Notable plantings: tropical and
subtropical species

Vizcaya
3251 South Miami Avenue
Miami, FL 33129
(305) 854-6559
Notable plantings: classical Italian garden

## Georgia

Atlanta Botanical Garden
Piedmont Park

Atlanta, GA 30309
(404) 876-5859
Notable plantings: over 3,500 species

Callaway Gardens
Pine Mountain, GA 31822
(404) 663-5186
(800) 282-8181
Notable plantings: azaleas; hollies;
chrysanthemums

State Botanical Garden of Georgia
2450 South Milledge Avenue
Athens, GA 30605
(404) 542-1244
Notable plantings: roses; wildflowers;
spring bulbs; azaleas

## Hawaii

Hawaii Tropical Botanical Garden
Onomea Bay
Hilo, HI 96721
(808) 964-5233
Notable plantings: over 1,800
tropical species

Honolulu Botanic Gardens
50 North Vineyard Boulevard
Honolulu, HI 96817
(808) 533-3406
Notable plantings: five separate
gardens; orchids

Harold Lyon Arboretum
University of Hawaii, Manoa
3860 Manoa Road
Honolulu, HI 96822
(808) 988-3177
Notable plantings: over 4,200
tropical species

National Tropical Botanical Garden
Halima Road
Lawai, HI 96765
(808) 332-7324

Notable plantings: Hawaii-native plants;
rare and endangered tropical plants

**Waimea Falls Park Arboretum and
Botanical Garden**
59-864 Kamehameha Highway
Haleiwa, Oahu, HI 96712
(808) 638-8655
Notable plantings: over 5,000 Hawaii-
native plants; thirty specialty gardens

## Illinois

**Chicago Botanic Garden**
Box 400, Lake–Cook Road
Glencoe, IL 60022
(708) 835-5440
Notable plantings: Illinois oak woodland;
greenhouse displays

**Garfield Park Conservatory**
300 North Central Park Boulevard
Chicago, IL 60605
(312) 533-1281
Notable plantings: over 5,000
plant varieties

**Lincoln Memorial Garden and Nature
Center**
2301 East Lake Drive
Springfield, IL 62707
(217) 529-1111
Notable plantings: Illinois-native plants

**Morton Arboretum**
Route 53
Lisle, IL 60532
(708) 968-0074
Notable plantings: flowering crab apples;
magnolias; lilacs

**Washington Park Botanical Garden**
Fayette and Chatham Road
Springfield, IL 63705
(217) 787-2540
Notable plantings: over 1,200 species

## Indiana

**Christie Woods of Ball State University**
200 West University Avenue
Muncie, IN 47306
(317) 285-8838
Notable plantings: orchids

**Eli Lilly Botanical Garden of the
Indianapolis Museum of Art**
1200 West 38th Street
Indianapolis, IN 46208
(317) 923-1331
Notable plantings: perennials and annuals

## Iowa

**Arie den Boer Arboretum**
Des Moines Water Works Park
408 Fleur Drive
Des Moines, IA 50321
(515) 283-8791
Notable plantings: flowering crab apples

**Des Moines Botanical Center**
909 East River Drive
Des Moines, IA 50316
(515) 283-4148
Notable plantings: begonias; bonsai;
orchids

**Dubuque Arboretum and Botanical
Gardens**
3125 West 32nd Street
Dubuque, IA 52001
(319) 556-2100
Notable plantings: All-America
Selections displays

**Ewing Park Lilac Arboretum**
3226 University
Des Moines, IA 50311
(515) 271-4700
Notable plantings: over 200 lilac varieties

Iowa Arboretum
Route 1, Box 44A
Madrid, IA 50156
(515) 795-3216
Notable plantings: rare and endangered
plants

Iowa State University Horticultural
Garden
Elwood Drive and Haber Road
Iowa State University
Ames, IA 50001
(515) 294-2751
Notable plantings: All-American Rose
Selections test garden

Stampe Lilac Garden
2816 Eastern Avenue
Davenport, IA 52803
(319) 326-7812
Notable plantings: over 170 lilac varieties

## Kansas

Bartlett Arboretum
301 North Line
Belle Plaine, KS 67013
(316) 488-3451
Notable plantings: tulips

Botanica, The Wichita Gardens
701 North Amidon
Wichita, KS 67203
(316) 264-0448
Notable plantings: Shakespeare garden;
xeriscape garden; juniper collection

Dyck Arboretum of the Plains
Hesston College
Box 3000
Hesston, KS 67062
(316) 327-8127
Notable plantings: prairie plants and
wildflowers

Meade Park Botanic Gardens
124 North Fillmore
Topeka, KS 66606
(913) 232-5493
Notable plantings: 6,000 annuals

E. F. A. Reinisch Rose and Test Gardnes
Gage Park
4320 West 10th Street
Topeka, KS 66604
(913) 272-6150
Notable plantings: All American Rose
Selection display and test garden; over
6,500 rosebushes

## Kentucky

The Bernheim Forest, Arboretum, and
Nature Center
Route 245
Clermont, KY 40110
(502) 543-2451
Notable plantings: azaleas; crab apples;
viburnums; redbuds

## Louisiana

American Rose Society Garden
8877 Jefferson Paige Road
Box 3000
Shreveport, LA 71130
(318) 938-5402
Notable plantings: old roses; camellias

Hodges Gardens
Box 900
Many, LA 71449
(318) 586-3523
Notable plantings: old roses;
herb garden

Jungle Gardens
General Delivery
Avery Island, LA 70513
(318) 365-8173

Notable plantings: azaleas; bamboos;
camellias; water lilies

Live Oaks Gardens and Joseph Jefferson
Home
284 Rip Van Winkle Road
New Iberia, LA 70561
(318) 367-3485
Notable plantings: Alhambra fountain
garden; camellias

Longue Vue House and Gardens
7 Bamboo Road
New Orleans, LA 70124
(504) 488-5488
Notable plantings: Spanish Court water
garden

Rosedown Plantation
State Highway 10
St. Francisville, LA 70775
(504) 635-3332
Notable plantings: formal French gardens

Zemurray Gardens
Route 1, Box 201
Loranger, LA 70446
(504) 878-6731
Notable plantings: azaleas

## Maine

Merryspring
Merryspring Foundation
Box 893
Camden, ME 04843
(207) 236-9046
Notable plantings: Maine-native plants

Wild Gardens of Acadia
Acadia National Park
Sieur de Monts Spring
Mount Desert Island
Bar Harbor, ME 04609
(207) 228-3338
Notable plantings: wildflowers

## Maryland

Baltimore Conservatory
Druid Hill Park
Gwynns Falls Parkway and McCulloh
Street
Baltimore, MD 21217
(301) 396-0180
Notable plantings: aroids;
orchids; tropicals

Brookside Gardens
1500 Glenallan Avenue
Wheaton, MD 20902
(301) 949-8231
Notable plantings: 2,000 taxa; 10,000
woody specimens

Cylburn Garden Center
4915 Greenspring Avenue
Baltimore, MD 21209
(410) 367-2217
Notable plantings: wildflowers;
perennials

Ladew Topiary Gardens
3535 Jarretsville Pike
Monkton, MD 21111
(410) 557-9570
Notable plantings: topiary

## Massachusetts

Arnold Arboretum of Harvard University
125 Arborway
Jamaica Plain, MA 02130
(617) 524-1718
Notable plantings: 15,000 north temperate zone trees and shrubs

Ashumet Holly Reservation
Massachusetts Audubon Society
286 Ashumet Road
East Falmouth, MA 02536
(508) 563-6390
Notable plantings: hollies

Barnard's Inn Farm
Route 1, Box 538
Vineyard Haven, MA 02568
(508) 693-0925
Notable plantings: over 1,400 species

Berkshire Garden Center
Routes 102 and 183
Box 826
Stockbridge, MA 01262
(413) 298-3926
Notable plantings: daylilies; primroses;
perennials

Garden in the Woods
New England Wild Flower Society, Inc.
180 Hemenway Road
Framingham, MA 01701
(508) 877-7630
(617) 237-4924
Notable plantings: wildflowers

The Lyman Estate
185 Lyman Street
Waltham, MA 02154
(617) 891-7095
Notable plantings: greenhouses

Newbury Perennial Gardens
65 Orchard Street
Byfield, MA 01922
(508) 462-1144
Notable plantings: perennials

Sedgwick Gardens
572 Essex Street
Beverly, MA 01915
(617) 922-1536
Notable plantings: hostas; peonies

## Michigan

W. J. Beal—Garfield Botanical Gardens
Michigan State University
East Lansing, MI 48823
(517) 355-0348

Notable plantings: over 5,500
plant varieties

Cranbrook House and Gardens
380 Lone Pine Road
Bloomfield Hills, MI 48013
(313) 645-3149
Notable plantings: formal gardens

Fernwood Garden and Nature Center
13988 Range Line Road
Niles, MI 49120
(616) 695-6491
Notable plantings: prairie plants

Grand Hotel
Mackinac Island, MI 49757
(906) 847-3331
Notable plantings: Victorian gardens

Matthaei Botanical Gardens
University of Michigan
1800 North Dixboro Road
Ann Arbor, MI 48105
(313) 998-7061
Notable plantings: roses; herbs; rock
garden; perennials

Anna Scripps Whitcomb Conservatory
Belle Isle
Detroit, MI 48207
(313) 267-7133
Notable plantings: formal gardens;
orchids

## Minnesota

Eloise Butler Wildflower Garden and Bird
Sanctuary
3800 Bryant Avenue South
Minneapolis, MN 55409
(612) 348-5702
Notable plantings: over 500 species

Minnesota Landscape Arboretum
3675 Arboretum Drive

Box 39
Chanhassen, MN 55317
(612) 443-2460
Notable plantings: hostas

Schell Mansion and Gardens
Jefferson Street South
New Ulm, MN 56073
(507) 354-5528
Notable plantings: formal
Victorian gardens

## Mississippi

Beauvoir
200 West Beach Boulevard
Biloxi, MS 39531
(601) 388-1313
Notable plantings: azaleas; camellias

Crosby Arboretum
1801 Goodyear Boulevard
Picayune, MS 39466
(501) 798-6961
Notable plantings: regional native plants

Mynelle Gardens
4738 Clinton Boulevard
Jackson, MS 39209
(601) 922-4011
Notable plantings: azaleas; camellias;
daylilies; roses; water lilies

## Missouri

The Missouri Botanical Garden
4344 Shaw Boulevard
St. Louis, MO 63166
(314) 577-5100
Notable plantings: roses; Japanese garden; water lilies

Shaw Arboretum
State Highway 100
Box 38
Gray Summit, MO 63039

(314) 742-3512
Notable plantings: prairie plants

Laura Conyers Smith Municipal Rose
Garden
5605 East 63rd Street
Kansas City, MO 64130
(816) 561-9710
Notable plantings: All American Rose
Selections garden; 4,000 rosebushes

## New Hampshire

Fuller Gardens
10 Willow Avenue
North Hampton, NH 03862
(603) 964-5414
Notable plantings: roses; hostas

## New Jersey

Leonard J. Buck Gardens
Somerset County Park Commission
Layton Road
Farills, NJ 07931
(201) 234-2677
Notable plantings: rock garden

Colonial Park
RD 1, Box 49B
Mettler's Road
Somerset, NJ 08873
(201) 873-2459
Notable plantings: 4,000 rosebushes

Duke Gardens
State Route 206 South
Somerville, NJ 08876
(201) 722-3700
Notable plantings: 11 greenhouse
gardens

George Griswold Frelinghuysen
Arboretum
53 East Hanover Avenue
Morristown, NJ 07962

(201) 326-7600
Notable plantings: azaleas; bulbs; ferns;
peonies; rhododendrons

Presby Memorial Iris Gardens
474 Upper Mountain Avenue
Montclair, NJ 07043
(201) 783-5974
Notable plantings: irises

Skylands Botanical Gardens
Sloatsburg Road
Ringwood, NJ 07456
(201) 962-7031
Notable plantings: daffodils; tulips

## New Mexico

Living Desert Botanical State Park
1504 Skyline Drive
Carlsbad, NM 88220
(505) 887-5516
Notable plantings: Chihuahuan
desert-native plants

## New York

Boscobel Restoration
Route 9D
Garrison, NY 10524
(914) 265-3638
Notable plantings: English garden; herbs;
orangery; roses

Brooklyn Botanic Garden
1000 Washington Avenue
Brooklyn, NY 11225
(718) 622-4433
Notable plantings: Japanese garden;
flowering cherry trees; roses

Mary Flagler Cary Arboretum
Institute of Ecosystem Studies
Box AB, Millbrook, NY 12545
(914) 677-5343
Notable plantings: ferns; perennials

The Cloisters
Fort Tryon Park
New York, NY 10040
(212) 923-3700
Notable plantings: three cloister gardens

Cornell Plantations
One Plantations Road
Ithaca, NY 14850
(607) 255-3020
Notable plantings: New York-native
plants

Highland Botanical Park
180 Reservoir Avenue
Rochester, NY 14620
(716) 244-8079
Notable plantings: lilacs; hollies

International Bonsai Arboretum
1070 Martin Road
West Henrietta, NY 14586
(716) 334-2595
Notable plantings: bonsai

New York Botanical Garden
200th Street and Kazimiroff Boulevard
Bronx, NY 10458
(718) 817-8700
Notable plantings: begonias; daylilies;
ferns; orchids; rock garden; roses

Old Westbury Gardens
70 Old Westbury Road
Old Westbury, NY 11568
(516) 333-0048
Notable plantings: cottage garden; 300
European beeches; evergreen garden

Planting Fields Arboretum
Planting Fields Road
Oyster Bay, NY 11771
(516) 922-9206
Notable plantings: azaleas;
rhododendrons; conservatories

Sonnenberg Gardens
151 Charlotte Street
Canandaigua, NY 14424
(716) 394-4922
Notable plantings:
ten turn-of-the-century gardens

Wave Hill
675 West 252nd Street
Bronx, NY 10471
(718) 549-3200
Notable plantings: English garden;
aquatic garden

## North Carolina

Biltmore Estate
One Biltmore Plaza
Asheville, NC 28803
(704) 274-1776
Notable plantings: formal gardens

Coker Arboretum
University of North Carolina
Chapel Hill, NC 27514
(919) 962-8100
Notable plantings: native plants; spring
bulbs

Sarah P. Duke Gardens
Duke University
Durham, NC 27706
(919) 684-3968
Notable plantings: Asian collection

Elizabethan Gardens
Manteo, NC 27954
(919) 473-3234
Notable plantings: Shakespeare garden;
camellias

North Carolina Botanical Garden
3375 Totten Center
University of North Carolina
Chapel Hill, NC 27599
(919) 962-0522

Notable plantings: native plants of the
Southeast, carnivorous plants, ferns

Sandhills Horticultural Gardens
Sandhill Community College
2200 Airport Road
Pinehurst, NC 28374
(919) 692-6185
Notable plantings: hollies

Tryon Palace Restoration
610 Pollock Street
New Bern, NC 28563
(919) 638-1560
Notable plantings: 18th-century ornamental gardens

## North Dakota

International Peace Garden, Inc.
Box 116, Route 1
Dunseith, ND 58329
(701) 263-4390
Notable plantings: perennials; orchids

## Ohio

Cox Arboretum
6733 Springboro Pike
Dayton, OH 45449
(513) 434-9005
Notable plantings: cacti and succulents

Falconskeape Gardens
7359 Branch Road
Medina, OH 44256
(216) 723-4966
Notable plantings: lilacs

Franklin Park Conservatory and Garden
Center
1777 East Broad Street
Columbus, OH 43203
(614) 222-7447
Notable plantings: orchids

Garden Center of Greater Cleveland
11030 East Boulevard
Cleveland, OH 44106
(216) 721-1600
Notable plantings: Japanese garden;
terrace garden

Stan Hywet Hall Foundation
714 North Portage Path
Akron, OH 44303
(216) 836-0576
Notable plantings: Japanese garden;
elliptical garden

Holden Arboretum
9500 Sperry Road
Mentor, OH 44060
(216) 256-1110
Notable plantings: lilacs

Kingwood Center
900 Park Avenue West
Mansfield, OH 44906
(419) 522-0211
Notable plantings: peonies;
daylilies; daffodils

Irwin M. Krohn Conservatory
950 Eden Park Drive
Cincinnati, OH 45202
(513) 352-4080
Notable plantings: rare and exotic plants

Toledo Botanical Garden
5403 Elmer Drive
Toledo, OH 43615
(419) 536-8365
Notable plantings: pioneer garden

Whetstone Park of Roses
4015 Olentangy Boulevard
Columbus, OH 43214
(614) 645-6648
Notable plantings: over 10,000
rosebushes and woody ornamentals

## Oklahoma

Will Rogers Horticultural Gardens
3500 NW 36th Street
Oklahoma City, OK 73102
(405) 943-0827
Notable plantings: over 1,000 varieties

Tulsa Garden Center
2435 South Peoria Avenue
Tulsa, OK 74114
(918) 749-6401
Notable plantings: roses;
chrysanthemums; irises; rock garden

## Oregon

Berry Botanic Garden
11505 SW Summerville Avenue
Portland, OR 97219
(503) 636-4112
Notable plantings: alpine and rock
garden plants; rhododendrons

Crystal Springs Rhododendron Garden
SE 28th and Woodstock
Portland, OR 97202
(503) 771-8386
Notable plantings: rhododendrons

Hendricks Park Rhododendron Garden
Summit Avenue and Skyline Drive
Eugene, OR 97401
(503) 687-5334
Notable plantings: rhododendrons

International Rose Test Garden
400 SW Kingston Avenue
Portland, OR 97201
(503) 248-4302
Notable plantings: roses

Leach Botanical Garden
6704 SE 122nd Avenue
Portland, OR 97236
(503) 761-9503

Notable plantings: Pacific
Northwest-native plants

Cecil and Molly Smith Garden
5065 Ray Bell Road
St. Paul, OR 97137
(503) 246-3710
Notable plantings: rhododendrons

## Pennsylvania

Arboretum of the Barnes Foundation
57 Lapsley Lane
Merion Station, PA 19066
(215) 664-8880
Notable plantings: peonies

Bartram's Garden
54th Street and Lindbergh Boulevard
Philadelphia, PA 19143
(215) 729-5281
Notable plantings: oldest botanical
garden in the US

Bowman's Hill Wildflower Preserve
Washington Crossing Historic State Park
Washington Crossing, PA 18977
(215) 862-2924
Notable plantings: Pennsylvania-
native plants

Hershey Rose Gardens and Arboretum
Hotel Road
Hershey, PA 17033
(717) 534-3493
Notable plantings: roses

Longwood Gardens
Route 1, Kennett Square, PA 19348
(215) 388-6741
Notable plantings: 350 acres of formal
gardens; water gardens

Pennsbury Manor
400 Pennsbury Memorial Road
Morrisville, PA 19067

(215) 946-0400
Notable plantings: ornamental courts;
herbaceous perennials

Phipps Conservatory
Schenley Park
Pittsburgh, PA 15219
(412) 255-2370
Notable plantings: orchids

## Rhode Island

Blithewold Mansion and Gardens
101 Ferry Road
Bristol, RI 02809
(401) 253-2707
Notable plantings: roses; rock
garden; water garden

Green Animals Topiary Gardens
380 Cory's Lane
Portsmouth, RI 02871
(401) 683-1267
Notable plantings: topiary

Roger Williams Park Greenhouse
and Gardens
Broad Street
Providence, RI 02905
(401) 785-9450
Notable plantings: Japanese garden; roses

## South Carolina

Brookgreen Gardens
US 17 South
Murrells Inlet, SC 29576
(803) 237-4218
Notable plantings: over 2,000 species

Cypress Gardens
Hampton Park
Charleston, SC 29403
(803) 553-0515
Notable plantings: over 8,000 varieties
of flowering subtropical plants

Magnolia Plantation and Gardens
Highway 61
Charleston, SC 29414
(803) 571-1266
Notable plantings: camellias

Middleton Place
Route 4
Charleston, SC 29407
(803) 556-6020
Notable plantings: oldest landscaped
garden in US; camellias; formal gardens

Swan Lake Iris Gardens
West Liberty Street
Sumter, SC 29150
(803) 775-5811
Notable plantings: irises

## South Dakota

McCrory Gardens
South Dakota State University
Brookings, SD 57007
(605) 688-5136

## Tennessee

Memphis Botanic Garden
750 Cherry Road
Memphis, TN 38117
(901) 685-1566
Notable plantings: twenty plant
collections

Tennesse Botanical Gardens at
Cheekwood
1200 Forrest Park Drive
Nashville, TN 37205
(615) 353-2148
Notable plantings: roses; daffodils;
perenniels; boxwoods

## Texas

Bayou Bend Garden
1 Westcott Street
Houston, TX 77219
(713) 529-8773
Notable plantings: eight gardens

The Dallas Arboretum and Botanical
Garden
8525 Garland Road
Dallas, TX 75218
(214) 327-3990
Notable plantings: perennials; azaleas

Dallas Civic Garden Center
Martin Luther King Jr. Boulevard
Fair Park
Dallas, TX 75226
(214) 428-7476
Notable plantings: watergarden;
bog garden; wildflowers

Fort Worth Botanical Garden
3220 Botanic Garden Boulevard
Fort Worth, TX 76107
(817) 870-7686
Notable plantings: begonias; roses;
Texas-native plants

McMurry College Iris Garden
Sayles Boulevard and South 16th Street
c/o Abilene Chamber of Commerce
325 Hickory Street
Abilene, TX
(915) 692-3938
Notable plantings: over 650 iris varieties

National Wildflower Research Center
4801 La Crosse Avenue
Austin, TX 78739
(512) 292-4100
Notable plantings: rare wildflowers

San Antonio Botanical Center
555 Funston Place

San Antonio, TX 78209
(512) 821-5115
Notable plantings: Texas-native plants

Tyler Municipal Rose Garden
420 South Rose Park Drive
Tyler, TX 75710
(214) 531-1212
Notable plantings: 30,000 rosebushes

## Vermont

Shelburne Museum
Route 7
Shelburne, VT 05482
(802) 985-3344
Notable plantings: lilacs; herbs

## Virginia

Bryan Park Azalea Gardens
900 East Broad Street
Richmond, VA 23219
(804) 780-8785
Notable plantings: 45,000 azaleas

Lewis Ginter Botanical Garden
7000 Lakeside Avenue
Richmond, VA 23228
(804) 262-9887
Notable plantings: seasonal floral displays

Gunston Hall
10709 Gunston Road
Mason Neck, VA 22079
(703) 550-9220
Notable plantings: 18th-century garden

Maymont Foundation
1700 Hampton Street
Richmond, VA 23220
(804) 358-7166
Notable plantings: Italian garden;
daylilies

Monticello
Thomas Jefferson Memorial Foundation
Box 316
Charlottesville, VA 22902
(804) 296-4800
Notable plantings: historic flowers

Mount Vernon
Mount Vernon Ladies Association
Mount Vernon, VA 22121
(703) 780-7262
Notable plantings: 18th-century gardens

Norfolk Botanical Gardens
Airport Road
Norfolk, VA 23158
(804) 853-6972
Notable plantings: azaleas; tulips;
camellias

Oatlands Plantation
Route 2, Box 352
Leesburg, VA 22075
(703) 777-3174
Notable plantings: roses; early-
nineteenth-century gardens

## Washington

Bellevue Botanical Garden
Box 7081
12001 Main Street
Bellevue, WA 98008
(206) 541-3755
Notable plantings: perennials;
rhododendrons

Bloedel Reserve
7571 NE Dolphin Drive
Bainbridge Island, WA 98110
(206) 842-7631
Notable plantings: Japanese garden

Ohme Gardens
3327 Ohme Road
Wenatchee, WA 98801

(509) 662-5785
Notable plantings: alpine and
rock garden plants

Pacific Rim Bonsai
Collection/Rhododendron Species
Botanical Garden
Weyerhauser Corporate Headquarters
2525 South 336th Street
Federal Way, WA 98063
(206) 661-9377
Notable plantings: bonsai; rhododendrons

## Wisconsin

Boerner Botanical Gardens
Whitnall Park
5879 South 92nd Street
Hales Corners, WI 53130
(414) 425-1130
Notable plantings: roses; forty-acre
English garden

Mitchell Park Conservatory
524 South Layton Boulevard
Milwaukee, WI 53215
(414) 649-9830
Notable plantings: orchids

Olbrich Botanical Gardens
3330 Atwood Avenue
Madison, WI 53704
(608) 246-4551
Notable plantings: All-America
Selections display garden

University of Wisconsin Arboretum
1207 Seminole Highway
Madison, WI 53711
(608) 262-2746
Notable plantings: prairie trees; viburnum
garden

## CANADA

### Alberta

Calgary Zoo, Botanical Garden,
and Prehistoric Park
St. George's Island
Calgary, Alberta T2M 4R8
(403) 232-9342
Notable plantings: hardy perennials;
conservatory

Devonian Botanic Garden
University of Alberta
Edmonton, Alberta T6G 2E1
(403) 987-3054
Notable plantings: alpine garden;
irises; peonies

### British Columbia

The Butchart Gardens
Box 4010
800 Benvento Avenue
Brentwood Bay
Victoria, British Columbia V8M 1J8
(604) 652-4422
Notable plantings: flowering plants

University of British Columbia
Botanical Garden
6804 SW Marine Drive
Vancouver, British Columbia V6T 1W5
(604) 822-4208
Notable plantings: alpines;
rhododendrons

VanDusen Botanical Garden
5251 Oak Street
Vancouver, British Columbia V6M 4H1
(604) 266-7194
Notable plantings: Sino-Himalayan flora

## Nova Scotia

Annapolis Royal Historic Gardens
Box 278
Annapolis Royal, Nova Scotia B0S 1A0
(902) 532-7018
Notable plantings: roses;
Victorian garden

## Ontario

Allan Gardens
19 Horticultural Avenue
Toronto, Ontario M5A 2P2
(416) 392-7288
Notable plantings: orchids; roses

Floral Clock and Lilac Gardens
River Road
Niagara Falls, Ontario L2E 6T2
(416) 356-2241
Notable plantings: 25,000
flowering plants

Royal Botanical Gardens
680 Plains Road West
Hamilton, Ontario L8N 3H8
(416) 527-1158
Notable plantings: clematis; climbing
plants; scented garden

## Quebec

Montreal Botanical Garden
4101 Sherbrooke Road East
Montreal, Quebec H1X 2B2
(514) 872-1400
Notable plantings: thirty gardens

# The Traveling Gardener

T HE NEXT-BEST THING to looking at your own garden is looking at someone else's. Gardeners enjoy traveling to see gardens and visit flower shows and other events. Travel agents who specialize in organizing trips for gardeners are listed alphabetically below. A state-by-state listing of the largest and best-known annual garden events in the United States and Canada follows. Of course, there are numerous smaller, local shows and festivals throughout the country, and local and regional plant clubs hold shows and plant sales throughout the year, but space does not permit listing them here. Contact the organizations listed in chapter 8 for information.

The exact dates of the flower shows and festivals listed below vary somewhat from year to year. The phone number listed for an event is generally that of the sponsoring organization or a professional exposition company. You can get additional information by contacting the Chamber of Commerce or Convention and Visitors Bureau for the appropriate state or locality (call the local information operator to get the phone numbers—the number is often toll-free). These organizations will happily send you free details about the particular event, along with free maps and other information about visiting the area. If you mention your interest in gardening, you'll also be sent free information about nearby botanical gardens, arboretums, display gardens, and other sites and events.

An excellent annual guide to gardening events is a paperback volume called The Garden Tourist, edited by Lois G. Rosenfeld. It's available from:

THE GARDEN TOURIST
330 West 72nd Street, Suite 12B
New York, NY 10023
Price: $12.95 plus $2.55 shipping and handling

## Garden Tour Operators

Border Discoveries
2117 Bobbyber Drive
Vienna, VA 22182
(703) 356-2826
Destinations: England

Coopersmith's England
Box 900

Inverness, CA 94937
(415) 669-1914
Destinations: Europe and elsewhere

Creative Travel Arrangers
36 Linaria Way
Portola Valley, CA 94028
(415) 854-4412
Destinations: worldwide

Elite Connections
(800) 354-7506
Destinations: London and the United
Kingdom

English Adventures
803 Front Range Road
Littleton, CO 80120
(303) 797-2365
Destinations: Lake District

Expo Garden Tours
101 Sunrise Hill Road
Norwalk, CT 06851
(203) 840-1441
(800) 448-2685
Destinations: worldwide

Family Society Tours, Ltd.
62 Weston Road
Weston, CT 06883
(203) 846-8486
Destinations: worldwide

Fugazy Travel
(800) 221-7181
Destinations: worldwide

Garden Adventures, Ltd.
(610) 444-6161
Destinations: worldwide

Geostar Travel
1240 Century Court
Santa Rosa, CA 95403
(707) 579-2420
(800) 624-6633
Destinations: worldwide

Horizon Travel
3520 South Osprey Avenue
Sarasota, FL 34239
(941) 955-6567
(800) 352-1036
Destinations: worldwide with
Dr. Ellen Henke

Horticulture Travel Programs
98 North Washington Street
Boston, MA 02114
(800) 334-2733
Destinations: worldwide

Ingatours
169 Bedford Road
Greenwich, CT 06831
(800) 786-5311
Destinations: Europe

J. E. G. Enterprises
26810 County Road 98
Davis, CA 95616
(800) 757-0404
Destinations: Scotland

Koelzer Travel
16971 Woodstream Drive
Huntington Beach, CA 92647
(800) 858-2742
Destinations: China

Limewalk Tours
444 South Union Street
Burlington, VT 05401
(802) 864-5720
(800) 426-5720
Destinations: the United Kingdom and
Europe

Lucas & Randall
(800) 505-2505
Destinations: France

New Zealand Australia Reservations
Office
6033 West Century Boulevard, Suite
1270
Los Angeles, CA 90045
(800) 351-2317
(800) 352-2323
Destinations: Australia and New Zealand

Port of Travel
9515 Soquel Drive
Aptos, CA 95003
(408) 688-6004
Destinations: worldwide

Reeve Garden Holidays, Inc.
Box 527
Hanover, NH 03755
(603) 643-5002
Destinations: worldwide

Sander Travel & Tours, Inc.
2760 Caraway Drive
Tucker, GA 30084
(404) 939-7818
Destinations: Europe

TOC
4208 North Freeway Boulevard
Sacramento, CA 95834
(800) 505-2505
Destinations: Europe

Travelworld
(800) 969-4194
Destinations: worldwide

# Gardening Shows, Flower Festivals, and Other Annual Events

## Alabama

Azalea Trail and Festival
Mobile
(205) 476-8828
Date: month of May

Birmingham Home and Garden Show
Birmingham
(800) 226-3976
Date: mid-March

Gulf Coast Home and Garden Show
Mobile
(800) 226-3976
Date: early February

North Alabama Home and Garden Show
Huntsville
(800) 226-3976
Date: mid-February

## Arkansas

Magnolia Blossom Festival
Magnolia
(501) 234-4352
Date: second week in May

## California

Alameda Country Home and Garden
Show
Pleasanton
(800) 222-9351

Camellia Festival
Sacramento
(916) 442-7673
Date: first two weeks of March

Contra Costa Home and Garden Show
Concord
(800) 222-9351
Date: end of April

Easter in July Lily Festival
Smith River
(707) 487-3443
Date: second weekend in July

Pacific Orchid Exposition
San Francisco
(415) 665-2468
Date: end of February

Pier 39's Tulipmania
San Francisco
(415) 705-5500

San Francisco Garden and Landscape
Show
San Francisco
(415) 750-5108
Date: end of April

Southern California Home
and Garden Show
Anaheim
(714) 978-8888
Date: mid-August

Ventura County Home and Garden Show
Ventura
(800) 222-9351
Date: mid-March

## Colorado

Colorado Garden and Home Show
Denver
(303) 696-6100
Date: end of January

## Connecticut

Hartford Flower Show
Hartford
(203) 727-8010
Date: end of February

Wildflower Festival
Storrs
(203) 486-4460
Date: second Sunday in June

## District of Columbia

Cherry Blossom Festival
Washington, DC
(202) 737-2599
Date: first week in April

Georgetown Garden Tour
Washington, DC
(202) 333-4953
Date: second weekend in May

U.S. Botanic Garden Spring Flower Show
Washington, DC
(202) 226-4082
Date: end of March–end of April

Washington DC Flower and Garden
Show
Washington, DC
(703) 569-7141
Date: early March

## Florida

Chrysanthemum Festival
Cypress Gardens (Winter Haven)
Date: month of November

Jacksonville Home and Patio Show
Jacksonville
(904) 730-3356
Date: end of February

Pensacola Home and Garden Show
Pensacola
(800) 226-3976
Date: end of March

## Georgia

Atlanta Flower Show
Atlanta
(404) 876-5859
Date: early March

Dogwood Festival
Atlanta
(404) 525-6145
Date: mid-April

Savannah Home and Garden Tour
Savannah
(912) 234-8054
Date: end of March–early April

Southeastern Flower Show
Atlanta
(404) 888-5638
Date: end of February

## Illinois

Chicagoland Home and Garden Show
Chicago
(800) 395-1350
Date: mid-February

Marigold Festival
Pekin
(309) 346-2106

## Indiana

Indiana Flower and Patio Show
Indianapolis
(317) 576-9933
Date: mid-March

Indianapolis Home Show
Indianapolis
(317) 298-7111
Date: end of January–early February

## Iowa

Des Moines Home and Garden Show
Des Moines
(612) 933-3850
Date: mid-February

Pella Tulip Time Festival
Pella
(515) 628-4311
Date: second weekend in May

## Kansas

Wichita Lawn, Flower and Garden Show
Wichita
(316) 721-8740
Date: mid-March

## Kentucky

Metropolitan Louisville Home, Garden
and Flower Show
Louisville
(502) 637-9737
Date: early March

## Louisiana

American Rose Society National Show
American Rose Center
Shreveport
(318) 938-5402
Date: mid-June–end of August

Christmas in Roseland
American Rose Center
Shreveport
(318) 938-5402
Date: month of December

First Bloom Festival
American Rose Center
Shreveport
(318) 938-5402
Date: end of April–start of May

Spring Garden Show at the Botanical
Garden
New Orleans
(504) 486-3736
Date: second week in April

## Maryland

Landon Azalea Garden Festival
Bethesda
(301) 320-3200
Date: first weekend in May

Maryland Home and Garden Show
Timonium
(410) 969-8585
Date: mid-March

## Massachusetts

Daffodil Festival
Nantucket Island
(508) 288-1700
Date: end of April

New England Spring Flower Show
Boston
(617) 536-9280
(617) 474-6200
Date: mid-March

## Michigan

Ann Arbor Flower and Garden Show
Ann Arbor
(313) 998-7002
Date: end of March

International Builders Home and Garden
Show
Detroit
(810) 737-4477
Date: mid-March

Kalamazoo County Flowerfest
Kalamazoo
(616) 381-3597
Date: third weekend in July

Meadow Brook Landscape and Garden
Show
Rochester

(810) 646-4992
Date: early June

Michigan Home and Garden Show
Pontiac
(616) 530-1919
Date: end of February

Spring Home and Garden Show
Novi
(810) 737-4477
Date: early February

Trillium Festival
Muskegon
(616) 798-3573
Date: second weekend in May

Tulip Time Festival
Holland
(616) 396-4221
(800) 822-2770
Date: mid-May

## Minnesota

Minneapolis Home and Garden Show
Minneapolis
(612) 933-3850
Date: early March

## Missouri

Builders Home and Garden Show
St. Louis
(314) 994-7700
Date: mid-March

Kansas City Flower, Lawn and Garden
Show
Kansas City
(816) 871-5600
Date: early February

St. Louis Flower Show
St. Louis

(314) 569-3117
Date: end of January or early February

## New Jersey

New Jersey Flower and Garden Show
Somerset
(908) 919-7660
Date: end February–early March

## New York

Buffalo Home and Garden Show
Buffalo
(800) 274-6948
Date: mid-March

Capital District Garden and Flower Show
Albany
(518) 356-6410
Date: mid-March

Central New York Flower and Garden
Show
Syracuse
(315) 487-7711
Date: mid-March

Greater Rochester Flower and Garden
Show
Henrietta
(716) 225-8091
Date: mid-March

Lilac Festival
Rochester
(716) 546-3070
(716) 256-4960
Date: last two weeks of May

Long Island Flower Show
Nassau Coliseum
(516) 293-4242
Date: early March

New York Flower Show
New York City
(212) 757-0915
(914) 421-3293
Date: early March

Rockefeller Center Flower and Garden
Show
New York City
(212) 632-3975
Date: mid-April

Tulip Festival
Albany
(800) 258-3582
Date: Mother's Day weekend

## North Carolina

Festival of Flowers
Biltmore Estate
Asheville
(800) 543-2961
Date: mid-April–mid-May

Southern Spring Show
Charlotte
(704) 376-6594
(800) 849-0248
Date: end of February–early March

## North Dakota

Sunflower Festival
Wahpeton
(701) 642-8559
Date: mid-August

## Ohio

Akron-Canton Home and Garden Show
Akron
(216) 865-6700
Date: end of February

Carnation City Festival
Alliance
(216) 823-6260
Date: first week in August

Central Ohio Home and Garden Show
Columbus
(614) 461-5257
Date: end of February–early March

Cincinnati Flower Show
Cincinnati
(513) 762-3390
(513) 579-0259
Date: end of April–start of May

Cincinnati Home and Garden Show
Cincinnati
(513) 281-0022
Date: end of February–early March

Greater Cincinnati Flower and Garden
Show
Cincinnati
(513) 579-0346
Date: end of April

Miami Valley Home and Garden Show
Dayton
(513) 258-2999
Date: end of February

National Home and Garden Show
Cleveland
(216) 529-1300
Date: mid-February

## Oklahoma

Azalea Fest
Muskogee
(918) 682-2401

## Oregon

Mother's Day Annual Rhododendron
Show
Crystal Springs Rhododendron Garden
Portland
(503) 771-8386
Date: Mother's Day weekend

Portland Home and Garden Show
Portland
(800) 343-6973
Date: end of February

Rhododendron Festival
Florence
(503) 997-3128
Date: mid-May

Rose Festival
Portland
(503) 227-2681
Date: month of June

Yard, Garden and Patio Show
Portland
(503) 653-8733
Date: end of February

## Pennsylvania

Acres of Spring Festival
Longwood Gardens
Kennett Square
(610) 388-1000
Date: month of April

Chrysanthemum Festival
Longwood Gardens
Kennett Square
(610) 388-1000
Date: month of November

May Market
Pittsburgh
(412) 441-4442
Date: mid-May

Philadelphia Flower Show
Philadelphia
(215) 625-8253
Date: early March

Pittsburgh Home and Garden Show
Pittsburgh
(412) 922-4900
Date: mid-March

## Rhode Island

Rhode Island Spring Flower and Garden
Show
Providence
(401) 421-7811
Date: end of February

## South Carolina

Charleston Festival of Houses and
Gardens
Charleston
(803) 723-1623
Date: third week in March–third week
in April

Charleston Garden Festival
Charleston
(803) 722-7527
Date: early October

Festival of Flowers
Greenwood
(803) 223-8431
Date: end of June

South Carolina Festival of Roses
Orangeburg
(803) 534-6821
Date: last weekend in April

## Tennessee

Dogwood Festival
Knoxville
(615) 637-4561
Date: mid-April

Home and Garden Show
Knoxville
(615) 637-4561
Date: end of February

Nashville Lawn and Garden Show
Nashville
(615) 352-3863
Date: early March

Spring Wildflower Pilgrimage
Gatlinburg
(800) 568-4748
Date: last weekend in April

## Texas

Abilene Iris Tour
Abilene
(915) 677-7241
Date: April

Bluebonnet Trail and Festival
Austin
(512) 478-9085
Date: first two weeks of April

Dallas Home and Garden Show
Dallas
(214) 680-9995
Date: early March

Fort Worth Home and Garden Show
Fort Worth
(214) 680-9995
Date: mid-February

The Gardener's Sourcebook

State Garden Show of Texas
Waco
(817) 772-1270
Date: mid-March

## Vermont

Stowe Flower Festival
Stowe
(800) 247-8693
Date: end of June

## Virginia

Apple Blossom Festival
Winchester
(703) 662-3863
Date: early May

Dogwood Festival
Charlottesville
(804) 358-5511
Date: mid-April

Historic Garden Week in Virginia
Richmond and statewide
(804) 644-7776
Date: third week in April

Maymont Flower and Garden Show
Richmond
(804) 358-7166
Date: end of February

## Washington

Daffodil Festival
Tacoma
(206) 627-6176
Date: third Saturday in April

Northwest Flower and Garden Show
Seattle
(206) 789-5333
Date: second week in February

Skagit Valley Tulip Festival
Mount Vernon
(206) 428-8547
Date: first two weeks in April

Tacoma
(206) 756-2121
Date: end of January–early February

## Wisconsin

Milwaukee Landscape and Garden Show
Milwaukee
(414) 778-4929
Date: end of March

## CANADA

### Ontario

Canadian Tulip Festival
Ottawa
(613) 567-4447
Date: third week in May

Garden Club of Toronto Flower Show
Toronto
(416) 447-5218
Date: early March

# A Gardening Miscellany

T HIS SECTION *contains, in no particular order, an assortment of interesting gardening sources and information that didn't quite fit elsewhere in this book.*

## Garden Designs

*For software that lets you design your garden on your computer, see chapter 11.*

Beckett Corporation
2521 Willowsbrook Road
Dallas, TX 75220
(214) 357-6421
Product: garden design kits
Catalogue: free

Design Works
6510 Page Boulevard
St. Louis, MO 63133
(314) 862-1709
Product: Gardener's Guide design kits
Catalogue: free

Garden Solutions
1950 Waldorf NW
Grand Rapids, MI 49550
(616) 771-9500
Product: garden designs
Catalogue: $1.00

Great American Green, Inc.
2981 Lower Union Hill Road
Canton, GA 30115

(404) 475-5537
Product: custom garden designs
Catalogue: $3.00

Landscape Design
15345 Terrace Road NE
Ham Lake, MN 55304
Product: landscape design kit
Catalogue: free

Perennial Graphics
Box 89B Hansen Road
Schaghticoke, NY 12154
(518) 753-7771
Product: custom garden designs
Catalogue: free

SeedScapes
Box 295
Edwardsburg, MI 49112
(616) 663-8601
Product: garden designs
Catalogue: $1.00

Silverbells & Cockleshells
Box 25244, Providence, RI 02905
(401) 941-6400
Product: garden designs
Catalogue: free

Springhill Nurseries
110 West Elm Street
Tipp City, OH 45371
(309) 689-3849
(800) 582-8527
Products: garden designs and plants
Catalogue: free

Swamp Fox Farm
Box 218
Gaylordsville, CT 06755
(203) 354-2659
Product: garden designs
Catalogue: free

## TV for Gardeners

*Home and Garden Television (HGTV) is a 24-hour cable network that started in January 1995. The network offers extensive gardening programming. For information on how to get the network through your cable provider, call (800) HGTV-ASK.*

*A syndicated half-hour program called Backyard America often deals with gardening topics. Check your local television listings for stations and times in your area.*

*Popular garden writer Derek Fell is the host of a gardening show on QVC-TV. Contact your cable provider or check local television listings for stations and times in your area.*

The Victory Garden, *hosted by Bob Thomson, is a long-running weekly program produced by WGBH, a public television station in Boston. Check with your local public television station for times in your area.*

## Plant-Finding Services

*If you can't find the plant you want from the sources listed in chapter 1, chapter 2, and elsewhere in this book, these fee-based plant-finding services may be able to help:*

Greenlist Info Services
12 Dudley Street
Randolph, VA 05060
Catalogue: long SASE

Inscape, Inc.
Box 1231
Brigantine, NJ 08203
(609) 822-6517
Catalogue: free

Rare Seed Locators, Inc.
Drawer 2479
2140 Shattuck Avenue
Berkeley, CA 94704
Catalogue: long SASE

## Gardening for Kids

*The GrowLab™ program from the nonprofit National Gardening Association consists of innovative resources for classroom instruction in gardening and botany. Funded by the National Science Foundation, this program offers a complete curriculum for grades K through 8. The NGA also sponsors the Youth Garden Grants program. For more information, contact:*

GrowLab™
National Gardening Association
180 Flynn Avenue
Burlington, VT 05401
(802) 863-1308
(800) 538-7476

*Another organization that promotes youth gardening is:*

National Junior Horticultural Association
401 North 4th Street
Durant, OK 74701
(405) 924-0771
Publication: *Going & Growing* (three times annually)

*Two good sources for children's gardening supplies and backyard nature study are:*

Gardens for Growing People
Box 630
Point Reyes Station, CA 94956
(415) 663-9433
Catalogue/quarterly newsletter: $4.00

Let's Get Growing
1900 Commercial Way
Santa Cruz, CA 95065
(408) 464-1868
Catalogue: free

*The Nature Company stores carry an extensive line of children's nature-study products. For the location of a store near you, contact:*

The Nature Company
75 Hearst Avenue
Berkeley, CA 94710
(510) 644-1337

# Horticultural Therapy

*Horticultural therapists are occupational therapists specially trained to work with people with disabilities and older adults. They help their clients enjoy the physical and psychological benefits of gardening. For information about becoming certified as a horticultural therapist, contact:*

American Horticultural Therapy
Association

362A Christopher Avenue
Gaithersburg, MD 20879
(800) 634-1603

Canadian Horticultural Therapy
Association
Royal Botanical Garden
Box 399
Hamilton, Ontario L8N 3H8
(416) 529-7618

# Flower Photography

*Slides of flowers, plants, gardens, and landscaping for private use only (not for reproduction in any way) are available from:*

Harper Horticultural Slide Library
219 Robanna Shores
Seaford, VA 23696
Catalogue: long SASE with two stamps

*The workshops listed below can help you move beyond garden snapshots to the specialized skills needed for serious flower photography. Costs, dates, and locations vary.*

California Natural Wonders
Photographic Workshop Series
Noella Ballenger & Associates
Box 457
La Cañada-Flintridge, CA 91012
(818) 954-0933

Center for Nature Photography
Allen Rokach and Anne Millman
Box 118
Riverdale, NY 10471
(914) 968-7163

Latigo Ranch Photography Workshops
Box 237
Kremmling, CO 80459
(303) 724-9008
(800) 227-9655

Lepp and Associates Seminars
Box 6240
Los Osos, CA 93412
(805) 528-7385

Natural Image Expeditions
13785 West 68th Drive
Arvada, CO 8004
(303) 420-7893
(800) 259-8771

The Nature Place
Colorado Outdoor Education Center
Florrisant, CO 80816
(719) 748-3475

Nature Photography Workshops
Edward and Lee Mason
8410 Madeline Drive
St. Louis, MO 63114
(314) 427-6311

Rocky Mountain Nature Association
Seminar Coordinator
Rocky Mountain National Park
Estes Park, CO 80517
(303) 586-1258

# Botanic Art

*A natural corollary to gardening is producing, looking at, and sometimes collecting botanic art. There are too many dealers in both contemporary and antique botanic art to list here, however. For information on finding a reputable botanic art dealer, contact:*
National Antique and Art Dealers
Association of America
12 East 56th Street
New York, NY 10022
(212) 826-9707

*Professional botanic illustrators may join:*
Guild of Natural Science Illustrators
Box 652

Ben Franklin Station
Washington, DC 20044

*The Hunt Institute for Botanical Documentation is a research center that studies the history of plant science, including iconography and art. The institute has an extensive collection of botanical illustrations.*
Hunt Institute for Botanical
Documentation
Carnegie-Mellon University
Pittsburgh, PA 15213
(412) 268-2434

*Software containing horticultural clip art is available from:*
Wheeler Arts
66 Lake Park
Champaign, IL 61821
(217) 359-6816
Program: Quick Art
Catalogue: $3.00

# Backyard Wildlife Habitat

*Your gardening efforts can make your backyard both more beautiful and more beneficial to wildlife. The organizations listed below provide information about creating backyard wildlife habitats and award certificates of merit:*
Backyard Wildlife Habitat Program
National Wildlife Federation
1400 16th Street NW
Washington, DC 20036
(202) 797-6800
(800) 432-6564

Urban Wildlife Sanctuary Program
National Institute for Urban Wildlife
10921 Trotting Ridge Way
Columbia, MD 21044
(301) 596-3311

# National Register of Big Trees

*Hundreds of champion big trees and their locations are listed on the National Register of Big Trees. To get a free copy, contact:*
National Register of Big Trees
American Forestry Association
Box 2000
Washington, DC 20013
(202) 667-3300

# Seeds from Famous Trees

*Kits containing seeds from famous trees (including those from the homes of presidents and other historic sites) and all you need to grow them are available from:*
Famous and Historic Trees
Box 7040
Jacksonville, FL 32238
(904) 765-0727
Catalogue: free

# Special Gardening Days

*April is National Garden Month. For information on events, contact the sponsor:*
Garden Council
10210 Bald Hill Road
Mitchellville, MD 20721
(301) 577-4073

*The second week of April is National Garden Week. For information on events, contact the sponsor:*
National Garden Bureau
1311 Butterfield Road
Downers Grove, IL 60515

*The first full day of spring is Master Gardener Day (see chapter 9 for more information about the*

*Master Gardener program). For information on events, contact:*
Jim Arnold, Master Gardener
543 Wagner Street
Fort Wayne, IN 46805
(219) 426-9904

*The last Friday in April is National Arbor Day. For information on events, contact the sponsor:*
Committee for National Arbor Day
Box 333
West Orange, NJ 07052
(201) 731-0840

*The second week in May is National Wildflower Week. For information on events, contact the sponsor:*
National Ecology Committee
107 Jensen Circle
West Springfield, MA 01089
(413) 737-7600

# Flowers of the Month

*Who decides this stuff, anyway?*

January: carnation
February: violet
March: jonquil
April: sweet pea
May: lily of the valley
June: rose
July: larkspur
August: gladiolus
September: aster
October: calendula
November: chrysanthemum
December: narcissus

## State and Provincial Flowers and Trees

| State | State Flower | State Tree |
|---|---|---|
| Alabama | camellia | southern pine (longleaf) |
| Alaska | forget–me–not | Sitka spruce |
| Arizona | saguaro | paloverde |
| Arkansas | apple blossom | pine |
| California | golden poppy | California redwood |
| Colorado | Rocky Mountain columbine | blue spruce |
| Connecticut | mountain laurel | white oak |
| Delaware | peach blossom | American holly |
| Florida | orange blossom | sabal palm |
| Georgia | Cherokee rose | live oak |
| Hawaii | hibiscus | kukui |
| Idaho | syringa | western white pine |
| Illinois | native violet | white oak |
| Indiana | peony | tulip tree |
| Iowa | wild rose | oak |
| Kansas | sunflower | cottonwood |
| Kentucky | goldenrod | Kentucky coffeetree |
| Louisiana | magnolia | bald cypress |
| Maine | white pinecone and tassel | white pine |
| Maryland | black-eyed Susan | white oak |
| Massachusetts | mayflower | American elm |
| Michigan | apple blossom | white pine |
| Minnesota | pink-and-white lady's slipper | red pine |
| Mississippi | magnolia | magnolia |
| Missouri | hawthorn | flowering dogwood |
| Montana | bitterroot | ponderosa pine |
| Nebraska | goldenrod | cottonwood |
| Nevada | sagebrush | single–leaf piñon |
| New Hampshire | purple lilac | white birch |
| New Jersey | purple violet | red oak |
| New Mexico | yucca flower | piñon pine |
| New York | rose | sugar maple |
| North Carolina | dogwood | pine |
| North Dakota | wild prairie rose | American elm |
| Ohio | scarlet carnation | buckeye |
| Oklahoma | mistletoe | redbud |
| Oregon | Oregon grape | Douglas fir |
| Pennsylvania | mountain laurel | hemlock |
| Rhode Island | violet | red maple |
| South Carolina | Carolina jessamine | palmetto |
| South Dakota | American pasqueflower | Black Hills spruce |
| Tennessee | iris | tulip poplar |
| Texas | bluebonnet | pecan |
| Utah | sego lily | blue spruce |
| Vermont | red clover | sugar maple |
| Virginia | dogwood | dogwood |
| Washington | coast rhododendron | western hemlock |
| West Virginia | rhododendron | sugar maple |
| Wisconsin | wood violet | sugar maple |
| Wyoming | Indian paintbrush | cottonwood |

| Province/Territory | Flower |
|---|---|
| Alberta | wild rose |
| British Columbia | Pacific dogwood |
| Manitoba | prairie crocus |
| New Brunswick | purple violet |
| Newfoundland | pitcher plant |
| Northwest Territories | mountain avens |
| Nova Scotia | mayflower |
| Ontario | white trillium |
| Prince Edward Island | lady's slipper |
| Quebec | white garden lily |
| Saskatchewan | red lily |
| Yukon Territory | fireweed |